NATIONALIZING THE RUSSIAN EMPIRE

RUSSIAN RESEARCH CENTER STUDIES, 94

Published under the auspices of the
Davis Center for Russian and
Eurasian Studies, Harvard University

Nationalizing the Russian Empire

The Campaign against Enemy Aliens
during World War I

ERIC LOHR

HARVARD UNIVERSITY PRESS

*Cambridge, Massachusetts,
and London, England   2003*

Library of Congress Cataloguing-in-Publication Data

Lohr, Eric.

    Nationalizing the Russian Empire : the campaign against enemy aliens
during World War I / Eric Lohr.

       p.   cm. — (Russian Research Center studies ; 94)

    Includes bibliographical references and index.

    ISBN 0-674-01041-8 (alk. paper)

    1. Russian—Ethnic relations—History—20th century.   2. Minorities—
Crimes against—Russia—History—20th century.   3. Political persecution—
Russia—History—20th century.   4. Forced migration—Russia—History—
20th century.   5. Minorities—Government policy—Russia—History—
20th century.   6. Minorities—Relocation—Russia—History—20th century.
7. World War, 1914–1918—Russia.   I. Title.   II. Series.

DK34.R9L64   2003
940.3'086'91—dc21   2002191913

To my parents

Contents

Figures

Tables

Acknowledgments

My research was supported in part by a grant from the International Research and Exchanges Board (IREX), with funds provided by the National Endowment for the Humanities and the United States Department of State, which administers the Russian, Eurasian, and East European Research Program (Title VIII). I am grateful to the Davis Center for Russian and Eurasian Studies for summer research grants in the early and late stages of the project, for a crucial semester-long postdoctoral fellowship, and for providing an ideal intellectual environment. I would also like to thank Mark von Hagen and the Harriman Institute for Russian Studies at Columbia for hosting me while I was writing.

Roman Szporluk has been generous with his time, advice, and support and has been an intellectual mentor in the very best sense. Richard Pipes organized an excellent seminar on Russia in 1916, in which I discovered this topic. Timothy Colton and Edward Keenan have provided much useful advice and support. Thanks also to David McDonald for inspiring me to enter the field of Russian history in the first place and for his help along the way.

Many friends and colleagues have read and commented on parts of the manuscript at various stages. I am particularly grateful to Richard Benert, David Brandenberger, Robert Geraci, Mark von Hagen, John LeDonne, Dominic Lieven, Terry Martin, Randall Poole, and Josh

Sanborn for reading versions of the manuscript and making many insightful comments. Grant Mainland and Kelly O'Neill provided excellent research and editorial assistance. Many thanks to Mark Baker, Patrice Dabrowski, Jonathan Daly, Benjamin Frommer, Peter Gatrell, Peter Holquist, Yanni Kotsonis, David McDonald, Kevin Murphy, Thomas Owen, Jeffrey Rossman, Serge Schmemann, Timothy Snyder, and Serge Troubetzkoy for reading and commenting on draft chapters. David Brandenberger's friendship and criticism helped every step of the way. Peter Holquist has been a model of collegiality, engaging with me in a voluminous correspondence on issues related to World War I and points of common interest. Elizabeth Wood and participants in her informal workshop on Russian History provided useful comments at an early stage in the evolution of the project, and workshops and seminars at the Davis Center were very helpful toward the end. Peter Gatrell generously shared his manuscript prior to publication. Thanks to Mark Baker, Alex Dillon, Scott Kenworthy, and Tom Trice for sharing and helping with documents. Thanks also to Kathleen McDermott, Kathleen Drummy, and Anita Safran at Harvard University Press for skillfully guiding me through the publication process.

A partial version of Chapter 5 was published under the title "The Russian Army and the Jews: Mass Deportation, Hostages, and Violence during World War I" in *The Russian Review* 60 (July 2001): 404–419. I am pleased to acknowledge the journal publishers' courtesy.

My Russian colleagues provided much advice and help in formulating and conducting research for this project. Viktor Mal'kov of the Russian Academy of Sciences, Institute of General History, was an excellent adviser and academic host in Russia. I would like to warmly thank him and all the members of the Association of Historians of World War I at the Academy of Sciences for their comments on my work. I especially wish to thank Evgenii Sergeev for his extensive help in both intellectual and practical matters of research. Aleksandr Kavtaradze, Igor Karpeev, Iurii Kir'ianov, and Sergei Nelipovich shared their knowledge of crucial archival holdings. Staff members at the Russian archives and libraries were consistently helpful and professional. In particular, I would like to thank Serafima Igor'evna Varekova and everyone at the Russian State Historical Archive (RGIA), Tatiana Iur'evna Burmistrova and the entire staff at the Russian State Military-Historical Archive (RGVIA), and Nina Ivanovna Abdulaeva at the

State Archive of the Russian Federation (GARF). Special thanks to Sergei and Violeta Ershov, Irina Kuptsova, and Andrei Maliutin for all their help.

I especially thank my wife Anya Schmemann for her constant support and for her patience while I worked in Russia and commuted between Cambridge and New York. Alexei arrived in time to provide many happy diversions. Most of all, the generosity and support of my parents—Richard and Joyce Lohr—made it all possible.

Nationalizing the Russian Empire

Introduction

A LITTLE-KNOWN but central aspect of Russia's participation in the First World War was a sweeping campaign directed against certain minorities suddenly recast by the regime and society as dangerous internal enemies. This campaign initially targeted enemy aliens, defined by international law as citizens of enemy states in time of war. This relatively narrow but economically and socially prominent category was subjected to wartime deportation, internment, and expropriation.[1] Russia was by no means the only country to take measures against enemy citizens,[2] but its campaign quickly swept up many others as well, from the empire's large population of ethnic Germans to Russian-subject Jews, Muslims, and others. The campaign resulted in the forced migration of roughly a million civilians, the nationalization of a substantial portion of the imperial economy, and the transfer of extensive land holdings and rural properties from the targeted minorities to favored groups.

Prior to World War I, few governments formally took measures against enemy subjects residing on their territory in times of war, and leading experts agreed that no rule of international law was more strongly held than the one protecting the person and property of foreign citizens in wartime.[3] But nearly all countries eventually interned at least some of the enemy subjects within their territory, and imposed extensive temporary restrictions on their property and economic activity.

1

Even states as far from the fields of battle as Australia, Brazil, the United States, Canada, and Cuba interned some enemy aliens.[4] The First World War introduced measures against enemy aliens and other civilians that became much more systematic and brutal both during and after the Second World War.

A number of long-term pan-European developments can help explain why enemy subjects came under such pressures when they did. The first was a gradual shift in the conception of war, dating from the time of the French Revolution, that transformed conflicts between armies into contests between their respective citizenries. One of the great military innovations of the French Revolution was the idea of the nation-in-arms, that is, of the whole citizenry fighting under a set of common ideals. During the nineteenth century, states throughout Europe—regardless of their political systems—expanded upon this idea by adopting universal military service and reserve systems. Inspired by the hope of creating a bigger, more patriotically inspired army, Russia introduced its version of universal conscription in 1874.[5] The links between reserve-based mass armies, the idea of modern citizenship, and the internment of enemy subjects in wartime were close. With the spread of reserve armies, military planners began to worry that if male enemy subjects were allowed to return to their countries of origin in wartime, they would end up in the opposing army.[6] Moreover, some military and police officials extrapolated from this purported threat to the notion that *all* enemy citizens would owe their loyalty abroad, and thus should be viewed as a source of recruits for spying and espionage. It is no coincidence that France, the birthplace of modern citizenship and the nation-in-arms idea, was also the site of the major nineteenth-century episodes of interning enemy subjects.[7]

Just as important as these developments was the great wave of internationalization in the late nineteenth and early twentieth centuries. With the help of the railroad and steamship, travel across borders expanded greatly in the decades prior to 1914, and the transnational movement of people and capital reached unprecedented levels. This dramatically increased the degree of concern about enemy aliens. By the turn of the century, anti-immigration nativist sloganeering appeared in many countries and precipitated legislation to curtail immigration of certain groups. Britain, France, Germany, and the United States all moved to establish new forms of oversight over immigrants and restrictions on immigration.[8] These developments were important, but the real shift toward a world bounded by citizenship with tight immigration controls and quotas came during the First World War, and the enemy-alien issue was an important part of this shift away from the internationalizing tendencies of the prewar world. This was particularly true for the continental empires along the Eastern front, which did not move so decisively toward making citizenship the crucial dividing line between members of the core community and those external to it until the war pushed them in that direction.

The Russian form of enemy-alien policies differed quite substantially from others in two important ways. First, while in many countries immigrants from enemy states were economically and socially marginal, in Russia enemy minorities held a highly disproportionate share of the leading positions in the economy as business owners, investors, managers, private landowners, store-owners, white-collar employees, engineers, foremen, and skilled workers. Thus from the start the stakes and potential impact of a campaign against enemy aliens were much greater in Russia than in countries like Britain, France, and Germany. Second, in Russia both official sanctions and the popular campaign quickly expanded well beyond enemy subjects to affect large numbers of naturalized immigrants and Russian citizens whose loyalty was questioned because of their ethnicity, religion, or former citizenship. This raises the question of terminology, as "enemy citizen" and "enemy subject" (*poddannyi, strany voiuiushchei s Rossiei*) technically refer only to noncombatant civilians holding passports from an enemy state (the Hohenzollern, Hapsburg, and Ottoman empires and Bulgaria after October 1915). Some of the restrictive laws and regulations added "Russian-subject immigrants from countries at war with Russia" (*vykhodtsy, Rossiiskie poddannye, iz stran voiuiushchikh s Rossiei*). Moreover, in practice, the army and government often extended sanctions even further to affect various other "suspect" or "unreliable" population categories. Incorporating these various categories under the English term "enemy alien" (which has no exact Russian equivalent), this book deals with all individuals and groups in the Russian Empire who were subjected to sanctions primarily designed at first to apply to enemy subjects.[9]

Accordingly, this study concentrates on the broader mobilization against aliens, paying specific attention to deportation, purge, expro-

priation of land holdings, and liquidation of businesses. More an investigation of administrative practices than a study of particular minorities, this study will argue that it was actually in part through the very
application of these sanctions that national distinctions were solidified
and made relevant.

From Imperial to Nationalizing State

The wartime campaign against enemy minorities was an important
event in the long-term history of the making and unmaking of the Russian Empire. One of the keys to the expansion and maintenance of the
empire was the co-optation of non-Russian elites. The dynastic imperial state incorporated Tatars, Poles, Lithuanians, Baltic Germans, and
others into its most prominent noble, bureaucratic, and military ranks
as it expanded from the sixteenth through the eighteenth centuries.[10]

Along with this extremely successful technique of imperial expansion
came a second crucial aspect in the formation of the empire: migration,
colonization, and settlement. This was the result of the remarkable demographic growth and migration of Eastern Slavs throughout the territory under imperial control, as well as the effect of official policies to
colonize border areas through the strategic settlement of Cossacks and
peasants. An important part of this policy from the mid-eighteenth to
the mid-nineteenth centuries was the programmatic encouragement of
immigration from Europe to settle the vast untilled lands of South
Ukraine, the Volga region, the North Caucasus, and other areas—both
to bring more land under cultivation and to consolidate imperial control over sparsely settled regions. The most numerous of the many
immigrant minorities encouraged to settle in rural areas were German
farmers, who settled in large numbers in Ukraine, Bessarabia, and
the mid-Volga, and grew into a population of over two million by the
1897 census.[11]

While the settling of open tracts of land led gradually to steps to
restrict immigration to rural areas, by the late nineteenth century the
regime was encouraging a new wave of immigrants to come to urban
and industrial areas. This immigration included managers, foremen,
white-collar workers, skilled and unskilled workers, tradesmen, technicians, and small- and large-scale entrepreneurs—and it was crucial to
the empire's modernization strategy. These cross-border migrations

Table 1 Net immigration from selected countries to the Russian Empire, 1828–1915 (in thousands)

Dates of immigration	Germany	Austria-Hungary	Turkey	Persia	China	Other Asian Countries
1828–50	24	13	2	15	–	.17
1851–60	64	43	25	41	–	66
1861–70	271	146	60	26	–	86
1871–80	328	268	53	91	.06	144
1881–90	447	287	33	73	−.02	106
1891–00	78	102	52	173	6	231
1901–10	188	−11	111	194	152	457
1911–15	59	41	58	214	132	404

Source: V. V. Obolenskii, *Mezhdunarodnye i mezhkontinental'nye migratsii v dovoennoi Rossii i SSSR* (Moscow: Ts.S.U. SSSR, 1928).

combined with large-scale internal migrations within the Russian Empire to contribute to a long period of the intermixing of peoples, a general characteristic of most empires during the "long peace" of the nineteenth century (1815–1914), and an important but often overlooked feature of late imperial Russian history.[12] The long peace contributed also to the intermixing of imperial economies, especially during the great internationalization of economic activity in the last decades before World War I, a process in which Russia was deeply involved.[13]

The old dynastic order accommodated to a fair extent the intermixing of domestic and international populations and economies, yet a number of distinct challenges emerged by the late nineteenth century. With the spread of literacy and the kind of social changes that came with industrialization, national movements began to arise among the empire's various ethnic groups. Partial democratization of politics and the relaxation of censorship in 1905 spurred a burst of nationalist activity, publication, and organization among the empire's various nationalities. But unlike the Hapsburg Empire, the Russian monarchy did not decentralize authority along national lines, and certainly did nothing along the lines of the Soviet Union's subsequent creation of institutions which propagated minority cultures.[14] The regime, in fact, consistently opposed all non-Russian expressions of nationalism right up to 1914.[15]

Instead, the monarchy began to embrace ideas of "official nationalism," with varying degrees of enthusiasm, most prominently through policies of Russification during the reigns of the last two tsars. Until the late nineteenth century, Russification primarily aimed to facilitate a more efficient administration, but by the 1880s it turned more sharply toward culturally assimilating minorities to remake the imperial state into a more homogenous, more national state. But the leading recent studies of Russification and of Russian nationalism take pains to point out how limited and contradictory these efforts were in practice.[16] Compromises were often made in education, hiring, language, and other policies. Moreover, the freedoms that came after the 1905 Revolution sharply curtailed Russification among all groups in the empire. Russification was among the most important ways the old regime began to act like a nationalizing state prior to 1914, but its limits point rather to the state's dilemma regarding Russian nationalism. This dilemma was based on the Russian rulers' fundamental conservative distrust of any autonomous form of nationalism—including Russian nationalism—insofar as any radically nationalizing program could profoundly undermine the imperial state and the legitimacy of its elites.[17]

Many of Russia's civilian officials retained this uneasy attitude during the early period of World War I. But they quickly came under serious pressure from two directions: public opinion and the army. The first chapter will examine the various slogans and ideas surrounding a nascent Russian nationalist movement that arose during the war to challenge the imperial, "anational" nature of the state, demanding that it be remade along more national lines. Specifically, the program of this movement centered on the idea of the *zasil'e* (dominance) of Germans, foreigners, immigrants, and Jews in imperial elites and in the imperial economy, and it drew upon the classically nationalist idea of emancipating the core nation from its purportedly dependent relation to the world economic system.[18] Its proponents aimed to free Russians (and other trusted core nationalities) from these forms of dominance, and lobbied for strong wartime measures to remake the empire along more national, more Russian lines, either by physically removing dominant minorities or at least by permanently removing their economic and social power over core national groups.

While the war heightened tensions with minorities, severed international economic ties, and encouraged a general shift toward greater economic autarky throughout all countries involved in the war, these trends took on particularly volatile form in relatively backward multiethnic empires. This was particularly true in the Ottoman and Russian empires, where the core nationality resented its lack of control over the imperial state, and where foreigners and minorities played prominent roles in the economic and other elites. Although Russia had much more political and legal control over the position of foreigners than either the Ottoman Empire with its capitulation treaties, or China with its outright spheres of influence for foreign powers, in terms of socio-economic structures and popular perceptions, the situation was comparable. In fact, the campaign against enemy aliens in Russia has much in common with the contemporary campaigns against the prominent roles of Armenian, Greek, and foreign commercial diasporas in the Ottoman Empire, and the "national products movement" against imports and foreigners' role in the Chinese economy.[19] Although most scholars of the role of foreigners and minorities in the Russian economy reject the notion that this role was exploitative, the conviction among many Russians that it was lent much dynamism to the entire campaign against enemy aliens.[20]

The wartime program broke with prewar Russification in that it no longer tried to nationalize individuals by assimilating them. Rather, it took identities as given and tried to nationalize larger abstractions, such as the commercial and industrial economies and the demographic make-up of the population, through the radical means of expropriation and deportation. There are two ways to think about this important transition. One approach, developed by Peter Holquist, draws on Foucault's notion of governmentality to correlate the emergence of a modern set of practices, including surveillance and sciences of statistical description of the population, to the activation of these practices during World War I as an applied science of population management. According to Holquist, such practices—many first developed by European powers outside Europe in colonial warfare and rule—mark a rapid shift toward the consolidation of the modern state, with all its pathologies about the demographic composition of the population and its determination to surveil and control the population.[21] I draw upon this framework to show a shift toward a "demographicization" of nationality disputes that began in the decades prior to World War I and proved to be a significant indicator of the kind of thinking about the population that had become established when the war gave the opportunity to exercise it. But, important as these broad shifts may have been, I put greater stress on the nationalizing practices adopted by the regime and the mobilization of society than on disciplinary foundations of power relationships.

Scholars of the end of the Ottoman, Hapsburg, Soviet, and German continental empires have established that the rise of nationalist ideas and practices among the core ethnic groups in each case proved to be among the most important challenges to the viability of the imperial polity. Thus we know how important Turkish nationalism was to the collapse of the Ottoman Empire, how German and Hungarian nationalisms contributed to the Hapsburg demise, and how central Russian nationalism was to the end of the Soviet Union.[22] This study shows that a type of Russian nationalism played a more important role in the last years of the Russian Empire than most scholarship has granted.[23]

Although the campaign against enemy aliens drew upon a strong kind of Russian nationalist program, the result was not the creation of a Russian nation or sense of national identity but—quite the contrary— the exacerbation of ethnic conflict throughout the empire. In fact, in the course of implementing the nationalizing agenda of the campaign, the state found itself unintentionally fostering what Mark von Hagen has called the "mobilization of ethnicity."[24]

So in one sense, by embracing the campaign against enemy aliens, the imperial state tried in a more radical fashion than ever before to "stretch the tight skin of nation over the gigantic body of empire."[25] But a second somewhat different conception of nationalization is just as central to this study. This draws on Rogers Brubaker, who stresses the role of "fields of practice" in nationality conflict, and suggests that nationalism be seen not so much as the result of long-term developmental trends as an "event" involving the "nullification of complex identities by the terrible categorical simplicity of ascribed nationality."[26] While the "events" central to his argument are the collapses of empires into new states which then strive to become national states, one can treat the experience of total war in a similar way. In this book I take up his call for empirical studies of events which bring the "sudden and pervasive nationalization of public and even private life," and nationality itself "as something that suddenly crystallizes rather than gradually develops, as a contingent, conjuncturally fluctuating and precarious frame of vision and basis for individual and collective action rather than as a relatively stable product of deep developmental trends in economy, polity or culture."[27] Hence this study stresses aspects of what Josh Sanborn calls the "mobilizational event" of total war, an unprecedented mobilization of the economy and the ethnic and political communities that comprise the nation.[28]

To the extent that policies applied to wartime enemy minorities have been touched upon in the secondary literature, the discussion has been largely within the nation-state paradigm, treating the individual histories of the nationalities affected.[29] However, the very nature of the enemy-alien category raises serious questions about this approach. One cannot write a history of the enemy alien in Russia. Like the "refugee," it was a category created suddenly on the outbreak of war.[30] While the most prominent and numerous members of the category were Germans, to write a history of the German minority during the war would not come close to dealing with the breadth and diversity of the nationality issues raised by the enemy-alien problem. The problem is much more one of the state, its practices, and the war as a "nationalizing event" than one of the specific long-term developments in the histories of Germans, Jews, foreigners, and other individual minorities in Russia. Thus the core of the book is organized as a series of studies of nationalizing state practices: the expropriation of landholdings and rural properties, the liquidation of enemy-alien businesses, and forced mass migrations. Focusing on the origins and implementation of these practices, this book investigates the ways in which the state judged and categorized its populations, sorting them into friend and foe, and the state's attempts to nationalize imperial society by manipulating its populations and economy.

1

Nationalist Challenges, Imperial Dilemmas

UPON THE OUTBREAK OF WAR, it appeared that Russia would hold to traditions in international law and its own practice by refraining from actions against civilian enemy aliens on its soil. Following the official declaration of war, an important July 26, 1914, Ministry of Internal Affairs (MVD) circular explicitly stated that "peacefully occupied Austrians and Germans who are outside any suspicion may remain in their places [of residence] and retain the protection of our laws, or they may leave the country."[1] Likewise, *Russkie vedomosti* predicted that the rights of enemy subjects would not be limited, and published Foreign Minister Sazonov's declaration: "in relation to the subjects of foreign governments, who find themselves on hostile territory at the moment of the declaration of war, no measures which would harm the person or property of them is allowed: they have full protection and are protected by the law as in peacetime."[2]

If initial declarations claimed that enemy subjects would be left alone, Russia's first full-scale general mobilization for war was also accompanied by calls to transcend national and social differences to unify the entire citizenry for the common fight. In the manifesto declaring war on Germany on July 19, 1914, Tsar Nicholas II declared: "In the terrible hour of trial, all internal differences will be forgotten and the union of tsar and people will be made even stronger, and Russia, rising like a single person, will boldly strike the enemy."[3] This sentence became a coda in publications and speeches of people with widely different political views.

10

Figure 1. Meeting of the State Duma on 26 July 1914 in support of the war. The meeting became a major symbol of the unification of the country behind the war effort. Source: *Velikaia voina v obrazakh i kartinakh*, vol. 1. By permission of the Houghton Library, Harvard University.

In urban areas throughout the country events on the streets reinforced the sense that internal differences were indeed being forgotten. On July 19, 1914, large crowds gathered in patriotic demonstrations of support throughout the country.[4] In the next few days, zemstvos, village assemblies, clubs, and associations sent telegrams of their dedication to a unified war effort.[5] Across the political spectrum, the press effused about the "historically unprecedented unification of all the peoples of Russia."

On July 26, the State Duma met in a grand ceremonial session. One after another, representatives of the empire's various parties and nationalities went to the podium and, in the name of their constituents, declared their full support for the war. Liudvig Liuts, speaking for the German farming communities, declared that "the hour has come for the Germans to show their loyalty, and that no one in Russia would

Figures 2 and 3. Demonstrations in Petrograd on the outbreak of World War I.
Courtesy of Tsentral'nyi gosudarstvennyi arkhiv kinofotofonodokumentov
Sankt-Peterburga.

be disappointed with their response."[6] N. M. Fridman spoke for the Jews and declared that although "we Jews have lived in exceptionally difficult legal conditions, nonetheless we always felt ourselves to be citizens (*grazhdan'e*) of Russia." Baron Fel'kerzam declared that the Baltic Germans would, as they always had done, discharge their duties in loyal service to the tsar. The leaders of the liberal Constitutional Democratic (Kadet) Party declared the official end of internal political struggle and full support for the government and tsar in the common fight against the external foe. The liberal chairman of the St. Petersburg city Duma, V. D. Kuz'min-Karavaev, enthusiastically declared that "now there are no nationalities, parties, differences of opinion; Russia stands before Germanism like a single person."[7] And the liberal paper *Rech'* triumphantly claimed: "They erred in believing the stupid slander about the incapacity of the Russian intelligentsia and people to display feelings of national patriotism for the defense of the honor and dignity of Russia."[8]

This period of public display of loyalty, dedication to the common struggle against the external enemy, and disavowal of conflict with others in society and with the government created a deep impression. The moment became a potent symbol and reference point in Russian discourse throughout the war, akin in some ways to the Burgfrieden in Germany and the Union Sacrée in France.[9] As Joshua Sanborn has argued, the mobilization for war created a real sense of nation and nationalism that seemed to transcend ethnic difference across the territory of the empire.[10]

The state faced a dilemma, however. It wanted to encourage patriotic public demonstrations and expressions of enthusiasm for the war, but it also wanted to maintain order. On July 22, after the gathering in Palace Square in St. Petersburg, several thousand members of the crowd proceeded to the German Embassy, breaking the windows of stores with German names along the way and destroying a German bookstore and the offices of the *St. Petersburger Zeitung*.[11] At the embassy, a crowd estimated by the police at several tens of thousands broke through a chain of policemen there and ransacked the building. Within two hours, the building and the nearby residence of the ambassador were completely destroyed and in flames.[12] Despite energetic police measures, including bans on further public demonstrations, the following evening a large crowd destroyed four more German stores.[13]

City governor Obolenskii banned all street demonstrations to prevent further violence. After several attacks on stores with German names on July 23 in Moscow, the city governor, A. A. Adrianov, responded quickly with a call for peace and order, declaring that "we should not forget that subjects of countries fighting us, who live among us, enjoy the full protection of the laws of the Russian Empire." He announced specifically that "no violence against foreign subjects who, trusting in the generosity and fairness of the Russian people, continue their peaceful pursuits in our midst, will be tolerated."[14] Even the Minister of Internal Affairs, N. A. Maklakov, widely regarded as a belligerent reactionary, instructed all the city and provincial governors in secret that they should try to maintain the unity of the country and avoid actions which would disturb the internal peace of the empire, including any violations of the person or property of enemy aliens.[15]

Parallel to these civilian events, orders for the mobilization of the army generated more enthusiasm and passed with fewer problems than expected. This too was portrayed as part of the great moment, part of a domestic unification against the external enemy. But the gathering of recruits was also accompanied by riots in a number of towns. In many cases, they were without clear cause or aim, often begun with attacks on local wine or vodka warehouses, followed by wanton drunken destruction.[16] But in a number of cases, most notably in Barnaul, where 20,000 reserve call-ups were temporarily present, the soldiers singled out German and foreign-owned stores and apartments for attack. Seven foreign firms in Barnaul suffered much of the total 200,000 rubles worth of damage.[17] Local authorities, including the army commanders present, could not halt the violence for several hours. When firemen tried to extinguish the fires started by the crowd, they were beaten and kept from the scene. Elsewhere in the empire, when troops stopped at railroad towns on the way to the front, a number of sizable pogroms against Jews and "mobilization riots" broke out and were subdued only with difficulty.[18]

The state's dilemma—whether to support patriotic demonstrations or order—was particularly thorny in non-Russian areas, especially in the Baltic provinces. There public demonstrations were frequent, large, and tense in the first month of the war. Latvians and Estonians turned out for marches and meetings in large numbers, and police noted with alarm that participants often were intensely anti-

German in sentiment, not distinguishing between the external enemy and Germans living in the area. The Latvian and Estonian papers included many articles accusing local Germans of disloyalty and blaming local officials for banning or halting demonstrations. The Russian authorities were not sure how to respond, wanting both to promote the patriotic expressions of the local populations and to avoid the rise of interethnic and social tensions such demonstrations often provoked.[19]

Alarmed by the reports of intense interethnic hostility, the minister of internal affairs sent his top assistant, Vladimir Fedorovich Dzhunkovskii, on a fact-finding mission. His report soberly outlined the dilemma in the Baltic region. During the 1905 Revolution, Dzhunkovskii wrote, the Latvians and Estonians had been largely affiliated with revolutionary parties, and right up to July 1914 they had been treated as the primary threat to state order, while the Baltic German ruling classes had been for the most part considered reliable. The war transformed the situation. Dzhunkovskii reported that the patriotism of the local populations was strong and appeared sincere, although its intense anti-German tenor was cause for concern. He concluded that German elites could not be trusted as before, and measures must be taken to prevent their spying, but that the Russian authorities needed to take a balanced approach, favoring neither side in what was a serious emerging nationality struggle. The priority should be on keeping order.[20]

Both in the Baltic provinces and throughout the empire, in the early stages of the war the government came down quite strongly on the side of order. The attack on the German embassy in Petrograd was energetically subdued by the police and troops in the city, and they successfully blocked a similar procession from reaching the Austrian embassy. Firm measures were taken to prevent future disorders in the capital. Police throughout the country were instructed to maintain order, and most cities reported successful measures to avert anti-German violence.[21]

Yet patriotic demonstrations recurred quite frequently during the first year of the war, and officials were not certain how to deal with them. Large spontaneous work stoppages and street demonstrations broke out to celebrate news of all the major Russian victories at the front in the first six months of the war. Such demonstrations were treated with tolerance or favor by the authorities, and by many employers.[22]

   Thus a pattern of going to the streets in response to news from the front was established, with uneasy police blessing. It applied to losses as well as victories. On October 9, 1914, shortly after news of the fall of Antwerp, a huge patriotic procession initially led by students from Moscow University first went to the Serbian consulate, then to the French consulate to demonstrate solidarity.[23] Later that night, the crowd, estimated at over 10,000, processed through the city, breaking windows of German-owned stores in various parts of town. The Einem confectionary stores owned by German nationals, which had been the object of an extensive press campaign, were among the worst damaged, along with the Mandel and Tsimmerman firms of mixed Russian and German ownership.[24]

   Within a week of the events, Minister of Internal Affairs Maklakov clearly indicated his preference for order over patriotic demonstrations in a letter to Adrianov, sharply reprimanding him for failing to take sufficiently energetic measures to prevent or stop the disorders.[25] Maklakov particularly criticized the Moscow city governor for not cracking down on the activities of the patriotic organization Za Rossiiu (For Russia), which had organized a boycott of German and Austrian firms. "Such activities," Maklakov unequivocally stated, "not only do not correspond to its basic goals—to support the dignity of the Russian state—but on the contrary, by adding to the already excited mood of the population and pushing it to illegal acts, undermine the authority of the government."[26]

   This communication demonstrated the internal affairs minister's preference for order over patriotic demonstration. Because of a later controversy over Adrianov's role in the May 1915 riots against enemy aliens, it is worth noting that Adrianov actually responded quite firmly to the October disturbances, quickly posting a declaration throughout Moscow which unequivocally stated his policy:

   It is with deep indignation that I must say that some people cannot find a more rational way to apply their energies than through
   attacks—under the cover of darkness—on commercial establishments, the owners of which, because of their non-Russian names,
   aroused the hatred of the crowd.
      Remember that the legal authorities of HIS IMPERIAL
   MAJESTY stand in protection of the interests of the motherland,

and the chance person on the street is not allowed to resolve the question of who is good or who is harmful for the state, or to accompany his decision on the spot through violent, illegal acts. It causes particular indignation when the crowd covers its criminal acts with patriotic songs. The national hymn is a prayer, and to combine a prayer with outrages is blasphemy.[27]

The declaration also stated that any individuals participating in further demonstrations would be brought to justice under the full penalties of the law. Thus early in the war, although the government wanted to "unite with the people and encourage patriotic demonstrations," it did not orchestrate or tolerate such actions if they turned violent.

The Army and Popular Violence

Whereas the civilian authorities' stand was initially quite clear in favor of maintaining law and order, the army's was radically different. As early as September 1914, incidents revealed that army commanders tolerated the participation of soldiers in pogroms, looting, and rape of Jews and other local civilian populations in the front zones. Often locals gathered just outside the towns with carts, and began to loot abandoned villages along with the soldiers even as forcibly expelled civilians were leaving the town. The army rarely intervened or punished participants in pogroms of Jews and Germans in areas under its control.[28] Already on August 15, 1914, the Russian governor general of Warsaw, describing a major Jewish pogrom within his jurisdiction that week, warned the Council of Ministers about widespread rumors of a massive impending pogrom.[29] The governor general stated that while he had taken all possible preventive measures, he already believed the local participation could not be controlled, "especially if soldiers participated." Indeed, the army's radicalizing role was by no means limited to areas near the front but extended through the entire empire by means of its mass deportations, much-publicized hunts for enemy-alien spies, and its sequestration and confiscation of property.

The army played such an important role largely because of the law which went into effect on the first day of the war, granting it extremely broad powers in all areas declared under military rule. This meant that all military circulars, declarations, and orders were made obligatory for civilian officials throughout the entire area under military rule, a vast territory including Poland, the Caucasus, Petrograd, the Baltic provinces, Finland, and large parts of Central Asia and Siberia (see Figure 10).[30]

At the highest level, Army Headquarters (Stavka) coordinated civilian affairs. By October 1914, it became clear that the tasks of civilian rule were complex and extensive, and a special section of Army Headquarters was set up to coordinate policies toward civilians (the Military-Political and Civilian Administration of the Commander in Chief). This institution was given a wide scope of powers to direct civilian affairs far behind the front, explicitly and prominently including "the limitation of enemy subjects." The Council of Ministers had no power to overrule Army Headquarters unless it gained the support of the tsar himself to intervene. One of the most important powers over civilians granted to the military was the nearly unlimited authority to deport "suspect individuals" or entire groups without trial. Moreover, the army exercised broad powers to requisition (demand goods or properties with payment) and sequester (take properties for state or army use without formally changing ownership).[31]

The army used its powers to launch a massive campaign against spying that overlapped with the mobilization against enemy aliens and had important repercussions on public discourse and the tenor of domestic politics during the war. Popular and professional concerns with spying had grown rapidly in the decade prior to 1914. Between 1905 and 1914, a large system of counterintelligence centers (*razvedyvatel'nye punkty*) was set up throughout the empire, concentrated in the border areas and western regions.[32] The army was determined not to repeat what it considered an abysmal counterintelligence performance during the Russo-Japanese War, and thus both the army and the police began to collect statistics on the numbers and locations of foreigners in the western borderlands as early as 1910, including information as to whether they owed military service in Germany or Austria.[33] Already in May 1914 a Russian law prepared for war by removing the right of court defense for *suspected* spies.[34]

As international tensions rose in the years preceding 1914, spy fever not only affected military and police practices, but also captured the imagination of societies throughout Europe.[35] But in the Russian case, public concerns with spying really rose to fever pitch only with the out-

Figure 4. Leaders of the Russian Army. From left to right, *top:* General N. V.
Ruzskii, General N. I. Ivanov, General A. A. Brusilov; *bottom:* General Radko
Dmitriev, Commander of General Headquarters General N. N.
Ianushkevich, General P. K. Rennenkampf. Source: *Velikaia voina v obrazakh i
kartinakh*, vol. 1. By permission of the Houghton Library, Harvard
University.

break of war. Stavka commander Nikolai Nikolaevich Ianushkevich ordered that both army and civilian officials should most vigilantly root
out spying among enemy subjects, Russian-subject Germans, and Jews,
and he offered monetary rewards to anyone providing proof of hidden
telephone networks, radio stations, signals, preparation of secret air-
strips, or any suspicious behavior.[36] An official army pamphlet that was
distributed widely among the troops warned that any ethnic German
was a potential spy, and the army press expanded such warnings to include Jews and foreigners in general.[37] The war statute gave military
authorities broad powers to deport individuals on the vaguely defined

grounds of "suspicion of spying." No evidence—not even a military court order—was required for such deportations, and the army made extensive use of these powers.[38]

Ianushkevich himself in many other ways proved to be a major force in the campaigns against spying and enemy aliens. Several members of the Council of Ministers claimed that he was obsessed with the idea of treason, and his actions and his correspondence alike reveal his belief that Jews, Germans, and enemy subjects were all traitors, and that strong prophylactic measures including mass deportation had to be taken against these "internal enemies."[39]

Moreover, Ianushkevich was by no means alone among army leaders in holding such views. In fact, his commander, Grand Duke Nikolai Nikolaevich, shared many of Ianushkevich's priorities and personally supported one of the most aggressive figures in the campaign against espionage and enemy aliens: the commander of the Petrograd Military District, Mikhail Dimitrievich Bonch-Bruevich (later a major figure in the Bolshevik Army and in Soviet military education). Nominally Bonch-Bruevich controlled only the Petrograd area, the Baltic littoral, and Finland. In practice, the Grand Duke secretly gave him informal control over the hunt for spies throughout the empire and ordered him to be his point man in the arrest and deportation of suspect enemy citizens and Russian-Germans.[40]

Not only the army engaged in the hunt for spies. Indeed, spy fever gripped society and was expressed in a flood of articles in the press. Periodic scandals dramatically heightened the mood of distrust toward enemy aliens. Army publications and the press played up stories of treason uncovered among Germans, Jews, Muslims, and others. For example, in late December 1914, *Novoe vremia* published an article claiming that German "colonists" near Akkerman in Southern Bessarabia harbored a landing party of five Turks and Germans dressed as Turks.[41] The article recounted in great detail how the German communities there purportedly hid them and even threw a festive dinner in their honor. The article created a sensation and in response the MVD ordered an investigation. The story turned out to be completely false, and *Novoe vremia* was ordered to print a retraction a month later.[42] During that month, however, the mass deportation of Germans from the western and southern parts of the empire began under clouds of suspicion and accusations of treason spurred in part by the spurious Akkerman Affair.

In April 1915, Colonel Miasoedov was hastily court-martialed and executed as a spy after his case caused a massive press scandal. Several historians who have reexamined the case have concluded that he was almost surely innocent.[43] Nonetheless, the Miasoedov Affair led to a wave of arrests of his associates and others accused of spying. It was but one example of how accusations of spying or treason became a major part of political discourse. Such accusations often focused on prominent individuals with German names. In January 1915, defeats on the Northwest front led to widespread rumors that the head of the tenth army, Sivers, and his chief of staff, Budberg, were guilty of treason, and they were nearly court-martialed.[44] General Rennenkampf was fired after his fall Prussian campaign failed in 1914, and in light of widespread rumors, an official investigation for treason was launched. Although the investigation completely exonerated him, the results were not publicized because public opinion had already condemned him and decided not only that Rennenkampf was a traitor, but also that other members of a "German clique" in the government were protecting him.[45] Rumors and stories of treason and disloyalty became a regular feature on the domestic political landscape. Officials and publicists alike turned the campaign against spying into an attack on entire population categories.

Russian press policies were to some degree responsible for the explosive nature of the spy scandals in particular as well as the more general wave of jingoism and chauvinism. In the first week of the war, the regime shut down nearly the entire range of publications that were critical of the war (mostly socialist periodicals) while subsidizing and encouraging all patriotic papers and articles—even if they openly incited against minority Russian subjects.[46] This said, the role of censorship can be exaggerated. Press campaigns against enemy aliens were common in nearly all belligerent countries—many with much less stringent wartime censorship regimes. In Russia, even the more tolerant and liberal mass circulation papers like *Gazeta kopeika*, whose editor had promoted tolerance, education, and enlightenment of the masses prior to the war, abruptly switched over to a singular focus on convincing his readers of the worthiness of the war and mobilizing the lower classes against the enemy. The main impact of censorship was to make it difficult for those who objected to the measures against enemy aliens to publicly register their opinions.[47]

Liberal and Nationalist Programs and Organizations

While the army and the press challenged the government's initial stand on enemy minorities, political parties and social organizations also posed serious nationalist challenges which they expressed in different ways. One of the most important challenges came from liberals and moderates who interpreted the "end of internal dissension" and the unification of all the peoples of Russia against the common enemy within their own political framework. For the Kadet Party leader Pavel Miliukov, the Russian nation was not defined by ethnicity or religion, but by citizenship.[48] For him and for most liberals, the consolidation and equalization of obligations (military service) and rights for all citizens was central to the concept of the nation at war. Much of the liberal political struggle can be seen as part of an attempt to create a modern citizenry, and many liberals wanted the same thing that the French Revolution and the Jacobins declared as their goal: "to assure equality among citizens and [thereby] to unite the whole nation in enthusiastic loyalty to the republic."[49] Of course, the main problem with this was that Russia was not a republic but a quasi-constitutional monarchy. Because individuals' standing before the law still depended upon their social estate and religion, Russia could not be said to have full citizens or citizenship as yet. But at the beginning of the war, many liberals hoped that the tsar and government would grant more rights and greater scope for public involvement in what was quickly described as a "peoples' war." Indeed, according to the liberal conception, a peoples' war required, if not the establishment of a republic, then at least the consolidation of a sense of citizenship; in other words, the expansion of rights along with obligations. From this world view the war was a struggle between citizenries (or in the Russian case, a citizenry-in-the-making).

This explains why the liberals did not necessarily oppose measures against *enemy citizens*. In fact, ideas of emancipating Russia from German trade and finance were quite popular. As long as such measures did not affect Russian subjects, they could be part of the "healthy Russian nationalism" actively sought by prominent liberal thinkers during the war.[50] Moreover, many Kadets supported measures to remove the privileges of Russian-subject Baltic Germans during the war, as long as they could be seen as moves toward establishing the equal rights and obligations inherent in universal citizenship.[51]

July 1914 became a symbol for the liberals: an idealized moment of possibility for the creation of civic and national unity, consolidation of universal citizenship, establishment of a "nation in arms." Thus liberal support for the government, the war effort, and even for measures against enemy citizens can be seen as conditional upon nationalizing the empire in the sense of consolidating a state based upon the civic nationalism of a bounded citizenry.

The Right

If liberals called for nationalization of the state in the civic nationalist terms of the French Revolution, members of the Right faction in the Duma and extreme Right organizations called for a very different kind of nationalization. Right-wing agitation against Jews, Poles, foreigners, Germans, and other aliens (*inorodtsy*) had a substantial prewar history. The war led to an intensification of such rhetoric; it also transformed the configuration of both domestic and foreign enemies and allies for the Right.

In the years leading up to the war, for example, there had been no strong consensus among right-wing politicians that Germans should be included among the suspect minorities. There was a sense among many on the Right that German farmers were a conservative pillar of autocracy in the countryside, that the Baltic Germans were more loyal and trustworthy than the revolutionary lower-class Estonians, Latvians, and Lithuanians, and that alliance with Germany better fit the conservative and monarchist principles of the Russian Empire than alliance with republican France and democratic Britain.[52] This conservative orientation in foreign affairs was often openly called "pro-German."[53] The rise of tensions with Germany and Austria led many politicians on the Right to move to open hostility against Russia's German populations. Even on the eve of the war, the original orientation still had influential defenders. Characteristically, former Minister of Internal Affairs Petr Durnovo wrote in a prophetic memo to the tsar in February 1914 that a war with Germany would lead to deep social unrest and the fall of the regime. In the memo he claimed that many Germans served the tsar loyally, that unlike other foreigners, they tended to establish permanent residence in Russia and invest in long-term projects, and that hostility against them would only undermine state authority.[54]

Once war broke out, however, such voices were no longer heard. The war created a burst of energy for the Right, and a flurry of new local branches formed during the first week and sent their resolutions to the tsar.[55] Many of them called on tsar and people to fight a vigorous war at home against all internal enemies. If liberals hoped for unity through the establishment of universal citizenship, many on the Right expressed an opposing vision of a smaller national community fusing around a Russian core, and unified in a common struggle against both the external enemy and internal enemies.[56] In the eyes of the Right, the main internal enemies prior to the war had been the Poles and Jews, but Germans quickly joined them and rapidly became the main focus of attention in right-wing declarations and press agitation.[57] For extreme right-wing organizations such as the Union of Russian People and its press organ *Russkoe znamia*, traditional anti-Semitic and anti-Polish themes merged seamlessly with new anti-German themes. Often Germans and Jews were listed as partners in conspiracies of sabotage, financial domination, and spying. Not long into the war, the paper began to stress the theme that the main threats to Russia were internal and denounced Yid, German, Polish, and foreign *zasil'e* (dominance) in the same breath in the context of a wider rejection of the agents of modernity, commerce, middlemen, and the like.[58] A theme on which the leader of the Right faction in the Duma, Aleksei Nikolaevich Khvostov, loved to expound in his speeches was the conspiracy and *zasil'e* of an international oligarchy controlled by Jews and foreigners in banking, finance, and international trade. When he was appointed minister of interior in September 1915, such ideas became the foundation of official policy.[59] The leader of one of the most extreme groups, Aleksandr Dubrovin, expressed his views in a memo to the tsar in May 1915, writing that the main domestic issue had become German dominance. To address it, he argued that the tsar should deport nine-tenths of the Baltic Germans to Iakutia along with the Jews, ban individuals of German origin—regardless of their citizenship—from all forms of state service, confiscate German "colonist" and Baltic German landholdings, and keep all the existing limits on the Jews.[60] The extreme Right Russian Monarchist Union expressed its conception of its role during the war quite succinctly: "the task we 'core Russians' [*korenniki*] face is clear—unite behind the tsar and Orthodox Church, and fight internal enemies."[61] Most remarkable was not that such opinions existed, but that the regime, despite declaring support for the theme of patriotic unification of the populace for the common fight, not only allowed the virulent incitations against minorities to be published, but even supported these groups and their publications with subsidies.[62]

The Russian Nationalist Party

A larger force than the extreme Union of Russian People or the Right faction in the Duma, the Russian Nationalist Party provided a somewhat broader base of active support and focused its campaign more specifically against enemy aliens.[63] Its members joined in the general enthusiasm on the outbreak of war, and "quickly forgot their internal disagreements and their equally profound dissatisfaction with the government" over its failures to take up the party's Russian nationalist program. On July 21, the Russian National Club passed a resolution in favor of ending all internal struggle and joining with government and society against the common external foe.[64]

The Nationalist Party derived the bulk of its support from the southwest, where the primary issue before the war had been the struggle against Polish dominance. Now the empire struggled to gain Polish support in the war, which was largely fought on Polish soil. Deprived of this internal enemy, the party enthusiastically turned to the questions of German and foreign dominance.

While the Nationalist Party supported all parts of the campaign, it focused its efforts on the issue of German colonist landholdings, which were quite extensive in the southwest. It was an issue which had appealed to the party before the war as a way to increase Russian and Ukrainian peasant landholdings without sacrificing gentry lands.

In their writings and speeches, Nationalists often condemned the state as unable and unwilling to take up a truly Russian national cause and thus unable to implement a full-scale fight against alien dominance. According to a Nationalist Party publication, the government would fail in this task because "arbitrary elements in our so-called 'Russian' (but in reality Teutonic) bureaucracy are ready to wipe out any traces of useful nationalism in our country."[65] In a general sense, the Right and Nationalists presented the government with a serious challenge—to transform itself into a nationalist government presiding over a state purged of alien influences. The challenge was presented in a volatile and emotional tone, and frequently implied that if the state failed, it would be nothing less than a matter of treason.

BUT THE REAL driving force of the campaign against enemy aliens did not come so much from the traditional monarchist Right or Russian National factions and organizations as from a broad press campaign and popular movement that gained prominent supporters from a wide range of the political spectrum, from the far Right to moderate liberals. While the far Right mixed agitation against Jews, socialists, liberals, Poles, and others with its agitation against enemy aliens, this broader movement focused on the largest and most influential subset of the enemy-alien category: the various ethnic Germans living within the empire. More than any other aspect of the mobilization against enemy aliens, it was the "internal German threat" which captured the public imagination and created the greatest volume of discussion.

Boris Suvorin, editor of the influential mass circulation conservative paper *Novoe vremia*, set the tone for the press campaign, conducted under the slogan "fight against German dominance" (*bor'ba s nemetskim zasil'em*). His editorial scorned the idea that any distinction should be made between German subjects and Russian subjects, and proposed that Germans be removed from any responsible post or management position, "even if they have been here for one hundred years."[66] During the first months of the war, *Novoe vremia* averaged nearly two articles per day on the issue of Germans living in the empire, and its campaign continued throughout the war. A flood of articles accused the internal Germans of spying, settling on lands according to a purported German colonization plan, grabbing all the most desirable positions in the economy, repressing Russian workers, and sympathizing with the enemy.

The turn of *Novoe vremia* against the "internal Germans" and its sharp criticism of the government on the issue reflects well what David

Costello has called the "conservative dilemma" of the paper, and one might add, of the regime. By embracing a Russian nationalist agenda on enemy aliens and other issues, *Novoe vremia* implicitly—and at times explicitly—directly challenged the legitimacy of the imperial monarchy. The editors were well aware of this dilemma before 1914, and often very self-consciously reined in its Russian nationalist writers. With the outbreak of war, however, the paper threw its full support behind the campaign against enemy aliens and often sharply criticized the government for any show of restraint in its anti-alien measures.[67]

Nationalist Challenges to the Imperial Economy

The most coherent and powerful set of Russian nationalist challenges to the imperial state came from proponents of the idea of making the economy less cosmopolitan, more national, more Russian. The most active proponents of such ideas came from Russian business circles, especially the Moscow Merchant Society, which had long espoused an economic nationalist program with a strong pro-Russian flavor. While its agitation to promote Russian business and Russian entrepreneurs against foreigners in the prewar decades had met with little official sympathy or support, the war suddenly transformed the situation by lending emotionally powerful patriotic arguments.[68] Already in the immediate prewar years, during the Balkan crises, the Moscow Merchant Society had used the foreign situation to promote its domestic program. In 1913, it subsidized the publication of a comprehensive list of all Austrian and German subjects and immigrants who had become Russian subjects three or fewer generations earlier along with a call to boycott their businesses.[69]

The Moscow Merchant Society energetically renewed its boycott of Austrian and German firms shortly after the declaration of war in 1914, and records of its organization indicate substantial public interest and participation.[70] The organization composed a declaration of measures for the "fight against German dominance" to create a "truly Russian economy," and sent it to other merchant organizations throughout the empire and to soldiers at the front.[71] It corresponded extensively with other merchant groups and helped them organize similar boycotts in Nizhnii Novgorod, Kostroma, Yaroslavl', and other cities.[72] These boycotts were not against imports (with the outbreak of war, direct imports from Germany were cut off), but rather against domestically produced goods, most produced by Russian subjects of German descent. The Moscow commercial and industrial groups also promoted the "fight against German dominance" by funding the publication of pamphlets and periodicals devoted to the issue.[73]

On the national political scene, the Progressist Party, which drew much of its core support from Russian entrepreneurs in Moscow, consistently and vociferously promoted the campaign. Shortly after the war began, a prominent member of this party, M. V. Chelnokov, the mayor of Moscow, led a personal crusade with strong support in the Moscow press against the Electric Company of 1886, the city's major provider of electricity. He maintained that it was controlled by Germans and should be transferred to municipal authorities.[74]

It is important to note that the Moscow Merchants and Progressists by no means limited themselves to Moscow and economic issues, but quite consciously framed their arguments for the emancipation of Russia from German and alien dominance as arguments on behalf of the entire Russian nation. With this in mind, they took an active interest in the progress of measures against enemy aliens throughout the country and in all spheres—landholding, Baltic questions, culture, and education. But German dominance in the economic sphere was clearly their central concern, and support for this aspect of the campaign tended to broaden as the war continued. For example, in September 1914, the leader of the moderate Octobrist Party, Aleksandr Ivanovich Guchkov, opposed the boycott of German goods "just because they are German." By May 1915, however, he and his party had become largely convinced of the need for a full-scale fight against economic German dominance and fully supported the boycott.[75]

The economic nationalist program of the Moscow Merchant Society found particularly strong support from a number of public organizations which arose during the war. The most active of the new organizations was the Society of 1914: For the Fight against German Dominance, which was founded in December 1914 and grew from its Petrograd base to become a fairly large organization, with 6,000 active members in nineteen chapters around the country by 1916.[76]

Several of its founders were members of the moderate parties, including its first chairman, the Progressist Duma member Mikhail Aleksandrovich Karaulov, and it quite insistently differentiated itself from the far Right, renouncing policies of pogroms and violence. The Society of 1914 included many small- to middle-scale businessmen and concentrated on the economic aspects of the campaign against German dominance. By no means did it limit itself to economic issues, however, and committees were formed to work on all aspects of the campaign, including trade and industry, consumer concerns, education, and landholding. Its founding charter outlined its goals broadly as "furthering the self-reliant development of productive and creative forces of Russia, its knowledge and enlightenment, and emancipation of Russian spiritual and social life, industry, and trade from German dominance."[77]

The society primarily engaged in lobbying and propaganda. It subsidized publications and public lectures to raise consciousness about German dominance and, along with propagandizing and lobbying on large national questions, it investigated and publicized quite specific local issues. For example, one local chapter devoted an entire meeting to the discussion of a local church's purchase of candles from an ethnic German supplier.[78] The organization's publications contain many bitter condemnations of the government for its "anational" approach and reluctance to fully take up its program.[79] The government, in turn, for the first year of the war kept a cautious distance from the organization. The police refused to allow it to post recruiting posters in Petrograd and was especially angry at its publication of attacks on individuals with German names in the state administration.[80]

According to its first-year report, the Society of 1914 spent much time in its meetings discussing the issue of "state nationalism." It saw the war as a chance for the government at last to take up an explicitly Russian economic nationalist program, which would permanently remove enemy aliens and promote Russians, most importantly, the proprietors of small- and middle-sized businesses. Its form of economic nationalism had much in common with that of the Moscow Merchants. Both claimed that Russia had become a colony of German and foreign finance and that a comprehensive campaign was necessary to create an independent Russia.[81] Most fundamentally, it proceeded from the assumption that the world economic system reproduced inequality among states, and that the Russian state needed to break with the system in order to emancipate its own productive energies. Thus it presented the war as an opportunity to achieve a long-term goal, and the program ultimately meant to reduce the role of all foreigners (not just the Germans), substitute domestic production for imports, and create a self-reliant, strong national state.

This program presented a major challenge to the old regime. It represented the most coherent and dynamic Russian nationalist program to emerge in late imperial Russia, and its underlying ideas appealed to many across the spectrum of Russian politics. Although economic resentments played a role in campaigns against aliens in Britain, France, and other nation-states, these forces never rose to the level of importance they took in the Russian case. As in the Turkish nationalist mobilization against "alien" Armenian, Greek, and foreign commercial diasporas, and the Chinese national movement's campaigns against foreigners and foreign products, a core nationalist challenge to an imperial status quo drew much power from the sense that the international economy and multiethnic domestic economy left the core nation exploited and in need of emancipation. These underlying sentiments created a tense atmosphere forecasting the storm that burst in May 1915 on the streets of Moscow.

2

The Moscow Riots

DESPITE STRONG PRESSURE from the public and the army, the government had many reasons to stay cautious about embracing the campaign against enemy aliens—including its potential for economic disruption, for undermining domestic unity, and for fostering national conflict. An outburst of popular violence against enemy aliens in Moscow in May 1915 dramatically demonstrated that the campaign could lead to a complete breakdown of order. Although the almost universal reading of the May riots both at the time and by scholars since then has been that the government cynically manipulated popular opinion and even instigated the riots, a closer look at the events reveals that government officials were acutely aware of the dilemma they faced throughout the crisis and saw the potential for the situation to slip completely out of control into a wider collapse of state authority.

EARLY IN THE AFTERNOON of May 26, 1915, about a hundred women, mostly wives and widows of rank-and-file soldiers, gathered on Tver' Street outside the headquarters of the Committee of the Grand Duchess Elizaveta Fedorovna; it was their weekly routine to receive there sewing work to do at home for the army. This time, the responsible official told them that there would be no work given out on that day owing to lack of material. Some burst into tears, and others began to shout at the official, claiming that the German Grand Duchess had given all the orders to the German sewing firm, Mandl'.[1] The crowd quickly grew to several hundred, and the frightened clerk locked himself inside the building. Several in the crowd suggested breaking in, but at that moment the police arrived on the scene and calmed the crowd by suggesting they go to the newly appointed military governor Feliks Feliksovich Iusupov's office to make a complaint. Iusupov—the head of the wealthiest family in Russia, father of Rasputin's assassin, and one of the most vocal proponents of a radical campaign against enemy aliens—received them personally and assured them he would investigate. With this the crowd dispersed.[2]

In another part of Moscow, also in the afternoon, workers at the Giubner printing factory went on strike, declaring they would not return until the administration fired all Alsatian employees.[3] (At the request of the French Embassy, all natives of Alsace-Lorraine had been declared under French protection and exempted from most deportation orders affecting enemy subjects.)[4] The entire workforce of 1,500 went on strike, demanding the firing of all Germans, enemy subjects, and Alsatians from the factory.[5] At 6:00 P.M., they gathered outside the factory with national flags, portraits of the tsar, and, alternating between singing the national hymn and shouting "down with the Germans," proceeded to the nearby Prokhorov munitions factory, where tensions were high as a result of a recent explosion and outbreak of cholera. Gendarme reports cite rumors common at the factory and among workers throughout the city that the explosion was the work of German saboteurs and the cholera outbreak had been caused by German poisoning of the factory's water supply. The Giubner workers tried to break into the factory to get the Prokhorov workers to join their procession, but were blocked by police. Within an hour, the crowd had dispersed, and the day's events came to a close.[6]

On the morning of May 27, the Giubner workers gathered again with flags and portraits and processed toward the Prokhorov factory. Joined by the workers of the Riabov factory, they instead turned toward the Tsindel' factory. There they demanded to be allowed into the plant to check if there were any German employees who had not yet been deported. Manager Karlsen, a Russian subject of Swedish origin, refused to let them in, but workers forced open the gate, broke into the factory, destroyed everything, and beat Karlsen badly. Then they carried him to the river and threw him in, to the shouts of "beat the German" from a large crowd gathered there. Soon the crowd began to throw stones at Karlsen and at the handful of police trying to get between him and the crowd. Two policemen dragged Karlsen to a nearby sailboat and pushed it off shore in an attempt to save him. But despite the pleas of the police chief, the crowd continued to throw stones until the boat filled with water, Karlsen fell into the river, and drowned.[7]

Meanwhile, a part of the original crowd went to the Zhako and Co. shoe polish factory and destroyed much of it, along with the apartments of the two directors, both French citizens absent at the time because they were fighting in the French army. Four workers of German origin were seized by the crowd, but police managed to save them by pretending to arrest them and take them off to prison. Later police used the same method to save the German subject Veber, owner of a wool mill and the Vinter steel works. He, his wife, and a foreman were beaten nearly to death before the police could intervene. Mounted police arrested sixty-three rioters, and used whips to hold back a crowd throwing stones at them.[8]

At the Shrader factory, the director, Robert Shrader, was severely beaten before the police, led by the Moscow chief of police, could surround him and drag him away, declaring that they would "take him to the station." At the station, a crowd tore him away from the police and kicked him violently. Mounted police again used whips to disperse the crowd.[9]

Meanwhile the crowd broke into the apartment of Ianson, the managing director of the Shrader firm (who was not there because he had already been interned as a German subject) and into the neighboring apartment of Betti Engels, where Ianson's wife Emiliia, his sister Konkordiia (a Dutch subject), and his aunt Emiliia Shtolle (a German subject) had all sought refuge. The workers threw Betti and Konkordiia into a drainage canal and drowned them. Emiliia Ianson was beaten to death on the spot, and the seventy-year-old Emiliia Shtolle died from injuries later in the hospital. The apartment was set on fire; when firemen arrived they were driven away from the scene, and police were beaten back when they tried to retrieve the corpses.[10]

That evening, Adrianov toured the worst-hit areas, ordered mounted police to disperse crowds with whips, and went to Iusupov's home for a meeting with the commander of the Moscow Military District, Oboleshev, Governor Murav'ev, Vice-governor Ustinov, and Procurator Tver'skii. Adrianov reported that a "patriotic mood" prevailed, and that it was still possible to calm the crowds with words. He called it an "ordinary street disorder which is now ending," claimed that the incidents of the day would not expand into more general disorders, and asserted that firm administrative measures against enemy aliens would satisfy the population. After the meeting, Adrianov sent out an order to fire all German employees from all factories in the city, and strengthened police forces in all factory regions. He remained reluctant to use bullets to stop demonstrations if they were "patriotic."[11]

No more incidents occurred that evening; however, early the next morning (May 28), crowds began to gather in the industrial region across the Moscow River from the Kremlin. Workers from many different factories joined the crowd, which processed toward the bridge to Red Square, again with flags and portraits of the tsar, singing the national hymn, gathering workers from factories, and destroying German firms and apartments along the way. Workers and youth from all parts of Moscow began to congregate in Red Square. By 2:00 P.M. Red Square had completely filled with people. Then the real mêlée began.[12]

The first stores attacked were the same ones that had been targeted in the initial anti-alien riots in October 1914—the Einem candy stores and Tsindel' retail outlets. But within an hour, not only German, but any stores with foreign names were under attack. By 5:00 P.M. the entire center of town was engulfed in chaos. Russian stores were looted along with foreign stores. The rioting quickly spread to other parts of Moscow, and by 7:00 P.M. all of Moscow was under siege. Stores and apartments were set afire after being thoroughly looted. An improvised market quickly appeared on Red Square, where one could buy Faberge eggs and Mozer gold watches for 5 rubles apiece. Carts and wagons full of loot openly moved through the streets. Stolen Moscow goods appeared the next day in neighboring villages and in cities as far away as Riazan' and Tula. The riot continued through the evening.[13]

At 11:00 P.M. the Moscow City Duma demanded that Adrianov and Iusupov appear to explain why the police were not acting. They reluctantly complied, and the packed and tense hall resounded with angry speeches during the midnight meeting.[14] The liberal Moscow mayor, Chelnokov, opened with a blistering attack on the government and police for their inactivity, and, he insinuated, approval of the pogrom. Iusupov certainly did little to dispel this notion when he launched into one of his usual tirades on German dominance and Petersburg's obstruction of his efforts to combat it, stating that he "could not undo ten months' inactivity in ten days."

Adrianov refused to speak, but his assistant, Sevenard, delivered a devastating and revealing statement. He openly claimed that the police were too few and could be easily routed if they were to intervene. Moreover, he declared that the troops of the Moscow garrison were unreliable and could very well join the rioters if ordered onto the streets. Hearing this, the commander of the garrison, Oboleshev, rose and indignantly declared that he would not stand for such libel on his troops, that the troops were reliable and had been ready to intervene for some time, but he had not yet received a request from the civilian authorities.[15]

This declaration proved decisive, along with another report delivered to Adrianov and Iusupov on the steps of the building, as they were leaving: the chief of the fire department reported that there were uncontrolled fires in thirty parts of Moscow. At this moment, Adrianov and Iusupov reportedly gave orders for the police to shoot and called in the troops of the Moscow garrison. It took several hours to plan and begin deployment. Meanwhile, the rioting continued through the night. On the morning of the 29th, troops appeared throughout the city and in three places shot into the crowd.[16] Calm soon returned to the city center, but in areas where troops did not appear, rioting continued until evening. Newspaper reports of arson and attacks on dachas and estates in the countryside near Moscow continued to appear as late as June 5.

The rioters killed at least eight civilians and seriously injured forty more.[17] When the troops intervened on May 29, at least seven soldiers were killed and an unknown number of casualties resulted when troops fired into groups of rioters. Although a few earlier Jewish pogroms had higher death tolls, the monetary damages were probably greater than in any other pogrom in Russian history, mainly because so many stores and factories were ransacked along with private apartments.[18] The Moscow fire chief reported that over 300 firms had been burned plus dozens of apartments, private homes, estates, and dachas.[19] A conservative estimate would put the total damages suffered by enemy subjects at roughly 40 million rubles.[20] But what made the pogrom such a widely deplored event shortly after it occurred was the fact that many Russian subjects suffered damages as well. At least 579 Russian subjects (most of non-Russian descent) suffered losses estimated at over 32 million rubles.[21]

Lines of Conflict

In the only study of the riot to date, Iu. I. Kir'ianov comprehensively refutes the usual Soviet line that workers were not involved, providing abundant evidence of the predominant role of workers in the violence.[22] According to the testimony of many eyewitnesses, these workers included unusually large numbers of women and adolescents. Drafting for military service had removed many male workers from Moscow and led to a massive influx of women and youth into the labor force. The proportion of women among industrial workers rose from 27 percent in 1914 to 43 percent in 1917.[23] Issues of military service and exemption created many tensions in the workplace, and moral-patriotic hostility over these issues could run high, especially when enemy aliens, exempted from service on account of their foreign citizenship, remained as bosses over women whose husbands were fighting at the front.[24]

Workers directed much of the violence and looting along class lines—against managers, owners, technicians, and foremen.[25] Yet it is also apparent that enemy-alien categories had influence and often trumped class. On May 26, workers specifically sought out Alsatian and German managers and employees. When the main pogrom began at 2:00 P.M. on the 27th, in the first few hours groups typically went to businesses and asked for documents from the owners. Those who could prove their Russian subjecthood were often spared. If the documents were not in order, the crowd would systematically loot the store or apartment. Several police reported success in guarding businesses by convincing crowds that the managers of the given firm were not enemy subjects, but full Russian subjects. One policeman was praised for successfully defending a store all day by explaining to periodically appearing bands of looters that the owner was a Pole, and that "the Poles are now our allies."[26]

Even if people were not quite sure which nationalities were or were not enemy aliens, they had absorbed the general ethos stressing loyalty and dividing the populace into two halves. For example, one witness testified that a group went from store to store carrying a portrait of

Kaiser Wilhelm. The group would pull people with foreign names out of offices, stores, and apartments and force them to spit on the portrait. Any who refused were beaten and their property destroyed. Similarly, potential targets devised their own demonstrations of loyalty. German and foreign store owners put flags and busts of the tsar in the windows. One desperate shopkeeper stood in the doorway holding a bust of Nicholas II on the 28th, singing "God Save the Tsar" every time a crowd appeared. Despite his heavy German accent, he avoided damage to his store all day.[27]

The official investigation team heard extensive testimony to the importance of enemy-alien categories in the violence. Participants in the worker processions carried lists with the addresses of enemy subjects. These lists had been compiled by the Moscow Merchant Society as part of its campaign for a boycott of enemy aliens, including naturalized immigrants up to the third generation. Witnesses testified that this gave the riot a purposeful (*ideinii*) character. The patriotic symbolism and targeted nature of destruction make it difficult to assert that the events were completely unfocused. Moreover, in the early stages, the crowds reportedly destroyed property rather than looted for personal gain, in some cases even forcibly taking items away from looters and destroying them on the street. The damage statistics provide perhaps the most convincing evidence that the events remained largely focused on enemy aliens (in the broadest of definitions). Only 90 Russian subjects with Russian names suffered losses out of 735 registered damage claims.[28]

Symbolic Meaning and the Role of the State

In addition to the material damage, the riot took on ideological importance as it became a powerful symbol and focus of contention in political discourse. That the pogrom became an uncontrollable melée affecting Russians along with aliens was crucial, for it raised larger questions about the possibility of a total breakdown of domestic order. Liberals and conservatives alike raised the specter of the *Pugachevshchina*, the uncontrollable, undirected violence of the dark masses, and Pushkin's words—"*Ne privedi Bog videt' russkii bunt, bezsmyslennyi i bezposhchadnyi!* [God forbid that one should experience the Russian riot, pointless and merciless]"—appeared as an epigraph for several articles and speeches.[29] Conservatives and police officials tended to present the revolutionary 1905 version of this image, while liberals stressed the established interpretive paradigm of the Jewish pogroms, which posited that the government inspired, passively allowed, or actively encouraged pogroms.[30] In either case, if it were true that the government participated, then this would be a damning indictment of its course. Letters intercepted by the military censors were full of comments that the riot had been akin to a full-scale war or revolution.[31] In the aftermath, the industrialist A. I. Putilov mused that "the days of tsardom are numbered . . . it [the fall of the regime] is only waiting for a favorable opportunity. Such an opportunity will come with a military defeat . . . a riot in Moscow."[32]

The assumption of state complicity was shared across the political spectrum. Liberals, moderates, and conservatives alike all blamed the government. As the prominent liberal Kadet Party member Fedor Rodichev declared in the Duma, "if the government did not want the pogrom, then it would not have occurred."[33] The liberal Moscow Duma officially declared that the pogrom had been "prepared and organized in advance," and that the authorities were to blame.[34]

But was the Moscow pogrom a creation of government officials? The accusation that the state was responsible for the pogrom rested largely on the actions of the most powerful figure in Moscow, the *gradonachal'nik* (city governor) Adrianov. His actions during the pogrom were indeed suspicious. He failed to order preventative measures on the 26th and failed to order police to intervene vigorously at the Shrader factory on the 27th. Moreover, *Vestnik Evropy* claimed that he passively watched the pogrom in progress and in one instance was even seen leading a group down a street. When the crowd stopped in front of one store, Adrianov reportedly said to the crowd, "he's not German. He's a Russian, let's go further." *Vestnik Evropy* indignantly commented that such words implied that if the owner were German, then it would be acceptable to the chief authority in Moscow to loot and destroy.[35] No orders were given to use troops or weapons to halt the violence until midnight of May 28–29; by then enormous destruction had already occurred, and the riot was already entering its third day. When this order was finally given, it was widely portrayed as a response to pressure from the Moscow City Duma. In articles and speeches, all this was presented as proof that the government had planned and participated in the pogrom.[36]

How could the top police official in the second-largest city of the empire have failed so signally to keep domestic order? The answer in the press was straightforward: Adrianov sympathized with the pogrom. In support of this assertion, many papers quoted the testimony of industrialist Nikolai I. Prokhorov. Upon hearing that workers from the Giubner factory were marching toward his plant, he called Adrianov at noon on May 27 and said "in the name of God . . . stop the crowd!" Prokhorov claimed that Adrianov replied that "according to my information, the crowd is peaceful, and when a crowd processes with portraits of the tsar and sings 'God Save the Tsar' and 'Lord, Save Your People'," then "I am not prepared to shoot into it or break it up."[37]

Adrianov's actions quickly became the primary focus of an official investigation, undertaken not only to calm public opinion, but also in response to the demands of several indignant ministers. Minister of Trade and Industry Shakhovskoi wrote angry letters to Maklakov and the Council of Ministers demanding a clear public declaration from the MVD that private property would be protected, with an explicit statement that any remaining enemy subjects would be protected on an equal standing with Russian subjects. Besieged by letters of protest from neutral and allied countries demanding compensation for their citizens, Minister of Foreign Affairs Sazonov likewise demanded a similar public statement. Already on May 29, Assistant Minister of Internal Affairs Dzhunkovskii was sent to Moscow to investigate, and within days, another leading MVD official, N. P. Kharlamov, joined him with two assistants. By June 10, realizing that an internal MVD investigation of its own actions would satisfy no one, the investigation was transferred to the widely respected Senator Krasheninnikov. He was given broad investigative powers, and his team worked independently of the ministries.[38]

On June 4, before the investigations had gotten under way, Adrianov was fired, and the following day Maklakov was forced to resign.[39] Suspicions mounted that state officials had been involved in the pogrom. While it is likely that Maklakov was forced from office for other reasons, his removal was widely interpreted as tacit admission that the Minister of Internal Affairs had conspired in the events.[40]

The investigation lasted several months and was held under conditions of great secrecy. Not even all the members of the Council of Ministers gained access to the final report.[41] The secrecy led the public to speculate, and thereby contributed to the idea that the government had sanctioned the riots.

To Shoot, or Not to Shoot?

The investigation concluded in favor of indicting Adrianov and Sevenard for dereliction of duty and failure to suppress the riots more quickly. But the evidence marshaled against these officials was quite different from the popular perception that leading officials had organized or at least been complicit with the rioters.[42] The first conclusion of the investigation was that not only Adrianov, but the MVD as a whole had, months before the riot, developed a general policy banning the use of firearms to subdue crowds, and allowed the use of whips (*nagaiki*) or other forms of force only in the most extreme instances. The policy was explicitly spread through the MVD by a series of circulars during an outbreak of demonstrations and riots against price increases in April 1915.[43] "Excess use of force by police" had been among the leading causes of public street demonstrations, both before the war and during its first nine months, and the ban on shooting aimed to reduce such conflicts.[44]

This policy helps explain the peculiar actions of Adrianov and the police during the pogrom. Deprived of the right to shoot—which the crowd sensed and probably knew—the police quickly lost control. The police were, however, far from totally inactive. Some were fairly successful at using their wits. A common technique was to announce that the managers and German employees at a store or factory under siege were being placed under arrest, then hustle them off to the safety of the station. Other police protected some stores from rioters by explaining that the owner or manager was Russian. The police were also not averse to using force within the established constraints. Adrianov authorized the use of whips and all levels of force (up to but not including shooting), and police often attempted to intervene. These attempts actually often ended in violent attacks on the police. Sixty-eight policemen were seriously injured during the riots before the order to shoot into the crowds.[45]

Adrianov himself appears to have been convinced that he, Iusupov, and other top officials could defuse the situation through persuasion, by convincing the crowd that they themselves would get rid of the enemy subjects and Germans through deportations and police arrests. This is what motivated him to drive around town and appear in the streets with the crowds, not—as many claimed—because he was the leader of the riot.

But why was he so reluctant to allow shooting? To fire into crowds of civilians, mostly women, adolescents, and widows with relatives at the front, was probably rightly seen by Adrianov as an extremely grave and politically risky step. Yet once mayhem broke out around 2:00 P.M. on the 28th, Adrianov's approach began to appear increasingly inappropriate. By evening it was clear that the city was engulfed in chaos, in conditions witnesses described as approximating civil war, and still Adrianov did not order his police to fire and declined Oboleshev's offer to send in the troops. Adrianov's reply, according to Oboleshev, provides some insight: the city governor exclaimed with emotion that he was "no novice in these affairs," and that he had successfully put down several uprisings during 1905. Adrianov firmly believed that if the police fired into the crowds, the conflict would explode into a full-scale rebellion or even revolution.[46] He also knew that the Moscow garrison was full of fresh, barely trained soldiers, and that many soldiers on leave were participating in the looting. He was far from certain that the troops would obey an order to fire into the crowds. Letters from soldiers in the garrison intercepted by the censor confirm that his fears were hardly paranoiac on this score.[47] It is no wonder then that the official report was kept as a highly guarded secret. It revealed not a strong state orchestrating a pogrom, but a weak state unable to control the streets, gripped with fear that the situation would spin out of control into general chaos or revolution.

Although the dilemma Adrianov faced was real and difficult, the government was quick to condemn his failure to fire into the crowds. Yet the dilemma did not disappear. The policy of banning the use of weapons against civilians was abandoned shortly after the pogrom, and already on June 3, twelve demonstrating workers were shot dead and fifty injured in Kostroma.[48] The shooting became a major scandal in the press and is still noted by scholars as a crucial event in the return of strikes after they had nearly stopped at the beginning of the war.[49] Hesitating to shoot, especially into crowds with large numbers of women and adolescents, appears to be far from unreasonable in retrospect. Moreover, it is questionable whether police or even the army could have quelled the disorders at their peak on the 28th. Riots were occurring throughout the city, and estimates of the number of participants range in the tens of thousands. Individual groups of rioters numbered from dozens to hundreds, while the police force was smaller than in peacetime due to call-ups to the front.[50]

Another factor may have been important in explaining Adrianov's hesitation to shoot and the alacrity with which he was fired. This was his reputation within the bureaucracy as a *zakonshchik* (law-abider), as a follower of Stolypin who believed in the rule of law and good relations with social organizations and moderate parties.[51] His reluctance to shoot was in good part based on this philosophy, which earned him the enmity of many on the Right and within the bureaucracy as weak and unwilling to use force to solve social problems. All this reveals quite a different form of cover-up from the one practically everyone in society assumed. The authorities did not organize the pogrom. Instead, the regime aimed to cover up the government's paralysis, fear, and real sense that it lacked enough reliable troops, police, and authority to keep Moscow from a complete collapse into anarchy and, perhaps, revolution.

Causes of the Riot

If the riot was not planned by the government, then what caused it? A number of factors may account for its outbreak. First, there were several immediate causes. The riots coincided with the much-publicized approach of a June 1 deadline for the liquidation of commercial and trade firms owned by enemy subjects. There may have been a sense that their property was unprotected and up for grabs. Another coincidence was the birthday of the tsarina, widely viewed as German in origin and sympathies. The Grand Duchess Elizaveta Fedorovna was intensely disliked; people believed she was of German origin, and this played an important role on the first day of events.[52]

Prince Feliks Feliksovich Iusupov was assigned to Moscow only 10 days before the riots as a military governor (*glavnonachal'stvuiushchii nad Moskvoi*), but the parameters of his authority were unclear. Although Moscow was not under military rule at the time, he was a member of the tsar's entourage, had high social standing within Moscow's elite, and exercised much informal influence in local affairs. His campaign of virulent public speeches on German dominance in Moscow included visits to factories where he asked workers to give him lists of suspect Germans and enemy subjects.[53] He conducted a large campaign of deportations of enemy subjects during the week leading up to the riots, releasing lists of names of the deportees to the press. *Moskovskie vedomosti* and *Novoe vremia* provocatively printed them daily. While there is little evidence to suggest that he directly approved a pogrom or helped organize it, he certainly lent legitimacy and prominence to the issue of German dominance in Moscow.[54]

The press and propaganda campaigns for vigilance against German spies and saboteurs encouraged a flurry of rumors. For example, Moscow gendarmes reported widespread rumors that Germans in the army command had sold out to Germany, and that Germans in Moscow were preparing a massive sabotage campaign.[55] An explosion at a munitions plant and at the Gatchina railroad were rumored to be the first signs of this broader campaign. Rumors likewise attributed a Moscow cholera outbreak to German employees poisoning the water.[56]

While all these specifically Russian conditions provide a number of immediate causes, a comparative perspective shows that the events were also driven by universal factors common to all powers. Here, the link between events at the front and anti-alien sentiment at home appears to have been crucial. After a string of frustrating losses, Przemysl came under siege, and the Russian retreat hit one of its worst points in late May. Germans began to use asphyxiating gas only a month before the riots, and on May 12, U-boats sank the passenger ship *Lusitania*, spurring massive anti-German riots in London and other cities throughout Britain.[57] Although there could be no question of sympathetic police attitudes in Britain, the British riots also raged for three days, and were almost identical in scale to the riots in Russia shortly thereafter. Smaller-scale anti-alien incidents were reported around the globe, usually coinciding with bad news from the front. For example, the outbreak of anti-alien riots in Britain, France, and Russia all coincided with the fall of Antwerp on October 10, 1914. The Moscow riot itself came on the heels of important military losses at Przemysl, L'vov, and Libava.

Figure 5. After the Moscow riot, the destruction at the firm Gergard i Gei.
    Courtesy of Rossiiskii gosudarstvennyi istoricheskii arkhiv (RGIA, f. 23,
    op. 28, d. 525, l. 19ob).

While all these factors help explain the outbreak of the riots, their
duration and extreme destructiveness can also be attributed to the dynamic of the events once they got underway. As studies of prewar Jewish pogroms have shown, the simple motive of loot could become decisive once order broke down. Likewise, by all accounts, a key moment in
the May riots was the breaking into several liquor warehouses—an extremely important factor given wartime prohibition. A number of letters intercepted by the censor, such as one written by a young man to
his friend Motia, illustrate how important these motives became for
some once order collapsed:

> On 28 May there was a pogrom of German stores here. Then, the
> poor became rich! Everyone carried away all they could manage.
> Many took stuff straight off in carts. Petushka and I went to Il'inka
> Street to the Vil'borna store and drank ourselves silly. We carried
> a lot home and also sold 25 rubles' worth. Mostly we drank and
> made off with cognac. We arrived home at seven in the morning
> stone drunk; with torn suits and without our caps. We rested a bit,
> sobered up and went to [the store] "Robert Kents." There we
> made off with a lot of stuff, but they took it all away since after

Figure 6. Empty vodka barrels from the warehouse of Gergard i Gei. Courtesy of
Rossiiskii gosudarstvennyi istoricheskii arkhiv (RGIA, f. 23, op. 28, d. 525, l.
21ob).

seven that morning there was an order to arrest and detain those
carrying stolen loot. Many were arrested and there were a lot injured and killed—drank themselves to death—and a few simply
sobered up in the barrels because they were drinking straight from
the barrel. That was some party! Like never before, almost all
Moscow was drunk.[58]

Several major alcohol storage facilities were broken into, and police reports indicate that the crowds became much more destructive and less

Figure 7. Another view of broken machinery and rubble at Gergard i Gei.
    Courtesy of Rossiiskii gosudarstvennyi istoricheskii arkhiv (RGIA, f. 23,
    op. 28, d. 525, l. 21).

discerning in their targets once the vodka began to flow. Witnesses
testified that by the evening of May 28, bodies of passed-out revelers
littered the streets.

A spokesman of a typical firm, the wholesalers Gergard i Gei, described the events to later investigators as follows: "At 4:00 on May 28,
a large crowd came, broke the windows and openly looted for four
hours. Items too heavy to carry were destroyed, and a fire then destroyed most everything else. By 9:00 P.M. all that remained were un-
conscious drunks who lay in the courtyard for a full day afterward."[59]

Consequences

Other than hangovers and thriving markets in stolen goods, the riots
produced important repercussions on the further course of enemy-
alien politics. While many liberals used the pogrom to denounce the
government's promotion of the campaign against Russian-subject enemy aliens, other influential figures claimed it was an unfortunate—but
understandable—expression of frustration from a populace that wanted

a more aggressive campaign against enemy aliens. One of the most in-fluential representatives of this view was Feliks Iusupov. Even during the riots, he blamed the excesses on the government's lax policies to-ward enemy subjects. In his speech before the City Duma late on the 28th of May, while the pogrom was raging, he claimed that the failure to deport all enemy aliens in the nine months before his appoint-ment had raised understandable alarm in society. Papers quoted him as promising workers that the state would resolve "the matter close to the hearts of the people of Moscow," that is, closing enemy-subject busi-nesses and firing all enemy subjects and "undesirable" Russian subjects of alien origin. Immediately following the riots, he provided the press with copies of his order to the police to arrest any enemy subjects found illegally residing in Moscow. He declared that all such individu-als would be imprisoned for three months, and intensified the deporta-tion of other enemy subjects from the city, ordering the internment of individuals who had been exempted for one reason or another in previ-ous sweeps.[60]

Most of the various proponents of the fight against German domi-nance supported this line of interpretation, that the best way to pre-vent riots was to act more strongly against enemy aliens, and they bitterly attacked the government for its inaction. Even some liberals, like the Progressist Party member and mayor of Moscow, Chelnokov, claimed that the government's soft line on enemy-subject-owned firms led to the pogrom. Moderate and liberal industrialist leaders, including Guchkov and Konovalov, expressed fears that further disorders could fatally undermine economic production and called for the deportation of remaining enemy subjects as a preventive measure.[61]

This interpretation quickly proved to have important repercussions on official policy. Iusupov comprehensively outlined the case for an ex-tension of extreme measures against enemy aliens in a report on the ri-ots to the Council of Ministers and the tsar. Citing several examples, he argued that Moscow authorities had been thwarted for months in their attempts to deport Germans by a flood of individual and categorical ex-emptions granted by Petrograd authorities. He claimed the MVD's wa-vering insulted the patriotic sensibilities of the population, and pro-posed "deporting all Germans, including Russian subjects, to special concentration camps for the duration of the war."[62]

Rather than reprove him for what several members of the Council of

Ministers privately regarded as demagogic and irresponsible attack—
not only directed against Russian subjects, but also against the government itself—the Grand Duke and tsar, both of whom held Iusupov in
their confidence, called a meeting to discuss his report. On June 14,
1915, the tsar presided over a special meeting at army headquarters
with the Grand Duke, all the major army commanders, and the entire
Council of Ministers. It was the first such gathering of all the country's
top leaders during the war, and the enemy-alien issue was the main
item on the agenda.

On the basis of Iusupov's report, the conference resolved, with the
tsar's immediate approval:[63]

1. To stop all acceptance of enemy subjects into Russian
   subjecthood, including subjects of neutral countries who
   entered Russian subjecthood after the declaration of war. To
   allow exemptions only under extraordinary circumstances, and
   only with the approval of the tsar in each individual case.
2. To deport enemy subjects, regardless of their sex or age, from
   their places of residence—most importantly from Moscow—to
   destinations determined by the Minister of Internal Affairs.
3. To apply the second measure with [case-by-case] exceptions for
   enemy subjects of Slavic, French or Italian origin, or for Turkish
   subjects of Christian faith—holding these individuals under
   close surveillance. To deport those whose presence in a given
   location is considered harmful to public safety and peace by
   local authorities of the Ministry of Internal Affairs or by the
   Department of Police in Petrograd.
4. Not to suspect of spying nor to consider dangerous for public
   peace all Austrian, Hungarian or German immigrants who
   acquired Russian subjecthood after January 1, 1880; if they are
   considered to be a threat to public peace, they may be deported
   to destinations determined by the Minister of Internal Affairs on
   a case-by-case basis. The destinations shall be chosen so that the
   deportees do not create a threat to public peace in their new
   places of residence.
5. Regarding all foreigners in general: when appropriate, to apply
   general measures of deportation from Russia of undesirable foreigners.

These rules, adopted and signed by the leaders of the three major sources of power—the tsar, army, and government—firmly established principles of deportation even in areas far from the front, and explicitly included naturalized immigrants and foreigners in general.

Points four and five officially recognized what was apparent in the actions of the rioters—that anti-alien suspicions extended beyond the relatively narrow enemy-subject legal category to incorporate more general anti-foreign and anti-immigrant sentiments. Perhaps the most significant change was the closure of the citizenship boundary. Russia was the only major power to ban naturalization of enemy subjects during the war. This ban led to the rejection of many clearly deserving cases and reflected a deeper problem, namely, that Russia lacked a strong sense of citizenship as a fundamental marker of national belonging. It also set the stage for liberal anger that the regime was including members of the Russian citizenry in its definition of enemy alien.

Another direct impact of the pogrom was its potential cost to the government in terms of compensation to the victims, and perhaps even more important, the loss of confidence among foreign lenders and investors in the Russian government's commitment to protecting foreign interests. In response to intense diplomatic pressure from neutral countries whose citizens had suffered losses, and domestic pressure from Russian businessmen who wanted a clear message sent that private property would be protected, the government reluctantly accepted the principle of compensation and set up a committee under the Ministry of Finance to adjudicate the claims of individuals and businesses. While the Ministry of Finance supported compensation, the Ministry of Interior, especially under A. N. Khvostov, did all it could to impede its work.[64] Ultimately, only a fraction of the claims were recognized and almost no payments actually made.[65]

But it was not the number of rubles that mattered the most. More important was the impact of the riot on both public and official attitudes. Rather than moderate policies, the riots seemed to intensify the belief of the tsar and regime that they needed to accommodate popular demands with a much more aggressive program against aliens. This interpretation was similar to the dynamic in other countries, where official measures to register and intern enemy subjects, sequester their properties, or other similar measures followed mass riots. This dynamic was most clear in Britain, which experienced remarkably similar riots in May 1915.[66] But for liberals and moderates, the notion that the government was to blame for the pogrom only added to their growing conviction that the government stood in the way of the unification of the people for the common effort against the external enemy.

Popular Anti-alien Manifestations after the Riots

Was the Moscow pogrom merely an isolated incident or did it express a widespread phenomenon of longer duration and significant public support during the war? A major problem in determining the answer is the way police officials at the time and later historians categorized strikes and protests. Strikes wholly or in part motivated by demands to fire enemy-alien managers and workers were not separately counted, and appeared only under general categories such as "other."[67] Yet there is plenty of evidence that tensions with alien personnel were an important part of social conflict throughout the war. From the pogrom until the February Revolution and beyond, local administrators and the MVD were deeply concerned by monthly reports from gendarmes on the mood of the population—many of which claimed that anti-German, anti-foreign, and anti-Jewish tensions were so high that pogroms and other anti-alien violence could erupt nearly anywhere in the empire.[68]

Strikes demanding only the removal of enemy-alien personnel were reported throughout the empire. The experience of the Khar'kov steam engine plant was common. Already in August 1914, 783 workers there struck, demanding the firing of a porter, master engineer, metalworker, and shop foreman because they were enemy subjects.[69] The four were fired on the spot, and the workers returned to work. When news of the Moscow pogrom arrived at the plant ten months later, tensions once again rose against other German-subject workers still present, and things did not calm down until they were all deported in early June 1915.[70] Factory inspectors and police throughout the country reported many similar incidents. Most were spontaneous, spurred either by news from the front or the actions of a German or foreign manager or foreman.

In some cases, press campaigns and agitation by workers or patriotic organizations preceded open conflicts. The Society of 1914 accepted complaints from workers and Russian personnel about very specific cases of individual Germans in factories and local administrations. The Society researched these cases, informed the press, and published a series of pamphlets attacking specific individuals. Gendarmes and factory inspectors reported that secret worker meetings calling for action against enemy aliens in the workplace were frequent.[71]

Such agitation particularly drew the attention of the police in the wake of the Moscow pogrom. Tensions remained high in Moscow for several weeks. Censors intercepted a number of letters such as one dated June 15, 1915, in which Zina A. wrote to Ivan Andreev that "there is much talk of the killing of Germans and Lutherans in the next week. The army will not move against them [the potential perpetrators] because they sympathize."[72] The police also reported secret worker meetings planning to renew the riots, including concrete plans to kill generals and police if the authorities tried to intervene.[73]

Strikes demanding the removal of Germans from factories and minor incidents were reported throughout the country in the weeks following the pogrom. At the factory of Eduard Shtolle, partly destroyed in the pogrom, all 250 workers signed a petition to fire the two remaining workers with German names.[74] Both were Russian subjects—one since 1862, and the other was descended from an immigrant who became a Russian subject in 1711. The two were fired in order to prevent a threatened strike. Although the director, Iulii Shtolle, was a full Russian subject, the MVD feared a renewal of violence there two weeks after the Moscow pogrom. In a letter to the Council of Ministers requesting liquidation of the firm even though it formally did not fall under existing laws, the MVD cited a gendarme report on a student who convinced all the riders of a bus that Shtolle was German and if there were further losses at the front, they should demonstrate at his factory. Later, the Committee for the Fight against German Dominance resolved that Shtolle ought to be fired in the interests of preserving public order, even though he did not fall under existing laws.[75]

The tension was by no means limited to Moscow. In Ekaterinoslav, gendarmes uncovered a movement to chase "Germans" out of a Russo-Belgian metal works. A series of anonymous denunciations claimed that Director Shliupp was "covering up his spying for the Germans with his Swiss citizenship." In addition, the gendarmes confiscated a "declaration of workers' parties" distributed among the workers which stated:

Brothers, it is time to drive the Germans from the factory—both Shliupp and all the others. Shliupp himself is an evil spy harmful both to Russia and to us workers . . . Brothers, we need to demand that no German be allowed here, even if we have to write to the Supreme Commander Nikolai Nikolaevich. The engineer doesn't pay any attention to us. It is clear that he is in league with the Germans. He pays no attention to the workers' complaints. Brothers, they are beating our brothers at the front, and they are beating us within Russia. Enough.[76]

In Kazan', anti-alien agitation became so intense that the governor ordered the temporary closure of all enemy-alien and German-owned stores.[77] There, in Kiev, and in other cities, rumors spread of a coming massive anti-German and anti-Jewish pogrom.[78] Gendarme reports from Petrograd throughout the summer noted that enemy aliens were blamed for every fire or explosion in factories.[79] The chief of gendarmes in Samara reported that throughout the city workers were gathering petitions for the removal of all enemy-alien managers and foremen, threatening strikes and violence if the petition were not honored. The Samara governor responded by ordering the firing of several employees and increasing police presence in the city with 140 extra police. But he feared that he could do little to keep the peace in the countryside, where tensions with German farmers and deportees were extremely high. The Arkhangel'sk governor only narrowly averted a major pogrom against foreigners and Germans through some aggressive arrests.[80]

Despite firm police action, there was a major riot in Astrakhan on 9–10 September, which included the looting of several large German-owned stores. Arrests of over a hundred people helped to subdue the riots, but they still could not be suppressed for two days.[81] Gendarme reports through the rest of 1915 and well into 1916 strongly suggest that without aggressive police measures, the summer of 1915 and beyond would have been filled with scenes similar to that in Moscow.[82]

The largely successful deterrence of riots and pogroms, however, also involved a good deal of preventive firings and deportations of enemy subjects. In part these were ordered by local authorities. But most often, private employers fired aliens in response to pressure from workers. It is therefore difficult to measure its extent, but it is clear that a large-scale popular purge of aliens spread through the country. All kinds of voluntary and professional organizations passed resolutions barring enemy-subject membership and expelling current enemy-subject members. For example, in early 1915, theater and music groups around the country swept out individuals of German origin.[83] Worker strike demands for the firing of enemy aliens were often met immediately.[84] In September 1915, even before Bulgaria officially entered the war, employers throughout Russia, especially in Ukraine, fired Bulgarians in such large numbers that the government repeatedly had to declare that such firings were unwarranted.[85]

Through 1915 and 1916 rumors and tensions continued to focus on Russian subjects with German names in positions of power, not only in business, but also in the army, government, and court.[86] But the firing of prominent individuals with German names often was perceived only as a confirmation of the rumors of German treason in high places. For example, in Moscow, a month before the riot, Colonel A. Modl' was attacked on the streets during a price riot and stoned by the crowd with cries "beat the German" (he was actually of French descent). Rather than issue a public statement condemning the action of the crowd, Modl' and another top assistant to the city governor were fired, with the explanation that it was impossible to have top police officials who lacked public respect because of their foreign names.[87] A witness claimed that during the Moscow riot there was much indignation about the "German" Vladimir K. Sabler holding the office of Procurator of the Holy Synod, and a large demonstration outside his Moscow offices demanded his removal.[88] In a number of provinces, governors ousted individuals with German names from their administrations, and officials with foreign names throughout the country came under often intense public pressure.[89] Typical was the case of Emil Shtempel, who had worked for the Ministry of Justice as a mid-level legal expert for ten years and presented letters from many of his superiors attesting to his value to the Moscow procuracy, yet his firing was not overturned by the Minister of Justice on account of his former German subjecthood (he had become a Russian subject in 1881).[90]

Both police and liberal politicians became concerned that the official campaign against German dominance was creating a "pogrom atmosphere," not only in factories and cities, but also among soldiers and peasants. Reports that the mood was filtering into army ranks caused

particular alarm. Gendarmes expressed concern that soldiers responded positively to the Moscow pogrom. For example, soldier K. I.
Vogan wrote that "when soldiers read about the Moscow riots, they
said 'thank god, finally the people are supporting us'."[91] In June 1915,
soldiers from the 177th Battalion in Novgorod reportedly expressed
great dissatisfaction with German spies allowed to stay in Russia. According to a gendarme report, they were saying in private meetings
that "a pogrom of Germans would occur in Petrograd any day. As the
troops were on the side of the pogromists, it would spread to all the cities of the empire." At one meeting, the soldiers resolved to shoot the
commander of the garrison and the governor if they ordered the soldiers to quell the planned pogrom in Novgorod.[92]

THE MOSCOW RIOTS starkly illustrated some of the dilemmas and tensions facing the government during the war. Total war required an unprecedented mobilization of the country's forces and raised the stakes
and immediacy of demands to make the imperial state more national.
But the Moscow pogrom showed how volatile and destabilizing a patriotic campaign against enemy aliens could be, and it raised the specter
of the collapse of the imperial state into uncontrollable national and social violence. Some officials understood the dilemma and urged re-
straining the campaign against enemy aliens, but most of those who did
were purged from the high ranks of the government by the fall of 1915,
and replaced with officials who promoted an all-out campaign.

3

Nationalizing the Commercial and Industrial Economy

MUCH OF THE POPULAR mobilization against enemy aliens focused on the crucial role foreigners and minorities played in the modernizing imperial economy. Because enemy aliens—especially Germans—accounted for such a large part of all direct foreign participation in the imperial economy and a significant proportion of all advanced economic activity in the empire, the campaign against them had extremely broad implications. Although the government at first acted cautiously, it eventually endorsed and began to implement an economic nationalist program that intended to emancipate Russia and the state from German and foreign domination, going beyond temporary restrictions toward a permanent reduction of the German and foreign roles in imperial economic life. The campaign shows how the old regime deeply undermined principles protecting private property and the rule of law, and exacerbated social tensions along class and national lines in its wartime attempt to forge a more national Russian economy.

Foreigners and Russian-subject Minorities in the Imperial Economy

To understand the stakes and popular resonance of the wartime campaign against enemy aliens in the economic sphere, a brief overview of the role of foreigners and Russian-subject minorities in the modernizing imperial economy is necessary. The industrialization of the Russian

55

Empire in the late nineteenth and early twentieth centuries was driven by a massive influx of foreign entrepreneurs, technicians, workers, and capital. Most scholarship on the foreign role has focused on the quantity of foreign capital, which was remarkable. Between 1893 and 1914, foreign investment accounted for approximately half of all new capital formation in industrial corporations, and in 1914 foreigners held at least 40 percent of the total nominal capital of corporations operating in Russia.[1] Among Russia's World War I enemies, Germany accounted for the largest portion of foreign capital (20 percent of all direct foreign investment in 1914). In 1914 there were 29 corporations with 38.5 million rubles capital, and another 256 nonstock firms with 42 million rubles capital, which were founded under German law and owned entirely by German subjects.[2] Austrian subjects, though numerous, were less prominent and brought less investment capital. Ottoman and Bulgarian roles in advanced economic activity were nearly insignificant. Thus wartime hostility focused predominantly upon Germans.

The quantity of foreign investment alone does not capture the full extent of the non-Russian role in advanced economic activity. Both foreign and Russian firms hired many foreigners, predominantly Germans, in managerial, administrative, and technical positions. Thus statistics on purely German-owned firms greatly underestimate the degree to which Germans and other non-Russians were an integral part of the Russian economic system. A few statistical highlights can give a sense of the multiethnic and international composition of the economic elite. Roughly a tenth of all founders of corporations in the Russian Empire during the century up to World War I were foreign citizens.[3] At the turn of the century, nearly a third of all technicians in Russian industry and a tenth of all administrative personnel were foreign subjects.[4] In addition, Russian subjects of German, Jewish, and Polish descent made up respectively 20, 11, and 11 percent of all founders of corporations (1896–1900. Russian-subject Germans and foreign subjects each comprised a proportion of corporate founders and managers which exceeded their proportion in the population as a whole by a factor of more than twelve. Russian founders and managers, by contrast, represented only 75 percent of their proportion in the population, and Ukrainians only 9 percent.[5] Data from a 1903 survey of managers in smaller but more numerous unincorporated enterprises reveal a similar pattern, indicating that 9 percent of 16,400 such managers were foreigners.[6]

Soviet scholars from the 1920s until the 1960s generally argued that imperial Russia was in a relation of colonial dependence upon the West.[7] But several Western scholars—and, since the 1960s, a number of Soviet scholars—have made a strong case to counter this interpretation. First, while foreigners played a large role in the Russian economy, Russian exceptionalism can easily be exaggerated. The long period of relative peace from 1815 to 1914 helped create the conditions for a historically unprecedented cross-border flow of trade, capital, and people. Nearly every major industrializing society in the nineteenth century made similarly extensive use of foreign sources of capital, entrepreneurship, and managerial and technical expertise. The foreign role in Russian industrialization does not appear so extraordinary when compared with the foreign role in French, German, Austrian, American, Australian, and Canadian industrialization drives in the nineteenth century.

Indeed, optimistic contemporaries and recent scholars have argued that Russia was already on the path toward the same "nativization" of foreigners and foreign firms that was so apparent in all the above countries as their industrialization entered a mature stage. Optimists saw no reason to think that the large foreign role in Russia created conditions of dominance, but rather that it enabled faster industrial growth, which in the end would make Russia stronger and more independent. In 1913, one such economist wrote that the Russian situation differed sharply from that in European colonies. In Russia, "the nationalization process of import industrialism began and continued more quickly than elsewhere. Hand in hand with this, although not so easily and quickly, began the nationalization of large capital itself, the naturalization and further also the denationalization, that is, the assimilation of foreign personnel in Russia."[8]

The same author used the example of the German firm Fitzner and Gamper to illustrate how this process typically occurred, showing that the percentage of foreign personnel in the administration had declined from 81 percent at its founding in 1880 to only 9 percent by 1898. The lack of case studies of foreign firms in Russia makes it hard to assert confidently that this was a universal process, but studies of foreign firms by several scholars have shown that many of the leading foreign firms displayed similar patterns of replacing foreign personnel and managers with Russians.[9] Thomas Owen's database of Russian corporations suggests that these case studies were typical of a general trend in the decade prior to the war. His data show a sharp relative decline in the share of foreigners among corporate managers from over 10 percent in 1905 to under 6 percent in 1914.[10] To be sure, much of this statistical "replacement" was a result of foreign subjects' naturalization. But the preponderance of evidence suggests that naturalization involved more than simply acquiring a new passport. Foreigners, especially Germans, tended to assimilate quickly into Russian society. A recent study of St. Petersburg, the area with the largest number of German and foreign entrepreneurs and businesses, supports this finding, suggesting that imperial Russian culture exerted a powerful assimilationist influence upon both foreigners and Russian-subject Germans. The author found that rates of naturalization, Russian language acquisition, and cultural assimilation among these business communities were very high.[11]

Some sectors of Russian society promoted tolerance of foreigners, immigrants, and non-Russians in the economy, and defended the cosmopolitan economic system as a whole even well into the war. For example, the influential main organization of Russian entrepreneurs in the relatively cosmopolitan Petrograd region, the Association of Industry and Trade (AIT), strongly supported free trade and opposed restrictions on non-Russian economic activity within the empire throughout the war.[12] In a memo to the minister of trade and industry, the AIT argued that while it was true that Germany pursued a conscious policy of capital export in order to penetrate foreign countries for political purposes, and that German nationals acquired 147 million rubles in Russian shares from 1904 to 1914, its plans to subjugate Russia were failures. German capital only strengthened the ruble and Russian state power by increasing its productive capacity.[13]

Observers such as Peter Struve pointed out that the only way to become a modern great power and retain the empire was to find a liberal constitutional means to define a citizenry that would incorporate immigrants and alien individuals into full citizenship. According to one observer, constitutional Russia was successfully moving in this direction. In his view, foreigners "were already throwing off their foreign citizenship, becoming an integral part of the new liberal Russian civil society." Moreover, foreigners' contributions to the growth of the Russian economy were helping it to become stronger and more independent in its relationship to more advanced economies.[14]

While such views existed in 1914, they were opposed by strong countervailing official and popular attitudes whose origins dated back to the beginnings of the industrialization drive. The Ministry of Internal Affairs led official opposition to the Ministry of Finance and its industrialization strategy throughout the late nineteenth and early twentieth centuries.[15] The MVD and the government imposed a series of economic restrictions on foreigners and certain minorities, at times styling themselves in patriarchal fashion as protectors of the peasantry against the intrusions of foreigners, modern capitalist development, and the corrupting influences of alien middlemen, moneylenders, and tavern keepers. Playing to purported peasant ideas that commerce and trade were unproductive activities which exploited the peasant, many MVD officials portrayed the abstract forces of commerce and modern economic development as embodied in the persons of the Jews and others engaged in exploitative trades. Here official policy fused with popular anti–Semitism and xenophobic rhetoric, and provided an important backdrop to the pogrom waves of the 1880s, expulsions of Jews from Moscow and Petersburg in the 1890s, and the pogroms and violence of the 1905 Revolution. Despite restrictions on Jewish enterprises and quotas on the entry of Jews into universities, the number of Jews entering economic and professional elites continued to rise.[16] Officials increasingly became concerned about the prominent commercial role not only of Jews, but also of other non-Russians. For example, the MVD began to keep detailed statistics by nationality on the number of employees in banks and corporations during the decade prior to the war. MVD officials pointed with alarm to the northwest region, where Germans held 26 percent, Jews 35 percent, Poles 19 percent, and Russians only 8 percent of all such positions, and pressed for further restrictions to change the balance there and elsewhere in the empire.[17] The conflict between the world views of the Ministry of Interior and Ministry of Finance continued right up to 1914.

Although the Council of Ministers and the tsar more often than not supported the Ministry of Finance, a constant tension continued to exist within the government between the proponents of modernization and the "police view." The result was a series of rules which left foreigners and certain minorities in a precarious position. The very principles of private property and the legal status of the corporation were still very much under contention in 1914—not only for foreigners and suspect minorities, but for all corporations in the Russian Empire. In business, the most important reflection of this was the concession system of incorporation.[18] The incorporation of a business required a charter with a set of conditions on the firm's operation. These charters often included provisions forbidding firms to hire Jewish, Polish, and/or foreign managers, and excluding these minorities from share ownership. Charters also often stipulated that firms that exceeded specified quotas of Jews, Poles, and/or foreigners among their owners could not acquire real estate.[19] The concession system also had a theoretical-legal aspect of great importance during the war, namely, that both Russian and foreign corporations, rather than becoming juridical entities with legal rights, were granted a conditional privilege to operate in Russia, which the government could withdraw at any time. During the war, the government explicitly used this legal principle to defend its withdrawal of the right of specific firms to operate in Russia.[20]

Such official attitudes and policies found strong popular support from proponents of Russian economic nationalist ideas. Public opposition to the prominence of foreigners in the economy appeared already in the 1860s, when the foreign influx was just getting under way. The reactions of the Russian bourgeoisie varied in the different regions of the empire.[21] Thus the Petersburg and Polish entrepreneurial organizations represented a relatively cosmopolitan outlook favoring free trade and a liberal policy toward foreigners and minorities, while the Moscow and Ural associations were more Russian in membership and outlook. Disputes between these regions raged in the press over issues of state orders, tariffs, railroad construction, and other matters from the 1860s to the end of the regime. In these disputes, the Moscow businessmen in particular often appealed to nationalist arguments, claiming that the state should favor native Russians over foreigners. Slavophile publicists and editors lent their support and developed a fairly coherent ideology of Russian economic nationalism, which they applied to many specific issues.[22] But proponents of Russian economic nationalist ideas rarely succeeded in influencing the government prior to the war. The Ministry of Finance was more interested in using all possible sources of growth to ensure rapid industrialization than in promoting the movement of Russians into the economic elite.[23]

But the idea was a powerful one. If nationalism is treated as an ideology, then the ideas of Russian economic nationalism can be seen as similar to those of nationalism's classic progenitor, Friedrich List, who rejected the cosmopolitan world economic system as inherently exploitative and called for the development of national economies.[24] The Russian economic nationalist program grew in importance as industrialization entered more mature stages after the turn of the century. As Russian entrepreneurs grew in numbers, wealth, and confidence, they increasingly claimed to speak for the nation rather than only their narrow social interests. The war gave them an opportunity to call on the state for support in their economic competition with foreigners and minorities, and to do so in the name of the national interest.

The Development of Wartime Policy

At the outbreak of war, Foreign Minister Sergei Sazonov declared that no measures would be taken against either the person or property of enemy subjects.[25] As Edwin Borchard argues, "probably no rule of international law [and practice] was regarded in 1914 as more firmly established than the rule that private property within the jurisdiction belonging to the citizens of enemy states is inviolable."[26] The Russian Empire followed this principle closely during the wars of the nineteenth century. According to a Russian legal expert on the issue of enemy property, "from 1812 on, none of the Russian wars were accompanied by any limitation of the private rights of enemy nationals."[27] The War Statute of July 28, 1914, gave the army and governors general in areas under martial law the power to requisition and sequester properties of any individual or organization, but did not single out enemy properties. As late as August 23, 1914, the Council of Ministers, responding to (false) rumors that Russian assets in German banks were being confiscated, ruled that

> while admitting the possible application of such emergency measures to money, deposits and securities belonging to enemy nationals, [the Council of Ministers] thinks it important to keep in mind the serious effect which the extensive use of such measures is bound to have upon home industry and commerce. It is hardly necessary to emphasize the fact that, as a result of the peculiar course of our national economic development, up to the present time a large number of the commercial and industrial organiza-

tions of Russia belong to foreigners, among whom the Germans are prominent. Upon these concerns, that is, upon their uninterrupted operation, intimately depend the interests of Russian industrial circles, of the workers employed by them, as well as those of government departments which have been accustomed to place orders with them . . . Under these conditions, one may well apprehend that the seizure of the aforesaid assets, and the consequent loss to these establishments and firms of their operating funds, would lead to their liquidation, or at least to cutbacks in production and failure to meet their obligations. This undoubtedly would have an adverse influence upon economic life and disturb the normal development of commerce and industry.

The Council concluded that it was not in Russia's interests to move against enemy subjects' property within Russia.[28]

This approach was abandoned within months, however, partly in response to the actions of other powers. In a series of measures from August to November 1914, which became known as the Trading with the Enemy Acts, Britain banned transactions with persons residing in enemy states and appointed inspectors who had the power to oversee the financial dealings of firms owned by enemy subjects to ensure that they were not making payments to enemy countries. Most of the other powers followed Britain's lead and imposed similar restrictions, including Russia.[29]

Already by September 1914, Russia began to move away from its original cautious stand on enemy subjects' property. A decree of September 22, 1914, prohibited enemy subjects from acquiring any property or business in lease, ownership, or management.[30] From that date to the end of the war the Russian measures consistently exceeded measures taken by other countries in severity and the permanence of their intentions.[31]

Seizure, Sequestration, and Confiscation

The official campaign against enemy aliens in the economy was driven not only by specific laws, but also by officials using their broad wartime emergency powers. The War Statute granted military authorities in areas under military rule wide powers over these vast territories.

Army powers ranged from requisition, which included payment, to the most extreme measure of confiscation, which brought no compensation whatsoever.[32] Seizure *(arest)* amounted to a freeze on the assets of the firm and a ban on its sale or realization of profits. Sequestration *(sekvestr)* involved the actual transfer of the business or property either to the direct control of a state body (most often the Department of State Properties), to institutions such as the local *zemstvo*, municipality, Red Cross, or to private individuals and businesses. Sequestration differed from outright confiscation only in that it was not legally a permanent transfer of property rights. In theory, the sequestered property would return to its original owner at the end of the war or when the sequestration was lifted.[33] The War Statute granted army officials the authority to use these tools in the broadest of terms, "whenever interests of social order or state security warranted."[34] In addition, the entire empire was declared to be under a state of extraordinary security in August 1914, giving governors throughout the empire similar powers to use sequestration and seizure.

The mass deportation of enemy subjects of military service age during the first weeks of the war left hundreds of small proprietorships without owners. Petitions from the Red Cross and the military first raised the question of transferring these properties for hospital and army use. In response, the MVD issued a circular on August 20, 1914, determining that firms whose owner entered enemy service "or displayed clear hostility toward Russia" should be closed and placed under seizure or sequestration.[35] A sense quickly grew among officials that all enemy-alien property was fair game. Reports of mass confiscations of valuable materials from occupied East Prussia whetted the appetites for enemy-subject property within Russia.[36] For example, Minister of Agriculture Krivoshein followed his requests for confiscated East Prussian agricultural implements and supplies with demands for the sequestration of enemy-subject firms producing seed within Russia.[37]

Prior to the war, property confiscation applied only to individuals convicted of treason. In September 1914 an MVD circular ordered the confiscation of all properties belonging to anyone *suspected* of belonging to a Pan-German organization.[38] This order signaled only the beginning of a wave of confiscation during the fall of 1914. Tens of thousands of individuals deported under "suspicion of spying" often had their properties confiscated even if there was no proof of their guilt.

This gave business competitors and petty opportunists a chance to flourish, as the wife of Fridrikh-Avgust Kail claimed happened to her husband. She claimed in a petition that a boarder in their apartment who owed Kail several months' rent and another man, a business competitor, had both quarreled with her husband and shortly thereafter denounced him to the local military authorities. On the basis of their concocted story about a secret meeting with an Austrian subject, Kail was deported and his business was confiscated and transferred to the Russian business competitor.[39] Russian firms and organizations throughout the country quickly began to petition to take over enemy-alien competitors and firms, adding a dynamic element to the politics of sequestration and confiscation.[40]

In the Baltic provinces, where anti-German sentiment and proximity to the front made for a tense atmosphere, the practices of sequestration were particularly extensive and contentious. A prominent Latvian, V. L. Kerkovius of the Riga Exchange Committee, complained to the MVD in October that the governor had ordered a freeze (*arest*) placed on all enemy-alien property and the police had begun sequestering properties of stores, commercial firms, and individuals. As a result, he claimed that tens of thousands of Russian subjects who worked in the firms or depended upon them were being thrown out of work.[41]

The attacks on enemy-alien property were not limited to areas near the front. Cases occurred deep within the empire, as in Tambov, where the local commander of troops ordered the confiscation of all "foreign eggs" for the use of the army.[42] A broad spectrum of the national press, including several relatively liberal papers, pushed civilian authorities to move to stronger measures of confiscation and sequestration against enemy subjects.[43]

Alarmed by the way official actions were creating a sense that the law no longer protected enemy-alien property and by the emerging "pogrom-like atmosphere regarding alien property," the MVD tried to restrain first the governors, then the army. Beginning in late September 1914, the moderate Assistant Minister of Internal Affairs Dzhunkovskii sent a stream of circulars to governors stating that they did not have the right to sequester enemy-subject property without cause. Chairman of the Council of Ministers Ivan Logginovich Goremykin wrote to Ianushkevich that reports of the mass confiscation of enemy-subject businesses and property in Riga, Pskov, and Vitebsk were creating an undesirable atmosphere toward private property and risked provoking German retaliation against Russian subjects in Germany.[44] As a result, Ianushkevich ordered his subordinates not to confiscate or sequester the businesses and properties of individuals of German nationality "without cause." He claimed in a response to Goremykin that in the future the army would only confiscate businesses and properties of individuals aiding or communicating with the enemy. These interventions checked the growth of orders to confiscate and sequester but did not stop the practices, which continued throughout the war. Only a month after Ianushkevich's commitment to moderation, he returned to an aggressive approach, stating in a letter to Danilov that while confiscation should only be undertaken if there was proof of communication with or assistance to the enemy, it should be applied whenever possible and was preferable to sequestration because it brought full, immediate, and permanent transfer of ownership.[45]

The army also played an active role in initiating actions against firms that ultimately led to liquidation. The Petrograd commercial firm Shvarts, Brandt and Company provides a typical example of the course of events in such cases. It was founded on a Russian charter in 1900 and had eight employees on the outbreak of war (three Russian subjects, four German, and one Austrian). The German co-owners were deported from Petrograd early in the war. The specialization of the firm in the grain trade and reinsurance made the army suspicious that its insurance of Russian ships might give it information valuable to the enemy on the activities of Russian merchant shipping. The commander of the Petrograd Military District ordered the firm searched in the night of November 23–24, 1914. Although nothing suspicious was found, the War Ministry requested the liquidation of the firm. As a result, the Council of Ministers assigned inspectors who immediately formed a liquidation committee on May 10, 1915. The firm was closed and dismantled shortly thereafter.[46]

The army led the way in applying seizure and sequestration even to large firms. For example, in February 1915, military authorities ordered the sequestration of the large and complex corporation providing much of the electricity to Kiev, Dvinsk, and Warsaw, the Obshchestvo Elektricheskikh Predpriiatii v Berline, and five of its subsidiaries with a total capital of 14.1 million rubles.[47] Sequestration often proved to be the first step on the road to permanent liquidation of firms with enemy-alien participation. By transferring temporary control to private individuals, state, or social institutions, sequestration created a strong lobby for permanent retention of the property. The scale of sequestration is hard to determine, but reports from governors indicate that in some areas it was applied quite extensively, especially in areas under military rule, where several governors each sequestered over twenty large businesses and dozens of smaller ones.[48]

Sequestration and confiscation became important new tools in the reshaping of the national economy. They were part of the larger move of the tsarist regime toward radical practices of nationalizing the economy. First, they brought about the *de facto* transfer of many firms and properties to state institutions. Second, they transferred a lesser but substantial number of firms to "reliable" Russian individuals and social institutions. But more important than these extraordinary measures was a set of decrees that created the legal basis for a more systematic campaign against enemy-alien businesses.

State Decrees

The Decree of January 11, 1915

Despite significant apprehension within the Council of Ministers over the potential consequences of a major campaign against enemy aliens in the economic sphere,[49] public and army pressures eventually convinced the government to act. Several members of the Council, led by Minister of Justice Shcheglovitov, by October 1914 began to speak of the war as an opportunity to emancipate Russia from German and foreign dominance. Even the Ministry of Finance, generally considered the most wary of moving toward the liquidation of enemy subjects, came to declare support for some measures, stating that the agitation of workers in factories against enemy-subject owners, managers, and foremen was becoming serious, and the government should not be seen as inactive on the issue.[50]

The first major law was enacted on January 11, 1915, and applied to full and limited partnerships and firms engaged primarily in trade, insurance, or retailing as well as corporations operating under charters issued in enemy countries.[51] The first clause of the law prohibited issuing commercial licenses to enemy subjects or to the representatives of firms incorporated under the laws of enemy countries. This clause affected individuals in a wide range of occupations, including shippers, brokers, notaries, insurance agents, salesmen in commercial houses, and other professionals. It effectively required that all such enemy subjects be fired from their firms. The other clauses required the liquidation of firms owned entirely by enemy subjects, partnerships where one or more of the partners was an enemy subject, and stock corporations determined to be of "enemy nationality" and engaged in the types of activity listed above. At this time, the charter defined the "nationality" of such stock corporations: if a firm was founded in an enemy country under enemy laws, then it was considered to be of enemy nationality, but if it was chartered under Russian law, the firm was considered Russian.[52] This requirement for the time being protected most of the larger industrial corporations with enemy-subject participation, since most of them had been founded under Russian law. Moreover, a paragraph of the decree allowed many of the larger industrial firms chartered under foreign laws to continue operations. Thus, in practice, this decree affected mostly small to medium-sized firms and partnerships, primarily in commerce and the professions.

The liquidation of firms owned entirely by enemy subjects was quite straightforward. The owners had to sell the firm by the deadline of April 1 (later extended to July 1) or face forced liquidation by local authorities. Firms with Russians among the owners were liquidated by a committee of the Russian part-owners, who decided whether to dismantle the firm and buy out the enemy-subject partners or part-owners, according to a complex set of rules which allowed them to pay far less than the current value of their part of the company. The payments could not go to the enemy subject being bought out but instead were sent to special frozen accounts in the State Bank, to be released at the end of the war. In practice, this procedure led to the breakup of prosperous firms and in effect converted the enemy subject's share of the firm into a frozen account. Approximately 3,054 firms were affected by the law. Just over half (1,665) were exempted upon appeal on grounds of the Slavic, French, or Italian ethnicity of the German and Austrian subjects or the Christian faith of Ottoman and Bulgarian subjects. Three-fourths of the remaining firms (1,360) closed voluntarily or changed hands, and the remaining quarter (479) were forced to liquidation by the state under the supervision of state-appointed officials.[53] Most of the firms affected were moderate in size; the average firm affected had 30 workers and a yearly turnover of 100,000 rubles.[54]

Two factors added to the severity of these measures and pushed the campaign against enemy aliens forward. First, a decision of the Ruling

Senate on February 9, 1915 made Russia the only warring power to deprive enemy subjects of the right to appear in court to defend their interests. Thus there was no way for those affected by the laws to challenge them or the specifics of their implementation, opening a broad scope for abuse in their implementation.[55] Second, the implementation of the January 11 law was accompanied by a furious spate of articles in the conservative press demanding more sweeping measures, and at times openly accusing the government of a lack of commitment to the "fight against German dominance." Owing to the complexity of the liquidation procedures, the April 1 deadline was extended to June 1. On the eve of the deadline the Moscow riots against German and foreign businesses broke out, and the government read this as a signal to intensify the campaign against enemy-alien businesses.[56]

The tsar's decision to abandon his moderate ministers in September and October 1915—especially the appointment of A. N. Khvostov to head the Ministry of Internal Affairs—was crucial. Khvostov, formerly the leader of the Right faction in the Duma, was one of the leading proponents of a comprehensive "fight against German dominance," and he was especially insistent that the struggle be carried into the sphere of big business. Believing in an international conspiracy of finance and big business controlled by Jews and Germans, he declared that the government should break the ties with foreign firms that maintained this system. He pressed for the government to move into the tangled sphere of large industrial and financial enterprises, where enemy subjects often owned only portions of Russian firms and where their interests were deeply intertwined with those of Russian subjects and Russian firms.[57] His views found support from all the succeeding chairmen of the Council of Ministers. Of Goremykin's successors, Trepov and Protopopov had served on the Committee for the Fight against German Dominance prior to their promotion, and Shtiurmer, sensitive to criticism of his German name, was also aggressive on the issue.

The Decree of December 17, 1915

This decree expanded the campaign to large industrial firms. Its provisions were similar to those in the January law, except that it did not allow enterprises to avoid liquidation through the withdrawal of enemy subjects from their positions, and did not allow Russians within the firm to conduct the liquidation and reorganization of the firm. This was to be done only by state inspectors, who formed special "liquidation committees" assigned to each firm.

The law also recognized, to a degree, that its inflexible implementation could be disastrous for wartime production. Therefore it allowed exemptions for firms working on defense contracts and for firms which the government had already seized through sequestration.[58] Such exemptions were not guaranteed, but could be granted if officials thought it to be in state interest.[59] In each case of exemption, however, state officials assigned to the firm were not withdrawn, and they continued to oversee all aspects of the firm's operation through a "temporary administration." If the decision was later taken to move to liquidation, the "temporary administration" was transformed into a "liquidation committee."

From the publication of the December 17, 1915, decree right up to the February Revolution, the campaign continued to expand. On January 2, 1916, the previous practice of allowing commercial firms subject to the decree of January 11, 1915, to continue their operations if all enemy subjects withdrew from the enterprise was retroactively reversed. All contracts and agreements between former enemy-subject owners and Russians or subjects of neutral or allied countries were declared void and subject to review by state inspectors. The intention was to uncover cases of "fictive transfer" whereby an enemy-subject former owner made an informal deal with a Russian to act as his front man in order to avoid liquidation.[60]

Liquidation committees were assigned to 460 large industrial firms, and by November 1, 1917, 59 of these firms had been completely liquidated and 75 were in the midst of liquidation proceedings. The Provisional Government did not slow the pace of the liquidations; in fact, the bulk of actual liquidations were completed during its short tenure.[61]

Enemy Shares in Russian Joint-Stock Corporations

The most complex operation of the campaign against enemy subjects in the economy involved the liquidation of their shareholdings in firms founded under Russian law. Press agitation against German dominance focused on large firms. As previously mentioned, the laws of January 11 and December 17 defined the "nationality" of joint-stock companies according to the country in which they were founded. Therefore neither enemy-subject shareholdings in corporations founded under Russian laws nor their holdings in corporations founded under the laws of neutral or allied countries fell under these decrees.

In order to deal with this category of firms, the government enacted a series of measures. First, a decree of July 1, 1915, empowered the Council of Ministers to close joint-stock companies incorporated under Russian law, if their "activities were deemed harmful to public interests." Toward this end, it assigned state inspectors to firms in order to determine the "nationality" of the firm, its stock, and the individuals who held the stock. This ruling fundamentally changed the principle upon which the nationality of a firm was determined. Previously, the laws under which the firm was chartered had defined the nationality of a corporation. Now, the fundamental principle of corporate law, that the corporation is a legal entity distinct from its shareholders and owners, was abandoned altogether for the principle that the corporation was defined by the nationality of its shareholders and managers. The state inspectors were also empowered to manage and oversee the daily operations of firms where enemy-subject participation was suspected, even in the smallest degree.

By the end of 1915, state inspectors had already been assigned to two thousand Russian firms, of which 364 were determined to have substantial enemy-subject participation. During 1916 and 1917 inspectors were assigned to at least another thousand firms, including many of the largest enterprises in Russia.[62] These officials entered deeply into the daily operation and management of these firms. They enjoyed full access and ultimate control over all the firm's financial records and accounts, could demand changes in production and personnel, and acted as the firm's legal representative in any disputes. This new intrusion of the state into the sphere of private enterprise was an important part of the general expansion of the state role in the economy during the war. Furthermore, the press made much of decisions to appoint administrators, portraying them as the first step toward the ultimate liquidation of the firms or enemy-subject involvement in them. Memos and instructions gave a similar impression to the state inspectors, stressing that "they should be vigilant because even relatively small shareholdings in the hands of enemy subjects could serve as a base for their new penetration into Russian industry after the war."[63]

Nevertheless the government was, with good reason, leery of acting to force the alienation of enemy-subject shareholdings. In quantitative terms, this form of enemy-subject involvement made up a major portion of enemy capital in the Russian economy. The Association of Industry and Trade warned that such actions would negatively impact the stock market, disrupt the operations of some of the largest and most important firms in the Russian economy, adversely affect the interests of many Russian shareholders and companies, and, if the state took over the shares, would amount to a massive expansion of the state role in the economy—something the Association staunchly opposed. If enemy subjects were compensated, with their payments frozen in State Bank accounts, then there would be a massive withdrawal of capital from the wartime economy, hardly desirable when all attempts were being made to maximize production.[64] Moreover, both the Association and the Foreign Ministry pointed out that because in many of the firms affected neutral and allied subjects owned substantial amounts of stock, such a law could create serious diplomatic difficulties and eventually damage Russia's postwar attempts to attract foreign investment. If the shares of enemy subjects were not compensated at full value, then the bill of damages during peace negotiations could be enormous.

Despite such arguments, the government went forward with a decree signed by the tsar on February 8, 1917. The law set up a complex procedure whereby shares belonging to enemy subjects were declared void, and identical shares issued in equal amount. The Ministry of Trade and Industry transferred these new shares to new owners, who could include Russian shareholders in the company, the Treasury, municipal authorities, or other state institutions. Enemy subjects were to receive compensation for their shares, but the methods of determining this amount ensured that it would be well below the current market value. The compensation price was set according to the balance sheet approved by the last prewar shareholder meeting. The substantial depreciation of the ruble, inflation, and the general rise in stock prices during the war all drove down the compensation value. In any event, the Committee for the Compulsory Alienation of Enemy Shares, set up under the Ministry of Trade and Industry to oversee implementation of the law, was empowered to reduce the price at its discretion. Moreover, the procedure called for lists of enemy shares to be published in the official journal *Vestnik finansov, promyshlennosti i torgovli*

Table 2 Implementation of the law of February 8, 1917, by industrial sector

Branch of Industry	Share of Stock Owned by Enemy Subjects		
	Founding Capital	in percent	in rubles
1. Metallurgy	56,700,000	11	6,355,050
2. Chemical	56,700,000	11	6,355,050
3. Fibers	88,582,800	16	14,488,200
4. Food Processing	9,207,000	23	2,164,195
5. Oil and Coal	44,200,000	7	3,042,800
6. Machine Tooling	46,892,000	10	5,107,625
7. Electric	65,600,000	17	11,363,000
8. Other	43,085,600	14	6,037,240
TOTAL	374,467,400	14	53,732,320

Source: RGIA, f. 23, op. 27, d. 689, l. 7. The identical figures for the metallurgy and chemical sectors likely indicate an error in the document.

and the owners were given only two weeks thereafter to present their shares. Shares belonging to any enemy subject not meeting the deadline were declared expired without any compensation.[65] Given the large numbers of enemy subjects who had been deported to the Russian interior, expelled from the country, or were abroad, many could not meet the short two-week deadline and therefore lost the full value of their shares. The bulk of shares affected were liquidated under the Provisional Government, which did not alter this or previous laws aimed at enemy subjects in the economy.[66]

Although there was little time to implement the complex procedures to liquidate shares held by enemy subjects, during the Brest-Litovsk negotiations, a balance sheet of liquidations completed prior to the Bolshevik coup indicated that over 50 million rubles of enemy-subject stocks had been liquidated.

To put these numbers in perspective, there were 2.8 billion rubles of total common stock capital in Russian industry in 1914, of which 1.3 billion was in foreign hands. Thus the program affected Russian firms with roughly 13 percent of the total capital in Russian industry, and resulted in the actual liquidation and transfer of roughly 4 percent of all foreign stock investment, or nearly 2 percent of all capital in Russian industry. These results were obtained within a matter of months after the promulgation of the February 1917 law, and represented only a part of the enemy shares due for liquidation under its provisions.[67]

Control and Liquidation

The implementation of the various decrees requiring the liquidation of enemy-subject firms not only resulted in the nationalization of many firms, but also brought about a broader increase in state intervention in the economy through the assignment of state inspectors to enterprises. An entire new branch of the Ministry of Trade and Industry was created to coordinate their oversight and liquidation activities.[68] Hundreds of officials were assigned during the course of the war to over 3,000 firms, the majority of which were founded under Russian law and had substantial—if not majority—Russian ownership and management.[69] The Ministry of Trade and Industry could assign these officials to practically any firm where enemy-subject participation was suspected in management or ownership, even to the smallest degree.[70] Even purely Russian firms were assigned state overseers if the firm was suspected of having close ties through credit or trade relations with enemy subjects or enemy firms.

The Ministry of Trade and Industry pressured the inspectors to accelerate liquidation procedures and overruled many of their protests that liquidation could be detrimental to economic production.[71] The inspectors—often referred to as liquidators once they began liquidation proceedings—also expanded the campaign against enemy subjects to broader categories of aliens in the Russian economy. Their reports show that they paid particularly close attention to the dealings the firms under their oversight had with Jewish firms and creditors, and in some cases required the firing of "unreliable" Russian subjects of Jewish, German, or Polish descent from the management of firms. In the Far East, these officials also became involved in a broad campaign to replace Asian workers with Russians and Slavic POWs.[72]

Inspectors were given vast powers over the firms they oversaw, including the right to make decisions on personnel, finance, and pricing. They could call in the police or military to enforce their decisions if necessary.[73] They were instructed to ban all payments of dividends to enemy subjects and to research Russian buyers of firms to ensure not only that they were not acting on behalf of former enemy subjects, but also that they were reliable from the point of view of state interests. Several inspectors were appointed to larger firms, forming a "temporary administration" which essentially took over the powers of the board of directors and management. Once inspectors and temporary administrations were assigned to such a large number of firms—a significant proportion of all firms active in Russia—the state began to use them to impose increasing regulatory control over economic production. Directives encouraged them to use all available resources to stimulate the highest possible levels of production, keep profits low, and direct production toward state orders. Thus the state inspectors, administrators, and liquidators assigned to firms played an important role in the general trend during the war toward greater state involvement in the economy.[74]

In addition to increasing state controls, the officials added to trends toward nationalizing production by increasing the state role in direct ownership of firms. Once inspectors had been assigned to a firm, state institutions petitioned for its liquidation and nationalization. One of the most contentious liquidations where the state took over part of a corporation involved the Electric Company of 1886. The company, with fifty million rubles in founding capital, had branches in Petrograd, Moscow, Kiev, and Lodz, and was one of the largest suppliers of electricity in each city.[75] Articles in several major papers shortly after the beginning of the war insinuated that the firm was German and should be sequestered or liquidated.[76] The MVD, basing itself on gendarme investigations, claimed that the firm was "undoubtedly German" and appealed to the military to use its powers to establish controls over it. The military obliged, imposing a freeze on the company's assets and accounts in August 1915.[77] The press and the Moscow and Petrograd city dumas then took up the issue, demanding the transfer of the firm to municipal control. The government appointed inspectors to the branches of the company, but, according to Minister of Trade and Industry Shakhovskoi, the Council of Ministers was reluctant to transfer the firm to the municipalities because it mistrusted the motives of its liberal members.[78] Moreover, the inspectors reported that the firm was not, after all, German. It was chartered under Russian law in 1886, and the majority of its shares had been acquired by a Swiss company before the war. The Swiss ambassador energetically defended the rights of the Swiss owners.[79] Only 21 percent of its shares belonged to German subjects. Nearly all enemy-subject employees and managers had been deported in the first months of the war, including the two German subjects among its six directors. The six members of the state inspectorate assigned to the firm unanimously opposed forced alienation of enemy-subject shares for these reasons, along with concerns that the firm would be forced to cease production.[80]

Nonetheless, under intense pressure from the city dumas and both the conservative and liberal press, the Council of Ministers resolved to close the corporation and transfer enemy shareholdings to state control.[81] The actual reorganization was conducted by the Provisional Government under the February 7, 1917, law on the liquidation of enemy shareholdings. In the final arrangement, the municipalities took over two-thirds of the shares formerly belonging to enemy subjects and the Treasury took the remaining third.

State institutions took over a substantial stake in a number of other liquidated firms. With smaller firms, state bodies at times became the full owner, while with large corporations the state typically took over a portion of the shares. For example, when the large Siemens electric companies (Simens Gal'ske and Simens Shukkert) were liquidated in November 1916, the Treasury took over 35 percent of the shares of a consolidated single new firm with 25 million rubles capital.[82] Several other large electric companies with German shareholdings were dealt with in a similar manner. City governments throughout the empire clamored for the right to acquire enemy shares of electric and tram companies—successfully in several cases. For example, Vseobshchaia Kompaniia Elektrichestva (General Electric Company), one of the most important providers of electricity, electric trams, and railroads in Petrograd, Moscow, Ekaterinburg, Samara, Tashkent, Vladivostok, Irkutsk, Tomsk, Khar'kov, Ekaterinoslav, Rostov-on-the-Don, Odessa, Kiev, Pskov, and Baku, was liquidated on July 1, 1917. The treasury took over 35 percent of its 24 million rubles' worth of stock and sold 34 percent to Russian financiers.[83] The Kiev Electric Company was first sequestered by order of the military governor in February 1916, then liquidated and transferred to the city administration a month later. Given the intense interest of various state ministries, *zemstva*, and municipalities in acquiring various firms in whole or in part, it quickly became clear that the only factor limiting the move to an even wider program of state acquisition was the expense. The acquisition of enemy-subject shares in the firms mentioned above cost the Treasury over 30 million rubles.[84]

To promote the long-term goals of Russian economic nationalism, officials running the liquidation program sought above all to transfer enemy shares to private Russian owners. The Ministry of Trade and Industry declared in a circular to the state inspectors, liquidators, and administrators that "the main goal [of the liquidation program] was to transfer firms and shares to new owners who would secure to a necessary degree Russian trade and industry from dependence upon and the influence of enemy subjects and capital."[85] The ministry explicitly stated on several occasions that it saw the liquidation program as a permanent means to Russify industry in Russia, not a temporary wartime measure.[86] In the few cases where subjects of neutral or allied countries were allowed to acquire former enemy-subject shares, the government imposed many obstacles, investigated the deals extensively, and established close state oversight over the reorganized firms.[87] The Committee for the Fight against German Dominance worked closely with inspectors and liquidators to coordinate such transfers as part of a larger program to Russify the economy. The Council of Ministers granted it the right to decide in each case whether acquisition by Russians or the state was more in state interests.[88]

An important aspect of the decrees was their encouragement of the participation of Russian businessmen. This was most apparent in a clause of the decree of February 8, 1917, by which only a quarter of the Russian shareholders of a firm had to petition to liquidate enemy shares for liquidation proceedings to be initiated. Moreover the rules on the pricing of enemy shares gave a significant profit incentive to Russians to opt for liquidation of their enemy-subject co-shareholders.[89] The large number of petitions to liquidate enemy-subject shares that the Ministry of Trade and Industry received from Russian part-owners underscores the general dynamism of wartime enemy-alien politics in the economic sphere.[90]

WHILE MOST OF the measures discussed thus far applied to enemy subjects and their businesses, they also affected a much broader range of Russian businesses. Once the practices of liquidation, sequestration, and control of enemy subjects became a sanctioned part of domestic politics, the tools could also be applied to broader categories. Two cases show, first, how Russian subjects could be targeted and second, how foreigners from neutral countries could be swept up in the campaign. Both cases reveal the dynamism of the campaign against enemy aliens and the radicalizing interplay of popular pressures, the army, and the government.

Kunst and Al'bers

One of the largest and most contentious cases during the war involved Kunst and Al'bers, a huge retailer mostly serving the Russian Far East. It had a yearly turnover of 17 million rubles, and held nearly half the market share for a wide array of consumer items sold in its broad network of retail outlets.[91] This case shows how important the press and competitors were in the general mobilization against enemy aliens in the economy, the importance of the army's role in domestic politics, and the complex knot of interrelated Russian and foreign interests in the imperial economy, even in the remote reaches of Siberia.

The firm was a commercial enterprise chartered under Russian law in 1864, and had thirty branches throughout the Far East and in all the major cities of the empire. Its directors and owners, Adolf Dattan and Alfred Kunst, became Russian subjects in the 1880s. As a firm owned by Russian subjects, it did not fall under any of the laws to liquidate enemy property. The attack on the firm, however, began shortly after the outbreak of war. Acting on the basis of an anonymous denunciation of Dattan for running an alleged spy operation through the enterprise, the general quartermaster at Army Headquarters ordered a midnight raid of the firm's headquarters and Dattan's private residence on September 11, 1914. All enemy-subject employees were arrested and deported to Irkutsk, including Dattan, even though the police report found "no evidence of spying." These actions encouraged the press to publish a flurry of articles arguing that Dattan was a spy, that the firm was German, and that it should be liquidated. Dattan's release a few weeks later spurred another wave of angry articles. Ianushkevich wrote to Minister of Interior Maklakov in December 1914 that Grand Duke Nikolai Nikolaevich took a personal interest in the case, and wanted Dattan deported and the firm liquidated. In January 1915, police searched the firm's branches again, and this time Dattan was arrested and deported to Narym, deep in Siberia. Ianushkevich ordered the seizure of the income and capital of the firm. Agitation for the liquidation of Kunst and Al'bers continued throughout the war. The editor of *Vechernee vremia*, a right-wing Petrograd paper, played a major role in inciting the press campaign, and claimed in a 1917 memo to have been the first to uncover the "treason" of Dattan and the firm.[92] The Society of 1914 lobbied hard for liquidation and claimed to have the support of all the major military leaders, declaring that the liquidation of Kunst and Al'bers would "unite the government with the living forces of the population, and contribute to the victory of healthy Russian nationality over the predominant influence of foreigners, clearing the path to the rebirth of our motherland."[93]

Reality proved more complex, however. The Khabarovsk, Vladivostok, and Nikolaev-on-the-Amur market exchange committees (*birzhevye komitety*) wrote that liquidation would put the entire population of the Far East in a difficult position and exacerbate existing shortages and inflation in consumer goods.[94] The senior ethnic Russian employees of Kunst and Al'bers wrote a joint letter defending the firm, stating that nearly all the senior positions in the firm were held by Russian subjects, that 200 of 752 employees were fighting at the front and continued to receive full pay, that 85 percent of the goods sold by the company were produced in Russia, and that the last thing the Far East needed was more inflation in the price of staples.[95] They also brought a suit against *Vechernee vremia* for slander and warned that the entire Siberian retail market depended on the Russian Churin Company and Kunst and Al'bers, and that liquidation of the latter would give Churin a monopoly. The fierce competition between the two firms was beneficial to consumers, keeping prices low. Kunst and Al'bers claimed that Churin was behind the entire campaign for liquidation, writing anonymous denunciations and bribing the press to print slanderous articles.[96]

Because the firm was entirely owned and managed by Russian subjects, the authorities could not simply apply any of the liquidation laws, but they did first place a freeze (*arest*) on its assets, then appointed state inspectors to oversee the firm. The Committee for the Fight against German Dominance discussed the issue in December 1916 and resolved that the firm should be liquidated. The Council of Ministers confirmed the decision in January 1917, but the February Revolution intervened before it could be implemented.[97] The Provisional Government reviewed the case and postponed liquidation proceedings.

The co-owner Alfred Dattan, a Russian subject of thirty years, spent most of the war in Siberian internment. Shortly after the February

Revolution he gained his freedom for a few weeks before he was arrested and interned again on April 7, 1917. His cosmopolitan lifestyle and links to Germany were too ambiguous for wartime requirements. Although he was a full Russian citizen, member of the Russian hereditary nobility, and had two sons in the Russian army, he also retained ties with Germany and traveled frequently to Berlin, where he maintained a branch of his company. No evidence that he or anyone in his firm engaged in spying was ever found during the war. The counterintelligence service did face serious challenges in Siberia and throughout the empire, and military counterintelligence was particularly concerned by evidence that Germany used bases in China to run a spy and subversion campaign in Siberia.[98] But Kunst and Al'bers was by no means the only firm owned by Russian subjects which came under intense pressures during the war. Many others, especially smaller firms, did not escape liquidation as Kunst and Al'bers did. But the controversy over the firm demonstrated how the campaign could spill over from a focus on enemy subjects to include long-naturalized Russian subjects and their enterprises.[99] It was also quite typical in that while on the surface the main issue was security, upon closer inspection, the real issue becomes the attempt to shift economic power to ethnic Russians.

Singer Sewing and Manufacturing Company

Another of the largest and most contentious cases of the war, that of the Singer Sewing and Manufacturing Company, also illustrates how the campaign against enemy subjects extended to larger categories of domestic enterprise. With 50 million rubles nominal capital, 27,000 employees, and hundreds of stores throughout the country, Singer was one of the largest firms in the empire.[100] More than most cases, the attempt to expropriate Singer was driven by the army and its accusations that the firm was engaged in spying. The impetus for the campaign against it began with the interception of an open letter from Germany to the company's headquarters promising payment for information on Russian internal conditions, mobilization, and troop movements.[101] This led Army Headquarters to send a circular to all the regional military commanders in December 1914 declaring that Singer was a German company and its employees and agents were spies.[102] Investigations ensued, led by military counterintelligence and the MVD.

According to their correspondence, one of the most important pieces of evidence was the Singer practice of requiring detailed reports from all its branches on the conditions of the local economy, demographic and age characteristics of the population, and the impact of military call-ups on the population structure.[103] They did not understand that this was a routine part of the sophisticated "Singer system" of market research—according to Fred Carstensen, one of one of the most advanced of its time in the world.[104]

Determined to find direct evidence of spying, the military moved the investigations from a secret to a highly public stage in June 1915. Bonch-Bruevich ordered a midnight search of 500 branches of the firm within the jurisdiction of his Sixth Army (the Petrograd region) on June 6, 1915. This created an immediate sensation. The press picked up the story, denouncing the firm as a German front for spies. Within the next month, military commanders in the Petrograd, Kiev, Dvinsk, and Caucasus regions conducted coordinated midnight searches of Singer stores throughout areas under their control. On July 31, 1915, Bonch-Bruevich ordered the immediate closure of over 500 Singer stores and froze their assets and accounts. This action displaced 6,000 workers and froze 12 million rubles worth of goods.[105]

The MVD closed Singer branches in other areas throughout the empire, including 94 branches in the Tiflis area and 119 in the Rostov-on-the-Don region. The press continued its attacks on the "German firm Singer" and demanded its immediate sequestration or liquidation. Governors throughout the empire, often quoting articles in *Novoe vremia*, demanded the right to close, sequester, or liquidate Singer branches in their jurisdictions.[106] The Kazan' governor warned that if Singer were not closed, he feared riots.[107] To protect itself against official attack, the company purged enemy subjects and Russian subjects of German and Jewish descent from its management and employee rolls.[108] Local officials also deported many German and Jewish employees.[109]

It quickly became public knowledge, however, that the widely held assumption that Singer was German was false. Angry interventions by the American ambassador and others led Prince L'vov, head of the Union of Local Government and Cities (Zemgor) to conduct a major unofficial investigation.[110] His report, published in August 1915, determined that of 30,328 employees before the war, only 131 had been enemy subjects, and extremely few were foreigners from allied and neutral countries. The report concluded that the firm, chartered in 1897 as a Russian company, was entirely American in origin and took all its orders from New York, not Berlin. One of the three founders of the Russian division of the company had been a German subject, but he was naturalized in 1902. Furthermore, Singer had 82 defense orders worth 3.6 million rubles. The investigations, closures, and sequestrations were endangering the fulfillment of these contracts. The American mother company ordered ships with crucial supplies for the production of airplane engines in the Podol'sk factory to turn around and return to New York until the closures, sequestrations, and bans on payments to New York were lifted. The sequestrations and bans on payments abroad not only posed a threat to Russian production and sales, but also to the 120 million rubles owed by Singer Russia to the mother company in New York. This in turn threatened economic relations with the United States, relations already strained by the mass deportations of Jews and civilian enemy aliens.[111] The press and official campaigns further exacerbated problems as many customers and firms refused to make payments to Singer. Current account debts rose precipitously, further endangering the ability of the firm to fill its defense orders and continue production for the consumer market.[112]

Despite the evidence of damage to the economy, defense production, and relations with the United States—including explicit threats from J. P. Morgan to withdraw from Russia completely and lobby against credits to Russia—the campaign continued. On September 26, 1915, all 94 stores in the Caucasus were closed by military order, and the war minister himself continued to demand the closure of all Singer branches throughout the country.[113] The regime allowed most of the closed stores to reopen only toward the end of 1915, under state inspector control amounting to the conditions of sequestration. The state administrators reported many difficulties in restoring operations and many conflicts with police and army officials, who continued to obstruct their efforts.[114]

The Singer affair, although it did not lead to outright liquidation of the firm, illustrates the dynamic nature of the campaign. The accusations of spying initiated by the military led to a sort of official pogrom against the firm that was quickly joined by the MVD, local officials, and the press and rapidly spread throughout the country. Some of the managers of Singer branches tried to escape the pressure by firing Russian-subject Germans and Jews even if not required to do so, illustrating the dynamic purge mentality apparent in wartime enemy-alien politics. Singer was by no means the only firm of foreign but not enemy origins which was swept up in the wartime campaign.[115]

UPON COMING TO POWER, the Provisional Government exempted Russian subjects from most of the wartime measures against enemy aliens, but it by no means ended the attack on enemy subjects and their property. In fact, the liquidation of enemy-subject participation in the economy actually accelerated, and there was a remarkable degree of continuity in the program through four very different regimes. The liquidation committees set up under the tsar kept working under the Provisional Government and later under the Bolshevik regime (with substantial change in staff). There is even evidence that the White governments during the early stages of the Civil War went to the effort of completing the liquidation of some German firms.[116] During the short tenure of the Provisional Government, enemy-alien shares worth the equivalent of roughly two percent of all common stock in Russian industry were transferred to Russians or state institutions. All 33 large corporations operating in Russia under German and Austrian charters were denied the further right to operate in Russia, and most were liquidated by November 1917. In all, 1,839 commercial firms and 59 large industrial firms were liquidated or changed hands. The liquidation of enemy shares in the 364 firms identified as having significant enemy-subject minority shareholdings had begun. In addition, dozens of firms, including some of the largest foreign enterprises in Russia, had been sequestered and transferred to the control of state or social institutions. By the time the Bolsheviks took power, the bulk of German and Austrian participation in the imperial economy had been liquidated, and the official practice of nationalizing properties belonging to enemy categories of the population had been institutionalized and brought into practice on a large scale.[117]

The Bolshevik regime did not abrogate tsarist laws against enemy subjects, nor did the new regime disband the liquidation committees introduced by the old regime. An additional 191 of the industrial firms to which liquidation committees had been assigned prior to the revolution were liquidated in the first months of Bolshevik power, before the renowned decree on the nationalization of all large industry was issued on June 28, 1918.[118] In fact, the question of enemy-alien property played a significant role in the genesis and timing of this fundamentally important declaration.[119]

Because the foreign role in the late imperial economy was so large, and because enemy subjects made up a large part of the foreign role, the state-sanctioned mobilization against enemy aliens in the economy had important implications for the domestic economy as a whole. Spurred on by the goal of creating a more Russian economy, officials entered the imperial economy in aggressive ways in an attempt to disentangle the complicated national mix of industry, commerce, and finance to identify and extract the enemy sectors. Their actions affected the tenor of domestic politics and attitudes not only toward enemy subjects strictly defined, but also toward larger categories, including foreigners in general and Russian-subject commercial diasporas. The state abandoned its role as protector of property rights, reversed its long promotion of foreign investment, and embraced a radical program to nationalize the economy by transferring ownership and jobs from enemy aliens to Russians, other "reliable" individuals, and the state.

4

Nationalizing the Land

ONE OF THE CORNERSTONES of the wartime campaign against enemy aliens in the Russian Empire was the program to expropriate landholdings and transfer them to Russians and other favored nationalities. In some respects, the focus on land ownership reflected the old assumption that it was the key to social and political power, and to a certain degree the implementation of the extraordinary wartime measures was influenced by old estate categories. But it also built upon and reflected shifting approaches to nationality and imperial rule in the borderlands. The wartime measures had several serious unintended consequences for the economy, rural stability, and the legitimacy of private property in the countryside.

Land Ownership and Nationality before the War

The Bans on Land Ownership by Jews

Long before World War I Russia had elaborated restrictions on the acquisition of land by certain nationalities, most importantly Jews and Poles. Although the tool of expropriation had been used only in a few instances, the limits on Jewish landownership set crucial precedents for the wartime measures.

Policies limiting Jewish landholding reach back to the late eighteenth-century partitions of Poland, when Russia acquired most of its Jewish population. Catherine II inscribed Jews into the merchant estate, attempting to facilitate the collection of taxes and aid the growth of towns. This led to a series of measures to force Jews from the countryside into the cities. In 1784 non-Christians were banned from owning serfs, and until 1800 members of urban estates could not own land. The application of these and other regulations led to the transfer of up to 200,000 Jews out of rural areas into towns by the 1840s. Although these developments in effect excluded an entire nationality from land ownership, the decrees and regulations were expressed in the language of estates. Jews were not forced from the countryside as Jews, but rather as individuals ascribed to urban estates. Despite the many restrictions imposed on Jews, many remained in rural Russia, and some were even able to take significant amounts of land in formal and informal lease from the gentry within the Pale.[1]

Harsher restrictions came after the emancipation of the serfs in 1861 and the Polish rebellion in 1863. In the wake of the rebellion, an important 1864 law banned all Jews from acquiring land from gentry or peasants. After the 1881 wave of pogroms, the government forbade Jews from taking up residence in rural areas and banned their acquisition of rural real estate through lease, purchase, or any other means. These most extensive limits on Jewish land use to date were decreed as part of the infamous Temporary Rules of 3 May 1881, which remained in effect until the end of the old regime in 1917.[2]

The restrictions were based in part on the assumption by government officials that Christian peasants could not compete with Jews in agriculture; that if the restrictions were lifted, a flood of Jews to the countryside would lead to "Jewish domination" of the uneducated and inefficient peasants in "nearly every sphere of life and labor."[3] The bans on Jewish land acquisition proved to be the linchpin of the myriad of other restrictions on Jewish residence, entry into professions, and economic activity. Even when the geographic restrictions on Jewish settlement to the Pale were abolished on August 4, 1915, the government could not bring itself to open rural areas to Jewish settlement and land acquisition.[4]

Land shortage in European Russia as a result of rapid population growth after the emancipation of the serfs was an important backdrop to maintaining and expanding the restrictions, but no less important were new attempts after the 1863 Polish rebellion to increase the percent of land held by reliable segments of the population in the western borderlands.[5]

While neither the government nor the army moved toward a formal

program to expropriate the few rural lands still owned or leased by
Jews during the war, all the old bans on acquiring land remained in
place. The pattern was so ingrained that during Russia's occupation
of Galicia, the occupiers could not fathom the idea of Jewish land
ownership (which was allowed under Austrian law) and took steps to
expropriate Jewish landowners. The implementation of this project
was only cut short upon Russian loss of the territory in the summer of
1915. Moreover, once the expropriation of German and enemy-subject
properties began within the Russian Empire during the war, officials
strove to make sure that they would not be purchased or managed
by Jews.[6]

Restrictions on Polish Land Acquisitions

The underlying assumptions and patterns of Russian limitations on
Jews provided one template for the limitation and then outright expropriation of enemy-alien landholdings during the war. Nineteenth-century limitations on Polish landholding created another important precedent for the wartime measures.

One of the most important elements of Russian imperial expansion
from sixteenth-century Muscovy through the nineteenth century was
the co-optation of local elites.[7] While elite landholdings were selectively expropriated and redistributed following the incorporation of
Novgorod, Kazan', Ukraine, the Baltic provinces, and Poland, such expropriations were selective, aimed at individuals rather than nationalities, and were accompanied by attempts to bring elites into the imperial
system. Prerogatives of both Baltic and Polish elites over their serfs,
lands, and societies were often left intact as long as the elites recognized imperial authority.

Following both the 1831 and 1863 Polish rebellions, a number of estates belonging to leading Polish noble participants were confiscated
and redistributed to "Russians."[8] These actions again selectively punished politically disloyal individuals. However, important changes in
the Polish national movement in the second half of the nineteenth century began to expand its base from *szlachta* (gentry) to all classes of society. As Polish national leaders began to include townsmen, small landholders, and the peasantry in their movement and conception of the
Polish nation, the Polish challenge to the imperial Russian system was

transformed from a problem of Polish elites (against whom imperial authorities could pit presumed anational and assimilable Polish peasants) into a problem of all Poles.[9] The broadening of the Polish challenge led to a fundamental shift in Russian ruling strategy expressed in a secret ordinance of December 1865, which became "the cornerstone of land policy in the Western Provinces" for the last fifty years of the imperial regime. The ordinance was explicitly intended to Russify the provinces by "attacking the very root of 'Polish domination'—landholding." It prohibited "individuals of Polish origin" from acquiring landed properties in the western region by any means except inheritance.[10]

The decree fundamentally abandoned the traditional approach of co-opting local elites by imposing restrictions on the basis of national origin, regardless of conversion to Orthodoxy, evidence of assimilation, or loyal service to the Russian Empire. As the decree and its implementation made clear, if an individual was an ethnic Pole, his rights to acquire land were limited.[11] According to decisions in 1866 and 1871, the limitations applied not only to gentry lands but to all rural landholdings, including those held by townsmen and peasants. These measures moved decisively beyond Russification in the sense of assimilating and incorporating Polish elites into the imperial system and culture to a different type of Russification, one in which identities were assumed to be immutable, and only the object of policy switched from people to the land they owned. In other words, the focus shifted from co-opting or assimilating individuals to nationalizing the land.

The implementation of these initiatives was far from smooth, but the nominally Russian share of landholding in the western provinces grew from 17 percent in 1865 to 40 percent in 1885. According to official statistics, by 1914 the Polish share of landholdings in the western provinces had fallen to about half.[12]

Although the Grand Duke declared shortly after the war began that an autonomous Poland would be created under the tsar, and despite later exemption of Polish enemy subjects from wartime expropriatory decrees, the restrictions on Polish land acquisition continued to be enforced until the Provisional Government abolished them in March 1917.[13] Governors in the western provinces also took great care to ensure that German lands expropriated during the war did not end up in Polish hands.[14]

Prewar Limits on German Acquisition of Land

Compared to the restrictions on Jewish and Polish landownership, the prewar history of official policy toward German farmers is much more closely linked to the availability or shortage of land. In fact, the first major waves of peasant immigration from Austria, the Balkans, Bulgaria, and most of all from the German-speaking states began in the eighteenth century, when the Russian tsars invited immigrants to help settle and bring untilled expanses in New Russia (South Ukraine), the mid-Volga, and elsewhere under cultivation. The open invitation to farming communities ended gradually in mid-nineteenth century as population growth made land more scarce. By the late nineteenth century, rapid peasant population growth led to a land shortage in all major areas of German settlement.[15]

While isolated voices on the Russian Right and in the government began to call for curbs on German immigrant acquisitions of land as early as the 1880s, the context for the first official limits on immigrant land acquisitions was the struggle over Polish land ownership rather than negative Russian attitudes toward Germans.[16] To the contrary, the 1865 laws limiting Polish land acquisition emphatically declared that if Germans bought up land at the Poles' expense, it would still further the main aim of state measures: "the weakening of the Polish element."[17] The restrictions on Poles and Jews even facilitated a major influx of German migrants into Volynia and other western provinces during the late nineteenth century.[18] In Volynia alone, immigration increased the German population from 70,000 to 200,000 during the 1880s, and their share of landholdings rose by an even greater proportion. Many leased from Poles or purchased lands at prices depressed by the artificial repression of demand from Poles.

An important edict of March 14, 1887, banned foreign subjects in Volynia, Kiev, Podolia, and the ten Wistula provinces from acquiring land in ownership or lease except through inheritance. While this law did curb German immigrant acquisitions, more important was its aim of preventing Prussian and Austrian Poles (who as foreign subjects ironically had more rights to acquire land than Russian-subject Poles) from acquiring land for themselves or their relatives in Russia. In addition to Germans, the laws affected Czechs, Poles, and Galician Slavs (Poles and Ukrainians), making up 13, 9, and 5 percent of the immigrants, respectively. The measures were aimed less against German immigrants than against their role in foiling the desired expansion of Russian landholding at the expense of the Poles. Officials were most alarmed that the immigrants "gravitated toward local Poles and Jews rather than to Russians."[19]

As relations with Germany deteriorated in the early 1890s, attitudes toward immigrants and rural settlements took on a more specifically anti-German character, especially within the military, which began to raise questions of security based on the concentration of German settlements in strategic border areas.

At least as important was rapid peasant population growth in the Russian Empire. While plot size declined for most peasants as population rose, the Germans continued to add to their landholdings—largely owing to the relative efficiency of their agriculture and their practices of inheritance.[20] Only one son received the inheritance, and, as family sizes averaged at least eight, many sons were left landless. The inheritor was obliged to pay cash to his brothers in compensation, and they often used it to purchase or lease new lands from neighboring gentry and peasants. The rapid development of mutual credit associations servicing German communities in the late nineteenth and early twentieth centuries gave these landless sons a source of credit for their land acquisitions.[21] These factors drove a remarkable growth of German landholdings. For example, in the provinces of New Russia (Kherson, Ekaterinoslav, Taurida, and Khar'kov), total German landholdings rose from 10 percent of the total (2.3 million *desiatin*) in 1890 to over 17 percent (3.8 million *desiatin*) in 1912. In Volynia, total German landholding rose from .6 percent (96,000 *desiatin*) in 1871 to 4.6 percent (685,258 *desiatin*) in 1909 of all land in the province.[22] In the Volga provinces, the number of rural Germans rose from 400,000 to 600,000 from 1897 to 1914, and the area of their landholding from 1.2 million *desiatin* to 2 million *desiatin*. All together, German farmers owned nearly 9 million *desiatin* (24 million acres) within the Russian Empire by 1914. The importance of these holdings was magnified by the fact that most of the lands were among the best and most productive in the empire.[23]

As the extent of the German land acquisition became apparent in the late nineteenth century, the issue moved to the center of emerging polemics against the Germans. By that time, conditions in Russia had changed. No longer was the government primarily concerned with peopling its lands; instead, the issue was providing land for its rapidly growing population. Moreover, as relations with Germany deteriorated at the end of the century, the rural Germans came under increasing public and official scrutiny. As a result, a law of 1892 for the first time applied limits on acquisitions of land by *Russian subjects* of "German origin" in Kiev, Podolia, and Volynia. The laws were weakened somewhat in 1895 and 1905,[24] but they succeeded in substantially slowing the growth of German immigrant shares of land in the three provinces.

Some government figures thought that the real problem in the countryside lay in the situation of the Slavic peasantry. First, former serfs, unlike the German colonists, were saddled with 49-year redemption payment obligations until these were finally abolished in 1907. Second, the traditional communal form of agriculture provided few incentives for capital accumulation and land acquisition. Attempts to revive and reinforce the peasant commune in the 1890s exacerbated these structural deficiencies. The prevalence of primogeniture in most German settlements created strong incentives for families to accumulate wealth so that the younger sons could acquire new lands. Such incentives were lacking under the partible inheritance and communal systems prevalent through most of the empire. Thus the problem of German land acquisitions could be seen as part of the more general problems of Russian agriculture. Ultimately, as many German farmers and Russian reformers argued, the solution lay not in the restriction of German land acquisitions, but rather in reform of the communal landholding that prevailed among Slavic peasants. The relative success of German farmers' methods was in fact taken into consideration by bureaucrats preparing the type of reforms later implemented by P. A. Stolypin.[25]

The shock of the 1905–1907 agrarian disorders led the state to move away from the idea that the commune was a conservative source of order in the countryside. The Stolypin reforms attempted to create consolidated landholdings and independent landowners, both of which German communities already practiced in far greater proportion than other groups.[26] If the Stolypin reforms aimed to create a sense of private property to combat the revolutionary seizures of land by and for the communes in 1905–1907, the rural Germans, with their consolidated holdings and much higher rates of individual *khutor* ownership, could be seen as crucial allies in the effort.[27]

It soon became apparent, however, that the attempt to change Slavic landholding to a pattern closer to that already extant in German communities could not fully succeed right away.[28] By the eve of the war, the problem of growing German land shares had again become a major issue of public debate and official concern. Several governors in areas with large German settlements and immigration rates again pressed the Ministry of Internal Affairs to limit German immigration and land acquisition. In 1909, the Chief Administration for Land Settlement and Agriculture responded by forbidding German immigrant purchases through state land funds (most importantly, from the Peasant Bank) and limiting all new leases from the state to a maximum of six years.[29]

In 1910, the MVD introduced a more drastic bill to stop land acquisitions by German immigrants—including those who had naturalized—in the three provinces affected by the 1887 and 1895 laws (Volynia, Kiev, Podolia). It failed to pass in the Duma. Some on the Right opposed the measure because it would limit gentry options to sell and lease their lands, but most importantly, the moderate Octobrist faction stated firm opposition to any limitations on property rights based on nationality.[30] After elections to the new Fourth Duma, in December 1912, the MVD reintroduced the failed bill of 1910 in a more extreme form, now including Bessarabia. The bill proposed banning the acquisition of any landholding in ownership or lease by all immigrants who had not acquired Russian subjecthood before 1888, and who had "not assimilated into Russian nationality."[31]

Again, even though the Fourth Duma had more right-wing deputies, support for the proposal was not forthcoming, and it drew sharp denunciations from both Octobrists and a fair, but smaller, number of Rightists and Nationalists. For example, the leader of the Nationalist faction, A. Savenko, continued to defend the German farmers, stating that Russia "should not turn its aliens (*inorodtsy*) into enemies." He proposed halting further immigration, but not going so far as to limit the rights of those already in Russia.[32]

The failure of the MVD bills indicates that before the war the Duma would not even go so far as to limit the rights of German immigrants to acquire lands in four borderland provinces. Yet the bills brought the issue to a degree of unprecedented prominence in public debate on the national level. Some members of the Right and Octobrist factions began to move toward support for limits on German landholding already before the war in the wake of the two bills, and agitation in the press against German colonists markedly increased.[33]

The committees drawing up the proposals in the MVD gathered extensive data about German and foreign-subject landholding in the western regions. Governors throughout the country began to compile statistics and compose detailed maps of German landholding and settlement patterns. The military increasingly depicted the immigrant and foreign populations as strategic liabilities in internal memos and on maps.[34] Even in the sparsely settled Omsk region, the governor drew up detailed maps and statistics on German landholding in 1911.[35] In 1913, the head of the Chief Administration for Land Settlement and Agriculture wrote a report raising alarm that 4,000 Germans had acquired nearly 20,000 *desiatin* along the main railroad in the Caucasus. The tsar, who reviewed the report, twice underlined the conclusion that: "luckily time has not run out, but we must hurry to settle the area with the Russian element."[36] The idea that the security of the state and maintenance of imperial rule depended upon the percentage breakdowns of populations and their landholdings became much more firmly established in official practice and public polemics alike.[37] This "demographicization" of nationality issues and the conclusion that the state needs favorable demographic balances of nationalities in order to control its imperial space were important developments that prepared the way for wartime actions.[38]

German Challenges

Similar transitions were well underway throughout Europe and the world. Most significant for our case are the parallel transformations of German practice in its own lands acquired in the partitions of Poland. While as late as 1848 the option to integrate into a general German citizenship remained a real possibility for Prussian Poles, by the 1880s German officials in Poznan had begun to pay close attention to demographic balances and landholding. In 1886 Bismarck founded the Royal Prussian Colonization Association with the aim of buying out Polish landowners and replacing them with Germans.[39] Frustrated by the lack of progress and decades of acrimony over the poorly funded colonization efforts in Prussia, Chancellor Bülow forced through a bill to expropriate Polish estates in 1908. Although Reichstag opposition prevented its implementation, and only four properties were expropriated before the war, Poznan Provincial President Wilhelm von Waldow's report indicated that a major conceptual transformation had occurred. The old Bismarckian perspective that identified the Polish *nobility* as the principal obstacle to Germanization had been abandoned for a new concern with demographic details of population and land ownership. As William W. Hagen puts it, by 1914 Germanization already "had less to do with the Poles than with the ground they stood on."[40]

The trend in German nationality practices and rhetoric toward the equation of ethnicity and citizenship, and toward efforts to nationalize its territorial space, had important effects upon Russian practices.[41] This new style of German politics, embodied in its distinctive ethnically defined conceptions of citizenship, which included Germans abroad in its citizenry and community, was perceived in Russia as a direct threat which claimed the loyalty of even long-naturalized Germans in Russia. A concrete manifestation of these conceptual shifts came with the debates over a new German citizenship law in 1913, in which the German Right lobbied hard to recognize the German diaspora outside German borders as citizens on the basis of their blood lines. While the actual German law was cautiously worded and ambiguous on questions of dual citizenship, the debate over the law gave much attention to the idea that Germany was thinking of the German diasporas abroad as members of the German nation, regardless of their formal citizenship.[42] Moreover, Russian commentators and military planners did not fail to note that German war plans included the tactical use of racial groups, and that the German Right made grand plans for the resettlement of Germans from Russia to create the foundation for a future new order with the Baltic provinces and parts of Poland remade as German colonies.[43]

The visions of conquest promoted by some on the German Right— along with the obvious sympathy of members of the German government—lent a degree of credibility to those in Russia who claimed that Berlin was directing German immigration for strategic aims. The Latvian and Lithuanian press fulminated against the migration of several thousand Germans from the Volga and South Ukraine to the Baltic areas, claiming (not entirely without reason) that it was part of a Pan-German plot to begin the "peaceful conquest" of the region.[44] The published claims of Paul Rohrbach and other prominent members of the Pan-German League that the Baltic provinces were to become part of the future German Empire made the issue a major one, not only in the local press, but also in national Russian papers.[45] The Russian General Staff wrote that immigration to Volynia and elsewhere was planned and funded in Berlin, and drew up maps to reveal the logic of such settlement, highlighting new settlements along coasts, railroads, borders, and nearby forts. Official propaganda gave such themes a prominent place throughout the war.[46]

The Development of Wartime Expropriation Measures

Even before the war, several measures had already limited the rights of both immigrants from abroad and Jewish, Polish, and German subjects of the Russian Empire to acquire land. But the step from limitations on acquisition to outright expropriation was a large one.

The belief that private property was inviolable and that states could not arbitrarily expropriate properties—especially landed properties—was supported by long legal traditions in Europe linked to the most fundamental principles of the rights of the individual and citizen. Such traditions were certainly much weaker in Russia, but it is important to remember that the concept was among the many fundamental principles under contestation circa 1914.[47] The 1906 Fundamental Laws for the first time explicitly gave state guarantees that land and property of a Russian subject could not be expropriated without compensation. According to article 77, "Property is inviolable, forced expropriation of real estate . . . is not allowed other than with fair and reasonable compensation"[48] Like the idea of citizenship itself, with its universal establishment of equal rights and obligations under law, the idea of property guarantees was one of the fundamental principles many moderates were fighting to establish.[49] In the countryside, one of the fundamental aims of the Stolypin reforms was conceptually and in practice to establish private property in the place of communal land. It is well known that the establishment of this principle was challenged by many on the Left, who advocated mass expropriation of gentry and state lands, but less well remembered that both the Right and the state itself fundamentally undermined the principle during the war.[50]

From Enemy Subjects to German Immigrants

Although the government had officially declared that the property of enemy subjects would be protected, it quickly moved against their landholdings. On September 22, 1914, the tsar signed a decree banning the *acquisition* of land or any property in ownership or lease by all enemy subjects throughout the empire for the duration of the war.[51] This decree marked a major expansion of all such prewar limits, which had only applied to a few provinces.

Pressure quickly grew to move beyond limitations on new acquisitions of property to more extreme measures of expropriation. Initially, the government took a cautious approach. Minister of Interior Maklakov responded to demands from the army on August 22 with a circular to governors in Poland reminding them that the MVD had "already before the war turned its attention to the artificial strengthening of German colonization in the Polish provinces and the serious dangers it posed to the Russian nationality and defense."[52] He retained, however, a degree of neutrality at this early date, pointing out that many of the Germans had come to Poland as early as the eleventh century, and that the colonists had been a reliable bulwark against the nineteenth-century Polish rebellions and social unrest in 1905. At the same time, he also pointed out that German acquisitions of land and population growth had caused concern, along with recent reports that they had been signaling the enemy and were generally sympathetic to the German cause. Maklakov requested reports from the governors on whether such claims were true, and if so, what measures they proposed to fight them. The responses varied. Most governors argued that the German colonists were unreliable, that they should be deported and their lands expropriated. Some officials were initially more reserved in judgment, reporting that the colonists were responding well to the military call-ups and were a positive conservative element.[53] Internal army communications were far less ambivalent. Nearly all major army commanders from the first days of the war expressed the opinion that the colonists were a dangerous internal enemy which had to be fought in all possible ways.

Pressed by the military and the media, the government quickly lost its initial ambivalence on the issue. In October the Council of Ministers set up a committee under A. S. Stishinskii to rework the failed 1910 and 1912 bills into a far more radical measure. The real turning point came when Grand Duke Nikolai Nikolaevich sent a telegram in October 1914 demanding extensive measures against enemy aliens throughout the empire.[54]

As a result, the Council of Ministers held a series of meetings to dis-

cuss the issue. In two meetings in October 1914, Minister of War
Sukhomlinov and Commander of the Sixth Army (deployed in the
Petrograd military region) Fan der Flit proposed a far-reaching program of deportation and limitation of enemy subjects and "so-called
Russian-subject Germans" throughout the empire. The ministers responded defensively, noting that they had already taken several temporary measures to limit enemy subjects and that they opposed taking
more categorical measures for fear of retaliation against Russian subjects in enemy countries and unfavorable reactions in neutral countries.
Furthermore, since enemy subjects played an important role in Russian
industry, categorical measures against them could be unbearably disruptive to the wartime economy. Such extraordinary measures as
outright confiscation and sequestration of properties would raise the
question of compensation at the end of the war, which could be very
expensive. Instead, Foreign Minister Sergei Sazonov, after an impas-
sioned speech rejecting general measures against enemy subjects, spoke
for a majority of the Council in favor of expropriating German colonist landholdings in the immediate front zones. Because this measure
would primarily affect mostly Russian subjects, Sazonov probably considered that the international repercussions would not be so damaging
as the proposals from Sukhomlinov and Fan der Flit aimed at enemy
subjects. By applying the initial measures only to areas near the front,
the ministers also in a sense were simply trying to bring some order to
what the army was already doing. The military had already begun the
expulsion of Russian-subject Germans from areas near the front, and
the War Statute gave it wide powers to sequester and requisition in areas under military rule.[55]

Army Policies

The army's first and most extensive use of its powers began in occupied
foreign territories. In the first months of the war, Russian occupying authorities in East Prussia undertook a broad program of requisition and confiscation of German machinery, livestock, and properties. Shortly after the occupation of Galicia, the Russian authorities
began a large program to sequester lands left behind by refugees retreating with the Austrian armies.[56] Chairman of the Council of
Ministers Goremykin strongly supported such measures. He replied to

Ianushkevich's plan to sequester vacated properties in occupied Galicia by suggesting that the authorities not limit themselves to sequester, but move instead to outright confiscation. He also stressed that the policy should apply to vacant properties belonging to Jews, Germans, and individuals suspected of spying on the territory of the Russian Empire.[57]

Army policies in occupied parts of the Ottoman Empire were even more aggressive in promoting Russians at the expense of unreliable minorities. There the authorities began to transfer vacant properties to Russian Cossack settlers. In addition to Cossacks, General Iudenich began a program to import Russian agricultural workers in brigades (*druzhiny*) to occupied Turkey in October 1915. By late 1916, over 5,000 Russian peasants and farm workers had been settled in occupied parts of Eastern Anatolia, and plans were in place for much larger colonization. Russian officials forbade Armenians to join the settlement program and prevented Armenian refugees from returning to occupied Turkey, in part to prevent confrontations between returning Armenians and the Russians, Kurds, and Turks who had taken possession of their homes and lands. Future plans included the settlement of demobilized Cossacks on the Armenians' land at the end of the war. On February 10, 1916, lands of Armenian refugees were officially declared state property, and even when the few refugees who were able to return did so, they were not allowed to reclaim their homes and lands. Instead, they were forced to take their lands in lease from the authorities, and this was only allowed in the areas of less desirable farmland. In the fertile valleys and along the border, Armenians were barred from their former lands altogether, because they had already been reserved for Cossacks and Russians.[58]

The Russian military authorities also applied sequestration to broad areas of the Russian Empire itself shortly after the outbreak of the war. The army shifted its policies between December 1914 and February 1915, from forced expulsion of Germans from front zones to the more specific targeting of rural German landowners, exempting urban German populations. When an important conference of army leaders met in January 1915 to define the categories of Germans to be deported, it resolved to include all individuals of German nationality owning property or engaged in trade or cottage industries outside urban settlements, as well as farm laborers and seasonal German workers in cities still registered in a rural community. These comprehensive deportation guidelines show how closely the army's deportation policies became linked to a broader intent to nationalize the land.[59]

The military leaders' conference also reported that there had already been "many cases of theft and occupation of colonist property and lands by local populations, who looked upon the property of the deportees as not belonging to anyone."[60] Fearing a breakdown of law and order, the conference resolved to sequester and transfer the properties of deportees formally to the local organs of the Ministry of State Properties, with the cooperation of the Peasant Bank.[61] The Chief Administration for Land Settlement and Agriculture cooperated closely with the military and began to implement a massive transfer of the lands of deported colonists to state control early in 1915. Few statistics are available, but the extent of the process can be seen in figures for Volynia, where in June 1916 over 90 percent of the properties identified as due for expropriation had already been sequestered.[62]

Army commanders pushed hard to make the transfer of enemy-alien lands to new owners permanent. Already in January 1915, the governor general of Warsaw sent a circular to ten governors of Polish provinces which ordered that during mass deportation, authorities should "facilitate the voluntary liquidation [of properties] toward the final end of German landholding."[63] In practice, such transfers were far from voluntary. Often the army moved directly to the outright transfer of lands through sequestration, thereby avoiding the slow expropriation procedures and their requirements of compensation to the former owners. In June 1915, the commander of the Southwest Front ordered that refugees be settled on the lands of deported Germans and Jews throughout the area under his control.[64] The July 1, 1915, army orders to deport rural Germans from Volynia gave them ten days to liquidate their properties or face compulsory sequestration without compensation.[65] In parts of Volynia Russia reconquered in June 1916, army authorities simply allocated 50,000 *desiatin* of land of deported Germans to 200,000 refugees (mostly from Galicia), 100,000 *desiatin* to 7,500 local peasants, and 12,000 to local peasant communes as common grazing land.[66] Similarly, when 11,000 German settlers were deported from the Girshengof settlement in 1916, their lands were sequestered and transferred to the Baltic office of the Ministry of State Properties. The army then settled Latvian refugees on their lands.[67] Such army actions rapidly brought about massive property shifts without any compensation.[68]

The army command further demonstrated its simplistic and radical approach to complex questions of interrelated German and Russian interests in its policies toward German leaseholders. General Mavrin wrote to Ianushkevich on July 8, 1915, during the implementation of a mass deportation, informing him that many German colonists held lands in lease, and upon deportation left planted fields, implements, buildings, and large debts to Russian landowners.[69] He inquired what status their leases should have and what should be done about their property. Ianushkevich, only two days later, responded that the act of deportation should be considered to be a formal breaking of the contract, and that the question of the homes, buildings, factories, mills, and implements on their lands "would resolve itself [!]." Thus, in cavalier fashion, he decided the fates not only of tens of thousands of Germans and their properties, but also the material interests of many Russian landowners. Moreover, leaving the question of valuable property to "resolve itself" was an open invitation to precisely the kind of unregulated seizures by peasants, local institutions, and soldiers which were subsequently reported by local officials. Ominously, reports that local peasants were carting off movable property and taking over entire farmsteads proliferated during the first year of the war.[70] State and social institutions also pressed the government and army to sequester or confiscate enemy-alien properties in order to supply them with land for various initiatives.[71]

In addition, the extreme requisition policies applied to Germans and Jews heightened the sense that deportees' property was outside the normal protections of the law. In June 1915, for example, Ivanov ordered that all but seed grain be requisitioned from Germans and Jews, and that hostages should be taken from their communities to ensure full deliveries.[72] Through its radical practices, the army brought the permanent status of enemy-alien properties into question. But extreme as the army's policies were, they only applied to occupied foreign territories and to areas under military rule within the country. Moreover, the army most often ordered *sequestration*, not expropriation. Although sequestered lands came under state control, they technically remained the legal property of the prior owners. The most important step toward unambiguously permanent transfer of enemy-alien properties came with three decrees of February 2, 1915.

The Decrees of February 2, 1915

Responding to intense pressure from the military and the press, a committee headed by A. S. Stishinskii drafted a set of three decrees which were signed by the tsar on February 2, 1915, under article 87.[73] The first decree applied to enemy subjects. It expanded the limitations on the acquisition of landed properties imposed in September 1914 to include the administration of properties and lands controlled by firms incorporated under the law of an enemy country. The decree also required that all enemy subjects serving in executive positions of organizations owning land be fired from their positions. These provisions applied to the entire territory of the empire.

The most important provisions of the decree required the alienation of land belonging to enemy subjects in a major part of the empire, including most of its western and southern provinces, the Caucasus, and the Amur region.[74] All lands and properties outside urban settlements were to be registered by local officials in lists to be published within two months. After the publication of the lists, owners faced a deadline ranging from six months to two years to sell their property. Failure to sell by the given deadline led to forced sale of the property by local officials at public auction.

Additionally, an important clause required all forms of lease—whether formal or informal—to expire within one year, including rentals of apartments, gardens, and houses. This requirement also applied to long-term leases "in perpetuity," which in practical terms differed little from outright ownership. Finally, lands held by societies and firms incorporated under the laws of enemy states and partnerships in which as few as one of the stockholders or partners was an enemy subject were to be alienated by the given deadlines.

The second and third decrees applied to the much larger population of Russian-subject German settlers. They affected any individual falling into one of the following categories: (1) members of a *volost'*, agricultural, village, or communal institution formed by former Austrian, Hungarian, or German subjects or by immigrants of German descent (*proiskhozhdenie*); (2) individuals registered in colonies in Kholm or the

Figure 8. Areas subject to land expropriation decrees affecting individuals of
   German or Austro-Hungarian ancestry who acquired Russian subjecthood
   after January 1, 1880.

regions under the governor general of Warsaw; (3) individuals who had
accepted Russian subjecthood after January 1, 1880. These decrees applied the ten Polish provinces (*Privislenskii krai*) and a band of territory
extending 150 *verst* (160 kilometers) to the interior of the empire's
western and southern borders from Finland to the Caspian Sea, and a
100-*verst* zone to the interior of the border with the *Privislenskii krai*.[75]

The Nationalizing Aims of the Decrees

Although the February decrees applied to a relatively limited area near
the empire's borders and could to a degree be seen as driven by security

issues, the large amount of land subject to expropriation quickly raised contentious questions about its redistribution. Already on January 28, 1915, days before the February decrees were published, Grigorii Lashkarev proposed in the State Council that colonist lands be transferred to injured soldiers who had received medals of distinction, and that they should be preserved for "members of the Russian nationality (*Russkoi natsional'nosti*)." This should include Polish war heroes and would be a good way to gain Polish peasant loyalty, but "should not include other Slavs, who were already too numerous in the western regions."[76]

The issue was quickly taken up in the press. Some conservatives argued that the land should go to the gentry, but they were far outnumbered by those to their left and right on the political spectrum. Those on the left tended to argue that landless and smallholder peasants should benefit, while many officials and right-wing publicists in the western borderlands stressed ethnic factors more than class.[77] For example, one official in Volynia argued in a widely circulated memo that the land should be given to Russian gentry, but justified it less in terms of class than in light of the ongoing Russian struggle to gain social and political power against the Poles. He wrote that the main problem in his region was the lack of educated large Russian landowners who could act as a social and political counterweight to the Polish landowners. He argued that expropriated lands in Volynia should go to Russian gentry rather than landless peasants or smallholders, because the latter would not substantially affect the social, political, or economic balance in the overarching struggle against Polish influence.[78]

The February decrees did not ensure the achievement of any of these aims, since they allowed sale to any buyer through auctions. But the issue of redistribution quickly overshadowed the measures' original, purportedly security-oriented goals. When the Council of Ministers met on May 2, 1915, to discuss the decrees and their future, the question of enemy-alien lands and their redistribution loomed large. The army pushed for the use of the lands to reward valorous soldiers, while a majority of the Council argued in favor of giving the lands to the Peasant Bank for redistribution to peasants.[79] Four members of the Council, including Sazonov, who had originally proposed the February decrees, privately stated their opposition to the new proposals, which in their view would fundamentally alter the goals of the decrees and

"encourage ideas among peasants that forced alienation of land was allowed and approved by the state." Their objections were overridden by
the majority in the Council and, most importantly, by the tsar, who
wrote in the Council of Ministers' journal of the meeting: "Necessary
and good. I fully approve and give my orders. The entire essence of the
question is in the wide purchase by the Peasant Bank of the colonists'
land. Move toward it immediately."[80]

The tsar's preference notwithstanding, the army command assumed
that its vision of using the lands to reward soldiers would prevail. On
May 26 Ianushkevich issued a decree banning all sales of colonist lands
into private hands to ensure that they would all end up under state control, and thus would be available at the end of the war for distribution
to soldiers.[81] This decree, which applied to all areas under military rule,
deprived all those affected by the February decrees of the option to sell
their lands, and denied officials the authority to sell lands at public auctions. Thus it in effect temporarily stopped implementation of the decrees—except for deportees, whose lands were sequestered and transferred to state control.

The opposition of the four dissenting members of the Council of
Ministers found increasing support within the Council as alarming re-
ports began to flow into the MVD, such as the following from an
Odessa gendarme headquarters:

> Among the peasants, there is constant discussion that at the end of
> the war, the land of each peasant will be significantly increased at
> the expense of gentry and German lands, although fears are being
> expressed about the latter that a significant amount of land will re-
> main in the hands of the colonists. Therefore, it is said that if
> their lands are not given, then, at the end of the war, soldiers will
> demand it as reward for their sacrifices for the good of the Moth-
> erland.[82]

In multiethnic areas, the goal of increasing the number of Russian
landowners often clashed with the goals of local non-Russian peasants.
For example, the Latvian press and Duma members responded indignantly to rumors that expropriated German lands would be given
to Russian soldiers. In this case, the Latvian position won the day, and
the bulk of the lands went to neighboring Latvian smallholders and ref-

ugees.[83] The same issue could exacerbate social tensions as well. Rumors that German colonists were evading liquidation by secretly leasing their lands to gentry spread rapidly and stirred resentment over gentry class privileges.[84] Partly in fear that the expropriatory decrees were creating such attitudes in the countryside, the government turned against the May 1915 proposals to expand the February decrees. In August Minister of Internal Affairs Shcherbatov went so far as to declare in the Duma that implementation of even the February laws would be slowed. He stated that "a law which affects millions of *desiatin*, the direct interests of hundreds of thousands of colonists, and the economic life of entire provinces should, understandably, be fully grounded and cannot be put into effect in a very short time."[85]

Expansions of the Expropriatory Decrees

Shcherbatov and other moderates in the government were replaced in September and November 1915. The new Minister of Internal Affairs, A. N. Khvostov, declared the "fight against German dominance" one of his top priorities upon his appointment. He accelerated the pace of implementation of the February decrees and introduced fundamental alterations.

On December 13, 1915, a new set of decrees expanded the expropriation of enemy-subject lands to the entire territory of the empire and extended the area where Russian subjects were to be expropriated to include 21 provinces of European Russia plus the Amur region.[86]

New decrees in August 1916 extended the expropriation of Russian-subject enemy aliens to several Siberian regions where German landholding had grown in the prewar decades and where large numbers of deported and expropriated Germans were sent to live. The extensions were in part a response to petitions from Siberian governors.[87] By the end of 1916, the Committee for the Fight against German Dominance had worked out even more radical legislation to extend the area of expropriation to cover the Volga provinces and the entire territory of the empire except for a few nonagricultural areas of Siberia. In a remarkable new twist, all individuals expropriated by prior laws were forbidden from renting homes, apartments, or buildings in any area—including cities. Thus expropriated colonists were in effect allowed to live legally only in restricted parts of Siberia. The committee's bill was signed by the tsar on February 6, 1917, without substantial changes.[88] The introduction to the decree in the journal of the Council of Ministers included a straightforward explanation of how the laws' intentions had evolved in only two years:

> At first, the idea of the law was mainly strategic and meant to apply to enemy subjects. The Committee [for the Fight against German Dominance] decided unanimously on December 22, 1916, that the liquidation of the lands of enemy subjects should cover the entire expanse of the empire. For immigrants [Russian-subject Germans], the committee found that the ban should apply to areas where their land ownership would be dangerous and harmful to state interests in the broad meaning of the word. A majority thought that in addition to state defense we must consider the urgent need to destroy the large German nests and liquidate that planned colonization which has turned large and various parts of our fatherland (*otechestvo*) into solid corners of the *Vaterland* hostile to us.[89]

These territorial expansions decisively changed the expropriatory legislation from a security-based measures applied to front areas to a nationwide program to nationalize the demographics of land ownership by permanently purging enemy aliens from the rural economy.

The December decrees stimulated greater state involvement in the purchase of lands. In May 1915 the Peasant Land Bank was officially authorized to purchase enemy-subject and German-immigrant lands. The December decrees greatly expanded the bank's role by giving it the right of first refusal on *all* sales of such lands. It could thenceforth reverse any sales to private individuals, whether "voluntary" or at forced public auctions. The intent was to concentrate lands in the fund of the Peasant Bank, which could then reallocate them at war's end according to state priorities.[90]

Purchase by the Peasant Bank created much greater hardship and immediate poverty than had forced sales. In practice, the bank set the price of lands at a hefty discount—on average about one-third of prewar levels. More importantly, payments were not made in cash, but rather in twenty-five-year nontransferable bonds, to be paid out at a rate of 4.5 percent per year. Thus, for example, a property with a 1913 value of 3,000 rubles would typically be appraised at 1,000 rubles, and the expropriated individual would receive only 45 rubles per year. The bonds were further devalued by inflation. Thus the prosperous owner of a property worth 3,000 rubles was turned into an impoverished homeless individual with only 45 rubles cash and a rapidly depreciating bond he was not allowed to sell.[91]

The landowners who were able to sell their properties "voluntarily" and those whose properties were forced to public auction received much lower than prewar prices owing to the depression of land prices during the war. For example, Iakov Zuderman in Taurida received only 90 rubles at the September 1916 auction of his estate, which prior to the war had been worth 900 rubles.[92] This depression was caused by the large number of soldiers at the front (which decreased demand) and by the large amounts of land flooding markets in German areas. Thus, while the decrees included compensation, it was in a form which led to the impoverishment of most individuals affected.[93]

The December 1915 decrees decisively abandoned previous wariness about violating property rights. The laws for the first time included the land originally granted to colonist communities in the late eighteenth and early nineteenth centuries in *vechnoe vladel'stvo* (permanent possession). This land, which had been excluded under the February decrees, accounted for roughly half of all land scheduled for expropriation by the end of 1916. Moreover, the December decrees required the expropriation of lands held in joint or communal ownership if *any* of the members of the commune or institution fell under the laws, thus bringing many direct descendants of original colonists and their lands under the decrees even if they had acquired subjecthood long before 1880.

Identification of Individuals Subject to Expropriation

The first task of implementation was to identify and publish lists of individuals who fell under the decrees. This proved to be enormously complicated and difficult. The February and December decrees allowed local officials only two months to publish lists of all relevant enemy subjects in local official publications, and ten to eighteen months to publish lists of Russian subjects. The MVD was quickly deluged with complaints from regional authorities that their staffs and funding were utterly inadequate for the task, and few provinces published their lists within the established deadlines. The publication of lists was delayed by several months in most cases, but the procedures improved during 1916 as the MVD granted extraordinary budget subsidies and personnel to complete the task.[94]

The Peasant Bank compiled the best, albeit incomplete, data on the number of properties and individuals published in lists of those due to be expropriated. By January 1, 1917, it had information on 2,906 enemy-subject properties with 296,351 *desiatina* and 41,570 Russian-subject properties with 3,223,559 *desiatin*.[95] By the beginning of 1917, over 44,000 enemy-alien properties were scheduled for expropriation with a total area of 3.5 million *desiatin* (9.5 million acres). Since the average rural German household had eight members, one can estimate that roughly 350,000 individuals were listed as due for expropriation.

These figures do not include the large areas under German occupation, areas which by the end of 1915 included all the Polish provinces, Lifland, and parts of Kurland, Kholm, Minsk, Podolia, Volynia, and Bessarabia. Prior to the retreat from these areas, army officials had already sequestered and transferred many German properties to new owners. Moreover, the MVD ordered that the expropriation process be undertaken even for areas still under enemy occupation. While this was obviously difficult, evacuated provincial authorities did what work they could with evacuated landholding records to prepare for ultimate expropriation in areas currently under enemy control. When some areas were reconquered during the summer 1916 Brusilov Offensive, many officials were therefore ready to move quickly forward with the expropriation procedures.[96]

The Peasant Bank figures also do not include the substantial displacement and *de facto* transfer of property caused by the requirement that all leases be broken off within one year of the issuance of the relevant February and December decrees. The Peasant Bank did not keep statistics on leaseholdings, but their number was substantial. In the four provinces of New Russia (Taurida, Kherson, Ekaterinoslav, and Bessarabia) alone, there were over half a million *desiatin* held in lease by 20,000 German settlers already in 1890.[97] Although there are no summary statistics, evidence from petitions and the press suggests that the requirement that leases be broken was implemented on a large scale.[98] It should be noted that while leaseholdings did not appear in official statistics, the breaking of a lease could be as devastating to the family and communities affected as the expropriation of lands held in ownership—perhaps even more so, as former leaseholders did not receive any monetary compensation at all. Most held very long-term leases, and thus had substantial investments in livestock, buildings, and improvements. In the absence of compensation, they were forced to sell their livestock, implements, and buildings at very low prices on local markets swamped with similar items by other colonists facing expropriation of their lands. A very rough estimate of the number of German leaseholdings affected by the laws yields a figure close to 75,000 leaseholders with 750,000 *desiatin*.[99] If areas under enemy occupation are included, this figure should be at least doubled.

Clearly, the Peasant Bank figures alone are inadequate as a gauge of the number of individuals explicitly marked for expropriation before the February Revolution. As a working number, a conservative estimate of 6 million *desiatin* and at least half a million individuals were explicitly marked for expropriation by early 1917. The expansion of the territory to be affected by the decrees of August 1916 and February 6, 1917, is not included in these estimates. These extensions brought German settler communities with at least 750,000 *desiatin* in Siberia and probably another million in the Volga provinces under the threat of expropriation, although the February Revolution intervened before the lands subject to the decrees could even be published in lists.[100]

The scale of the planned transfer was impressive. To put the figures in some perspective, over the entire course of the Stolypin reforms from 1907 to 1915, approximately two million peasant households transferred roughly 14 million *desiatin* from communal to private ownership.[101] While the people actually expropriated before February 1917 were far fewer than those included in the lists, one should not underestimate the significance of inclusion itself. The process of collecting data and the publication of the lists had important impacts on local communities. In order to gather data for the lists, appraisers and local police officials came to German settlements and individual farmstead households, surveyed the boundaries of the property, perused household and community records, and noted in detail the size and value of the landholding, the number of cattle, implements, buildings, and other items of value. Such visits contributed significantly to panicked community and individual decisions not to plant seed for the next crop, to sell off milk cows, livestock, and implements, and to dismantle the equipment in mills, textile factories, and other enterprises and cottage industries on their lands for sale.

Another effect of expropriation decrees was to bring all the disparate German communities under a common threat, helping to consolidate a growing sense of unity and national identity defined more explicitly against the state than ever before in the long history of Germans in Russia. The *Volgadeutsche Zeitung*, for example, explicitly argued that the February 6, 1917, extension of expropriatory legislation to the Volga proved the need for a unified national organization of German settlers.[102] Likewise, a study of German charity in the Omsk region found that mass deportations and liquidation of lands and lease-holdings spurred a sharp increase in German financial assistance from areas throughout the empire to help deportees and expropriated colonists who appeared in the province in large numbers during the war.[103]

Finally, it should also be noted that in the provinces where German settlers made up a substantial part of the population, the program affected a significant portion of the total land in the area. For example, in the provinces of New Russia (Taurida, Kherson, Ekaterinoslav, Khar'kov, and the Don), 6 percent of all tilled land was marked for expropriation.[104] Dissenting government officials and many moderates in the Duma warned that the expropriation of German colonists would encourage peasant hopes for the expropriation of broader categories—from ethnic minorities to all *khutor*-owners and landlords. Miliukov's declaration in the Duma that "if you start with the colonists' lands they will end with yours" appeared increasingly apt.[105] Ironically, it was the liberal Kadet Party—which had supported expropriation of gentry lands with compensation—that proved to be the only consistent voice in defense of the principle of private property rights of the German farmers, while the government most enthusiastically undermined the same conservative principle.

Defining Enemy-Alien Categories

State identification of individuals subject to expropriation involved a massive operation to sort and categorize large populations according to various criteria into the opposites of reliable and unreliable, acceptable and unacceptable landowners. This sorting process took place both on the categorical level, which set the parameters, and on the individual level, as various committees and officials ruled on thousands of individual petitions for exemption from the laws.

Traditional *soslovie* and religious markers remained important in making these decisions. Although the colonist estate was abolished in 1871, and the term *sobstvennik-poselianin* (landowner-settler) was used officially thereafter, colloquially the term *kolonist* (colonist) remained in wide use, even among the German settlers themselves. The major decisions on expropriation separated rural Russian-subject Germans from the equally numerous individuals of German origin in urban areas. The exemption of German members of gentry, merchant, and other nonpeasant estates from the expropriatory decrees further indicated the way the legislation went along old *soslovie* lines.

The expropriatory decrees also exempted individuals who became Orthodox prior to January 1, 1914, another old criterion in defining the enemy-alien category. But it is remarkable how quickly and extensively ethnicity and citizenship joined these older markers of difference.

The February decree affecting Russian subjects applied only to individuals of "German descent." A specific clause exempted individuals in rural communities who were able to prove their Slavic ethnic origins, leading to the exemption of the substantial number of Russian-subject Czech, Bulgarian, Serb, and Greek settlers living in rural "colonist" settlements in southwest Russia. So while the enemy-alien category in some sense reasserted an old *soslovie* category, it was sharply delimited by ethnic criteria.

Moreover, the decrees affecting enemy subjects eventually brought ethnicity to bear in the definition of the enemy-alien category. There were few categoric exemptions—even the generally most favored Czechs, Slovaks, and Greeks were officially exempted only in the summer of 1916.[106] In practice, though, officials allowed most individual petitioners to avoid expropriation if they could prove "favorable" ethnic origins. Czechs and Slovaks received the most favorable treatment, while Polish and Bulgarian enemy subjects were more often denied their petitions.

The various exemptions in effect constituted a constructed enemy-alien category along the old *soslovie* lines of "colonist," further delimited by factors of ethnicity, citizenship, and immigrant status. Puzzling as the enemy-alien categories were to some, they quickly became reified as the most crucial markers defining distinct enemy populations. Just as Peter Gatrell argues that refugees can be seen as a distinct new population and identity created by the war, so too can the expropriated enemy-alien landholders be seen as a distinct newly created category, based on an amalgam of old *soslovie* and newer ethnic and citizenship markers of identity.[107] Once marked as enemy aliens, the stigma followed those so labeled even after they had lost their farms, and thus their identity-defining ties to the land. Provincial and city governors, claiming that expropriated colonists were flooding into cities and buying up properties and businesses, strove to ban them from acquiring property in cities.[108] The December 1915 decrees in part responded to such concerns by requiring that enemy aliens originally from rural communities be fired from all firms, social institutions, and civil service posts, even if they now lived or worked in urban areas. The August 1916 extensions of the expropriatory decrees to areas of Siberia were in part motivated by an attempt to prevent and reverse the acquisition of lands by expropriated and deported enemy aliens even in these distant areas where land was not in short supply.[109] Finally, by banning colonists from acquiring any property in urban areas or even from renting apartments, the February 6, 1917, decree recognized in law what many local authorities had already been doing for months.

The sudden creation of an enemy group with stigmas and legal limitations gave rise to the use of a term more commonly associated with the *lishentsy* (individuals deprived of voting rights) of the Soviet period—namely, *byvshie liudi* (former people). The term was colloquially used in reference to expropriated enemy aliens deprived of their rights and lands but allowed temporarily to remain on their lands or in the area by special exemption for a defined period.[110]

Problems and Effects of Expropriation

In practice, expropriations quickly ran into serious problems of implementation. Lack of personnel and funding to implement the complicated and large-scale program prevented the rapid execution of the expropriatory decrees. The complex and shifting rules on exemptions created a huge backlog of cases. The most important barrier to rapid implementation, however, proved to be the unforeseen scope of dam-

age the program wrought upon local economies and the national economic system as a whole. It proved very difficult to isolate and remove
perceived enemy-alien "dominance" in the agrarian economic sphere
without causing severe declines in wartime production and serious difficulties for the imperial economy as a whole and for the interests of
"Russians" throughout the empire. The economic effects of the expropriation program became most apparent in early 1916, shortly after the
December 1915 decrees vastly expanded its scope and news about the
current and potential impacts of the program began to arrive from the
provinces.

The German farmers used to run a highly productive, export-ori-
ented agriculture. In the four provinces of the Black Sea region alone,
Germans tilled three million *desiatin*, approximately 14 percent of the
land under cultivation. Their capital-intensive methods and advanced
techniques of breeding, seed innovation, crop rotation, fertilizer, and
implement use all contributed to much higher yields than the imperial and regional average. Their productivity proved a major reason
why these provinces were important surplus grain producers which ex-
ported not only abroad, but also to other Russian provinces. This became a crucial factor by early 1916, as the grain supply for the empire
suffered critical shortages. By 1916, nearly half of all marketable grain
was going to the army, and serious regional problems of grain market-
ing had emerged.[111] State-imposed price ceilings, transportation problems, and a sharp decrease in marketed grain as peasants and grain sell-
ers built up stocks in the expectation of higher prices in the future all
contributed to the shortage of grain in key regions.[112] The expropriation program should be added to these factors.

While during peacetime land hunger had been the major problem,
during the war the call-ups for military service caused a shortage of agricultural laborers. In 1915, some of the shortfall was met by sending
prisoners of war to work the fields and by directing refugees capable of
work to areas of labor shortage. By early 1916, however, the War Ministry reported that over 700,000 POWs and internees had been allocated for work in agriculture, industry, and construction, and that no
more labor was available. Several tens of thousands of Asian agricultural workers were allowed into the country during 1916, but military
and Ministry of Internal Affairs opposition to their entry into the country limited their numbers.[113]

In early 1916, just when the shortage of workers in agriculture became most severe, the expropriation schedules began to take effect on a large scale. Military officials exacerbated the problem. For example, the commander of the Caucasus Military District decreed that all enemy aliens had to leave his region once expropriations were completed, thereby ensuring that they could not continue to work on their former properties or engage in agricultural work for others. A May 1915 military order banning the sale of lands in order to reserve them for military heroes also greatly complicated the work of authorities and made it much more difficult to ensure that expropriation would not lead to fallow fields. The order was not officially retracted until July 10, 1916, after many letters of complaint from MVD officials.[114]

More important even than the expropriations themselves was the wave of panic which swept through German areas as the lists of those due to be expropriated under the December 1915 decrees were published. Many of the expropriation schedules came due before the fall 1916 harvest. As a result, many farmers had no incentive to plant their spring crops in 1916. The publication of lists according to the February 1915 decrees and a decision of the Council of Ministers in March 1915 to deny credit to farmers of German descent had already caused many to forego planting spring and winter crops in 1915.[115] The denial of credit was particularly damaging, as many German farmers operated capital-intensive farms and depended upon yearly short-term loans to buy seed, fertilizer, and essential tools. According to one widely disseminated report, 1.5 million *desiatin* of colonist lands went unplanted during 1915, resulting in a decline of 150 million poods of grain (1 pood (*pud*) = 16.38 kilograms = 38 pounds).[116] This would account for over half of the entire decline in seeded area in that year.[117]

The December 1915 laws worsened an already bad situation. On March 24, State Council member P. V. Kamenskii claimed that nearly two million *desiatin* would go unseeded in Ekaterinoslav, Kherson, Khar'kov, and Taurida provinces.[118] It was estimated that such a decline in seeded area would lead to a decline of 200 million poods of grain in the four southern provinces alone. To put such figures in perspective, the entire decline in grain output during 1915 had been 344 million poods.[119]

The publication of the lists also induced a mass sell-off of implements, seed, livestock, and other movable property.[120] Facing payment by the Peasant Bank in illiquid bonds, the targeted farmers logically tried to convert whatever they could into cash. Sales of land to private individuals were risky, as the bank could and often did overturn them by exercising its right of first refusal, a right it retained for three months after private sales or auctions. Not surprisingly, Germans sold off the contents of their farms. Meat canneries sprang up in areas of German settlement, and cattle, sheep, pigs, and even dairy cows were sold to them at a fraction of their value. In the Mennonite Molchan *volost'* of Crimea, 37 percent of the horses and 18 percent of all dairy cattle were sold in the first months of 1916.[121] As a result of these sell-offs, when properties were transferred, the new owners often lacked many of the essential implements, draft animals, and crucial equipment in mills, dairies, and other firms. Even when such property stayed with the land, officials reported that the new owners often lacked the means and expertise to operate machinery and to manage the dairy, milling, breeding, and other farm-related enterprises on the properties.[122]

In addition to the expropriation of landowners, the December decrees moved toward a comprehensive purge of enemy aliens in all prominent positions and types of activity in rural Russia. An important provision of the decrees forced the rapid liquidation of all firms on rural lands if any of the owners was in a category subject to the laws. This included hundreds of grain mills, food processing plants, wineries, and other businesses that serviced both the needs of German areas and those of the surrounding communities.

Small, medium, and large agricultural firms located in rural areas were all affected. The Ministry of Trade and Industry reported in March 1916 that it had already identified and begun liquidation proceedings against 400 firms in rural areas, and that the list represented only a fraction of the number which would be closed according to the December 1915 decrees.[123] Among these firms were 26 factories producing agricultural implements, with an annual prewar production of 116 million rubles, and mills which processed 14 million poods of flour per year.[124] In some areas, entire industries went out of production. For example, in Podolia the entire large textile industry shut down in mid-1916 following to the mass firings and expropriations of enemy aliens and the panicked sell-off of looms and equipment.[125] A ruling of the Council of Ministers in August 1916 that all buildings owned by German colonist communities were to be confiscated and transferred to the Peasant Bank caused further damage.[126]

Among the more serious effects of these disruptions of rural industries and services was a sharp rise in the price of milling throughout South Russia, Volynia, and other areas with substantial enemy-alien populations.[127] The owners of enterprises in rural areas facing liquidation sold off movable equipment and parts rather than wait to receive compensation at heavily discounted prices in the same nontransferable 25-year bonds used to compensate landholders.

Moreover, a clause of the December decrees required the firing of German enemy aliens from a list of twenty specific positions in firms, social organizations, and the civil service, and sanctioned the firing of others at employers' discretion.[128] An additional decree of February 20, 1916, required the firing of all Russian-subject immigrant Germans and enemy-subject estate managers. These measures applied to the numerous Germans in cities as well. There are no statistics on such firings, but anecdotal and archival evidence indicates a broad scale, as a purge mentality spread throughout the country.[129]

The impulse was easily transferred to other populations. About 220,000 Bulgarians lived in rural settlements in Ukraine on the outbreak of war. After Bulgaria entered the war against Russia in October 1915, the Council of Ministers applied all expropriatory decrees to Bulgarian enemy subjects. Soon thereafter, local administrations, factory managers, and social institutions throughout the south began to spontaneously fire Bulgarians from their jobs, even if they were Russian subjects. The process took on such magnitude that the Council of Ministers was forced to act to slow down the reaction. Noting that many provinces with large Bulgarian populations were in dire straits for lack of workers, the Council decreed that further firings and deportations should only be applied to those deemed "truly dangerous" and to those in nonagricultural pursuits.[130] In practice, the MVD had to send repeated reminders that enemy-subject Bulgarians were temporarily exempted from the laws, and also that Russian-subject Bulgarians did not fall under the decrees.

Firings of German immigrants from their jobs in cities also took on a large scale. Only in early 1917, long after the disruptive results had become clear, did the Committee for the Fight against German Dominance begin to draw back from its earlier encouragement of this practice.[131]

The economic impacts of the campaign could not be contained to the targeted communities alone. For example, a single *volost'* in Crimea reported that the factory of G. Shreder (the first producer of oil pumps in Russia); the mill of G. Vilems (which produced 6,000 poods of flour per day, serving an area much larger than the *volost'*); the mutual credit society; the consumers society; and fifty other factories and mills with 5,000 workers were all being liquidated.[132] Of course, many of the workers in these firms and consumers from surrounding areas were not enemy aliens.

Likewise, the liquidation of enemy-alien participation in credit institutions led many of them to bankruptcy, bringing down many Russian individuals and organizations along with them. The impoverishment of enemy aliens in turn led to a wave of defaults on their bank loans, a fact which Russian bankers made abundantly clear in correspondence with the authorities. A group of banks in Taurida province reported that it alone had 2 million rubles of outstanding loans to colonists, but saw little hope of recovering the debts in view of the expropriation program.[133]

The campaign led to other unforeseen ripple effects upon Russian individuals, communities, and national interests. Karl Lindeman, who gathered extensive data on rural German financial affairs in South Russia, pointed out that these relatively prosperous communities had given substantial contributions to the Red Cross and the army, and contributed time and money to help refugees.[134] Such donations dropped off considerably in 1916. Schools, hospitals, orphanages, and voluntary associations providing funds and services for the war effort were hit hard; many were forced to close in 1916, whether because of loss of income or because of the laws requiring the closure of social institutions founded or managed by rural Germans or enemy subjects.[135]

Evidence of the scope of damage being caused by the expropriatory decrees—especially the seeding crisis in early 1916—provided the immediate impetus for the mobilization of liberal and moderate Russian opinion against the program. The Duma debated the issue several times, and prominent members of the Octobrist Party who had either supported or tolerated the expropriatory program moved into opposition. The Progressive Bloc issued a statement that the laws were causing economic problems and that measures should be taken to ensure that lands stayed in production.[136] In May 1916, Prince L'vov sent a series of appeals on behalf of the Special Committee on Defense, arguing that the closures and firings of employees were affecting many firms producing defense orders and thus were hardly in the national interest. He cited evidence from one district (*uezd*) in Ekaterinoslav where twenty factories producing solely for defense orders were scheduled for liquidation.[137]

Many individual Russian landowners who leased land to enemy aliens also sent petitions for exemptions, claiming that the forced ending of leaseholdings would seriously affect their own economic well-being. Such petitions were rarely granted, even when sent by prominent, well-connected gentry who vouched for the good farming and complete reliability of their leaseholders.[138]

Officials, faced with evidence of serious damage to the national economy and defense production, attempted to limit the negative effects while continuing the campaign. On May 1, 1916, the MVD sent a circular to all governors asking them to send lists of mills and firms due for expropriation that in their opinion were essential to defense or the local economy and thus should be exempted. The governors responded with lists of hundreds of mills and firms producing for defense needs or otherwise of "social or state significance."[139] The MVD directed that such firms, and the amount of land necessary for their operation, could be exempted, but all lands not necessary for the firms' production were to be expropriated on schedule. Significantly, when exemptions were allowed for such firms, they were typically granted as temporary postponements "until conditions would allow the expropriations to proceed." By no means were all firms exempted, but this substantial retreat revealed a partial recognition of the impossibility of completely removing enemy aliens from the rural economy in rapid fashion.[140]

In an attempt to halt the sell-off of movable property, the Council of Ministers decreed in June 1916 that if owners had sold any livestock, implements, or other movable property prior to expropriation, the value of such property would be deducted from the price paid by the Peasant Bank, or if forced to auction, the owner would be forced to pay fines of up to 5 percent of the value of the landholding. There is little evidence that this stopped sales of movable property, for the fundamental incentive of selling for cash continued to outweigh the loss of value in illiquid 25-year bonds.[141]

With similar coerciveness, the government tried to address the seeding crisis by imposing fines of up to 10 percent of the value of the landholding on any enemy alien who did not plant—even if he was scheduled for expropriation before the next harvest. By July 1916, faced with labor shortages and practical difficulties in implementing such a broad transfer of properties, the government issued a cynical decree allowing new owners to keep expropriated enemy aliens on their former lands as wage laborers or leaseholders for up to a maximum of one year in order to bring in the next harvest and plant fields.[142]

It is difficult to measure the effects of the many initiatives to expropriate and purge enemy aliens and German colonists from their participation in the rural Russian economy. The evidence cited above is but a small part of the large body of anecdotal and local evidence that the actual and projected impacts were important, not only upon German communities, but also upon surrounding populations and the Russian national economy.

Despite the increasing evidence of the program's economic damage, few officials adopted a lenient approach by granting exemptions. One of the main reasons was the vigilance of the conservative press over their daily decisions. Officials across the country were very sensitive to reports in *Novoe vremia*, *Vechernee vremia*, and other mass circulation papers that they were soft in the fight against German dominance. According to N. P. Kharlamov, several officials of German descent, such as Governor Grevenits of Kherson, were especially aggressive and inflexible in their implementation of the various decrees, confiding to him that they wanted to counter accusations that they sympathized with Germans. Officials with Russian names also felt pressure. Kharlamov himself recalled that he rejected many worthy petitions for exemption in order to avoid seeing his name in the pages of *Novoe vremia*.[143]

Exemptions that were granted usually came in the form of temporary postponements rather than comprehensive alterations to the long-term goals of the program: they were given either to individuals proving membership in a favored nationality or to those proving that their enterprise was essential to the war effort. Ironically, the last category contradicted the purported goals of the program—to remove unreliable individuals from sensitive positions in the economy where they allegedly engaged in sabotage, and to remove alien individuals from influential positions where they allegedly dominated Russians economically. The right-wing press was quick to point out these anomalies in vicious attacks upon government officials for treasonous "protection" of influential Germans and foreigners. Thus although officials implemented a quite radical version of the anti-alien program, this still did not gain for the government the public support of the Right, which saw no possibility for compromise on an issue it framed in the emotional terms of treason and patriotism.

Statistical Results of Expropriation

The actual expropriations of landholdings were conducted rapidly and completely for enemy subjects. Reports from governors indicate that in most provinces every single enemy-subject landholding had been expropriated by summer 1916. But enemy subjects held a relatively small portion of the lands slated for expropriation (2,906 properties with 296,351 *desiatin*).[144]

The expropriation of Russian subjects did not begin on a large scale until late 1916 because several deadlines in the February decrees stretched the implementation process over many months. For individuals within the 150- and 100-*verst* zones, deadlines stretched ten or sixteen months, respectively, from the date of publication of lists of properties to be expropriated. Most of the lists were published between April and June 1915, so expropriation could not begin until February 1916. The December 1915 decrees accelerated the schedule, giving Russian subjects ten months after the publication of lists before compulsory expropriation was to begin. Since few lists were published before March 1916 for the areas newly affected by the December 1915 decrees, expropriation could not begin in these areas until early 1917.

Given these schedules, it is hardly surprising that only a small portion of those on the lists were actually expropriated before the February Revolution. There are no statistics available for the large number of "voluntary" sales by farmers trying to sell before the expropriation deadlines and only incomplete figures on compulsory auctions. Once the Peasant Bank was granted the right of first refusal to purchase enemy-alien lands in December 1915, it began to keep the most complete records on expropriations. By January 1, 1917, according to its data, 1,923 properties belonging to Russian subjects with 665,892 *desiatin* had been forced to public auction and sold for 123 million rubles. In addition, the Peasant Bank itself had resolved to acquire 1,127 properties with 516,749 *desiatin*, and had actually completed the acquisition of 431 properties with 144,894 *desiatin* for 22 million rubles by January 1, 1917.[145]

The expropriations accelerated during the first two months of 1917 right up to the February Revolution. Large sales by public auction were reported in the press during the two months, including 100,000 *desiatin* in Kherson during January and 130,000 *desiatin* in Bessarabia in a single day.[146] Lindeman reports that by February, 20 to 30 auctions were taking place every day in the southern provinces.[147] The Peasant Bank also rapidly increased its acquisition activity in early 1917. By March 1, it had acquired a total of 920,000 for 140 million rubles.[148]

BY THE EVE of the February Revolution, the regime had publicly declared its intention to expropriate the landholdings of over half a million of its citizens amounting to well over 6 million *desiatin* (15 million acres), and had begun the process, forcing the alienation of nearly 2 million *desiatin* with many more lands *de facto* transferred in areas under military rule.[149] Building upon prewar administrative patterns of restricting land ownership rights according to ethnicity and citizenship, the projects undertaken during World War I expanded the politics of land and nationality to additional groups. The program aimed for a radical transformation of the demographics of land ownership and settlement by permanently removing a population category and replacing it with favored nationalities.

The government's embrace of this campaign takes on particular significance in light of the growing tensions in the countryside over private property in general. In some areas of heavy German settlement such as Volynia, Germans made up the bulk of the population practicing *khutor* (separate individual farmstead) agriculture.[150] Marking Germans as enemies to be expropriated thus also gave official endorsement to the powerful idea among the peasants that *khutor* and other forms of private ownership were illegitimate.[151] On the macro-level, the expropriation of private landholders of precisely the type Stolypin had aimed to create, on a scale comparable to the Stolypin reforms themselves, indicates an important shift in the government's role.[152] During the war, the regime switched its support from a grand program to create and protect private ownership to a program of comparable scale to nationalize the land by expropriating private owners.

5

Forced Migrations

OF ALL THE PRACTICES that define the concept of the nationalizing state, forced migration has been the most dramatic. The forced population exchanges following the Balkan wars shortly before World War I, the deportations of Armenians in 1915, population exchanges in the wake of World War I, and the even more massive population exchanges and mass killings of World War II and its aftermath show how integral the forcible movement of peoples has been to the the remaking of imperial and postimperial space into national states. In this broad context, forced migration in the Russian Empire during World War I has an important place as one of the earliest cases of large-scale state-sponsored forced migration in the last century. It marked an important early step away from the world of empires and the mixing of populations during the so-called long peace of the century prior to 1914 toward population division in the age of nationalizing states and war.

At first, the army's mass operations seemed to focus on security issues raised by the nature of total war, especially the idea that the war was one being fought between citizenries. Thus the first mass operation of the war aimed to intern all male enemy subjects of service age in order to prevent their departure to join their respective armies. But the categories affected widened until they amounted to nearly all enemy subjects—including men of all ages, women, and children—and the operation then swept up large numbers of Russian subjects of German, Jewish, and other backgrounds as well. Each roundup quickly became enmeshed with the nationalizing agendas of expropriating

121

landholdings, businesses, and properties, further changing the intentions and nature of the operation as it was being implemented. In this chapter I examine the forced migration of each of the major groups affected: enemy subjects, Russian-subject Germans, and Russian-subject Jews, then look at a few cases of smaller minority groups.

The Deportation and Internment of Enemy Subjects

The provisions of martial law explicitly granted the army the authority to order civilian officials throughout the area under military rule to deport any individuals or groups out of the country or into the interior. The army began to use these powers quickly after the outbreak of the war. On July 25, 1914, the acting Chief of the General Staff, M. A. Beliaev, ordered the deportation of all "enemy-subject males of military service age" residing in areas under military rule and their internment in camps in Viatka, Orenburg, and Vologda.[1] Internal correspondence of the commanders involved shows that this was seen as a straightforward military-strategic operation intended to prevent the departure of enemy-subject males to enemy armies. Because it proved difficult to distinguish males who were actually in the reserves or otherwise would be drafted for army service, the army and the Ministry of Internal Affairs established that "all German and Austrian males age 18–45 who were deemed physically capable of carrying a weapon" were to be interned.[2] The Ministry of Interior took over responsibility for the oversight of these deportees and distinguished them from POWs by creating a new classification for them—"civilian deportees" (*grazhdan'skie vyselentsy*)—and within days of the military order, expanded the operation to the whole empire.[3]

To carry out these first mass deportations of the war, the Ministry of Internal Affairs set up a series of staging points in major cities throughout the empire, using jails, guarded barracks, or makeshift camps. From these points, the deportees were sent in sealed freight cars under armed guard to one of the designated provinces.[4] On October 18, 1914, the day before Russia declared war on the Ottoman Empire, the Council of Ministers and the army extended all measures affecting German and Austrian subjects to Ottoman subjects.[5]

The internment of this relatively narrow category of enemy subjects living in areas of the Russian Empire under military rule affected about

50,000 individuals (out of an estimated 600,000 enemy subjects with permanent residence in the empire).[6] The operation can be in large part attributed to the development of mass reserve armies throughout Europe; hence men of service age were potential enemy soldiers if allowed to leave the country. All the other major powers took analogous measures, and this category made up the bulk of enemy aliens interned throughout the world during the First World War. Although the internment of this category was closely linked to straightforward security concerns, scholars have noted that it already marked a major worldwide departure in the practice of warfare, creating a new category of prisoner: the civilian enemy alien.[7]

When war broke out, there was little expectation that other enemy-subject civilians—women, children, and men who did not owe military service in enemy countries—would be affected at all by the state of war, much less deported. Indeed, a July 26, 1914, MVD circular explicitly declared that "peacefully occupied Austrians and Germans who are outside any suspicion may remain in their places [of residence] and retain the protection of our laws, or they may leave the country."[8] An indeterminate number of enemy subjects were able to leave the country in the first few days of the war, but by the end of the first week, the army had effectively sealed the borders. Although the Ministry of Foreign Affairs negotiated several agreements with Germany and Austria on the exchange of enemy-subject civilians, the army and the Ministry of Internal Affairs were able to block the implementation of these agreements. It is unlikely that more than 10,000 enemy-subject civilians were allowed to leave the country during the war, less than four percent of the number of enemy subjects ultimately interned in Russia and two percent of the total number of enemy subjects living in Russia prior to the war.[9]

Some military commanders rapidly extended the definition of security. In isolated instances, a few began to order the *polnoe ochishchenie* [full cleansing, or clearing] of all enemy subjects without exception from areas near the front already in the first weeks of the war. On July 27, 1914, Commander in Chief Grand Duke Nikolai Nikolaevich ordered the deportation of "any foreigners who raise suspicions" from areas where troops were actively engaged.[10] The extensive powers of military authorities made such broad directives possible, and led to the rapid expansion of deportations beyond the initial category of males owing military service in enemy countries. Already in September 1914, the army included women and children in the deportation of 7,000 enemy-subject civilians from Riga. The operation was so complete that only eighty were allowed to remain.[11]

At first, in August and September, deportations occurred sporadically at the front. But a telegram on October 3, 1914, from the Grand Duke Nikolai Nikolaevich to the Council of Ministers, proved to be one of the chief turning points in the move toward a broad and systematic program of deportation and internment. The Grand Duke told of German and Austrian atrocities at the front, and demanded in response the "strictest and most decisive measures toward the subjects of enemy powers without regard for their social position, on the entire territory of Russia."[12] This led the Grand Duke's Chief of Staff, Ianushkevich, to issue a series of orders to clear all enemy subjects *without exception* from areas near the front.

The operations then quickly spread to areas under military rule well to the interior of the front lines. In November 1914, General Sivers ordered the governors of the Baltic provinces to deport all remaining enemy subjects from the Riga district and the entire Kurland province, and requested permission to deport them from other points along the coast, claiming that there had been cases of signaling from German ships. During the first three days, women and children were deported along with the men. In response to a flood of complaints, on the fourth day, the commander of the operation reluctantly allowed the exemption of women—but only if their loyalty was not under suspicion.[13]

On December 13, 1914, the army orders expanded to a truly mass scale. The commanders of the Northwest Front coordinated the deportation to the east of all Austro-Hungarian, German, and Ottoman subjects from all of the Wistula provinces (the ten provinces of the former Kingdom of Poland within the Russian Empire), allowing exemptions only for Slavs "who were in no way suspected of spying."[14] In the course of the next three months, a series of additional decrees from the highest levels of the military command ordered the complete clearing of all enemy subjects without exception, including women and children, from Volynia and parts of the Baltic provinces. Ianushkevich berated those commanders of military districts behind the front whom he regarded soft in their treatment of enemy subjects and demanded that they implement all deportation orders fully and punish any lenient subordinates.[15]

While the army expanded the deportation and internment of enemy subjects from zones along the front to cover the entire huge area under military rule, it also pressed the civilian government to extend the operation to areas outside military control. The civilian authorities had already paved the way through two September 1914 MVD circulars, which removed the right of enemy subjects to defense in any court civil action, voided all international agreements and conventions protecting enemy subjects, and banned local officials from granting any enemy subject the right to leave the area of his or her residence without written permission from the police.[16] On December 12, 1914, Ianushkevich wrote to the head of the Petrograd Military District that "the clearing of the many subjects of countries at war with Russia from the theater of military activity, including our capital, is [a matter] of first-order military significance."[17] On December 20, 1914, he ordered Lieutenant General Manikovskii to "clear out/cleanse in a most careful manner" [*ochistit' samym tshchatel'nym obrazom*] the area in a 100-*verst* band of territory along the Finnish coast, as well as a complex of zones within the Petrograd region along rivers, near factories working for defense, and other places covering a large part of the capital city.[18] Ianushkevich ordered that no exemptions be made for social position, Slavic origin, or any other reason.[19] On January 7, 1915, Fan der Flit expanded this exclusion zone to include all of Estland, Lifland, most of Petrograd, and parts of Novgorod and Vyborg provinces.[20]

In April 1915, under army pressure, the Department of Police added its own network of security zones throughout the country, including twenty- to fifty-*verst* zones on both sides of strategic railways, around hundreds of factories working for defense, and along coastlines and rivers. Civilian authorities were required to deport all enemy subjects—including Slavs, women, and children—from these zones. Any excluded individual appearing in the zones could be charged with treason and tried by military court. As the war progressed, the zones tended to expand to include more areas farther behind the front.[21]

By the summer of 1915, deportation orders encompassed all enemy subjects without exception in most areas under army rule and within a broad set of exclusion zones throughout the country, as well as all males of military service age throughout the empire. But several influential military officials were not satisfied and pushed for a maximalist program—what might be called the "hard line" on deportations. For example, Prince Feliks Iusupov, who presided over the May–July 1915 deportations of several thousand enemy aliens from Moscow, wrote a memo to the tsar in June 1915 excoriating deportation policies in areas under civilian rule as insufficient. He proposed constructing concentration camps to which all enemy subjects without exception (and also Russian subjects with German names) would be sent for the duration of the war. Although this proposal was not implemented, Iusupov was granted permission to continue his deportations of enemy aliens from Moscow.[22] An internal memo within the headquarters of General Staff expressed a version of the hard line on deportations:

> Not a single German or Austrian subject alive can or should be considered harmless. All must be investigated, and this will be expensive for the government and likely unsuccessful. The Russian population reserves for itself the role of observer of foreigners harmful to us and many of their declarations have the character of a cry: "save our Motherland in such a difficult moment from compromise." The only solution is deportation without exemptions [*pogolovnoe vyselenie*].[23]

Indeed, in the first half of 1915, exemptions on the basis of age or gender became increasingly rare. On June 21, Ianushkevich ordered the immediate deportation of all enemy subjects regardless of sex or age who had been allowed for whatever reason to remain in a 100-*verst* zone along the front and the borders.[24] The military strove for the most complete possible removal of enemy subjects from the area under its control and pressed the civilian government to follow suit elsewhere. In practice, this operation, potentially involving the identification and relocation of over a half million permanent residents of the empire, proved to be much more complex and problematic than expected, principally because "enemy subjects" included large numbers of Slavs (Czechs, Poles, Slovaks, Serbs, and others) who demanded exemption from the deportations. Even with the exemptions granted to many of these nationalities, the internment program affected a remarkable proportion of the total number of enemy subjects resident in the Russian Empire. Summary statistics are difficult to determine because of the dispersal of authority to order deportations. The military branch responsible for railroad evacuations alone reported a quarter million enemy subjects deported and placed under police oversight during the war (see table 3).

Table 3   Enemy subjects deported by train during the war, according to the
Military Railroad Transit Division

1914	68,000
1915	134,000
1916	41,278
1917	11,511
Total	255,789

Sources: Sergei Nelipovich, "Repressii protiv poddannykh 'tsentral'nykh derzhav'," *Voenno-istoricheskii zhurnal* 6 (1996): 41; RGVIA, f. 400, op. 8, d. 697, l. 242; d. 704, ll. 1–163; RGVIA, f. 400, op. 8, d. 707, ll. 1–8.

These statistics include only some of the tens of thousands who were expelled from Moscow, Petrograd, and the network of security zones throughout the country. Nor do they count individuals who traveled by their own means to avoid deportation under guard. Including these individuals would bring the total number of enemy subjects deported or expelled during the war to roughly 300,000. This estimate does not include the nearly equal number of civilian foreign citizens deported to the Russian interior from occupied territories.[25]

Thus approximately half the 600,000 enemy subjects registered as permanent residents of the Russian Empire in 1914 were deported, then interned in camps or assigned to live in specified areas and placed under police oversight during the war.[26] The vast majority of those exempted were Slavs, while the deportation of German, Jewish, Turkish, and Hungarian enemy subjects was remarkably thorough. For example, by June 1915, 14,890 enemy subjects had been deported from Warsaw, and 7,199 allowed to stay, nearly all of whom were Polish.[27] Likewise, by early 1915, just over 10,000 German and Austrian subjects had been deported from Petrograd province. Of the 3,227 remaining at that point, 1,858 were Slavs and another 635 were from neutral countries.[28] Governors of several western and southern provinces reported that every single German and Jewish enemy subject had been deported.[29]

Although Russian deportation and internment of enemy subjects preceded analogous actions in most other European countries and exceeded them in scope, they were also part of a worldwide shift in the practice of warfare. Already on July 20/August 2, 1914, France declared that enemy subjects had one day to leave the country, after which date they were required to notify the police of their whereabouts, and those residing in fortified areas throughout northwestern

Figure 9. Major internment sites of enemy-subject civilians.

France were required to leave.[30] Britain passed an Alien Restriction Act on August 3/16, 1914, requiring all enemy subjects to register, and prohibiting them from living in or entering nearly one hundred strategic areas, mostly near the coastline. Actual internment began in both countries in mid-1915, and by the end of that year, each country had interned nearly 50,000 enemy subjects. Germany and Austria began their internment programs four months into the war. The number of civilian enemy subjects in German camps rose from 48,000 in June 1915 to over 110,000 in October 1918. Even states as far from the areas of fighting as Australia, Brazil, and the United States deported and interned significant numbers of enemy subjects.[31] An important aspect of the processs leading to the internment of enemy subjects throughout the world was an international chain of actions and reactions, and the Russian actions played a key role in this dynamic. The deportations were part of the general blurring of the line between combatants and civilians and the sharpening of the distinctions between "core" populations and immigrants which the First World War brought about.

Within the Russian context, the deportation and internment of over a quarter of a million enemy subjects was particularly significant because of the number and prominence of enemy subjects in economic elites. While in most countries interned enemy subjects retained ownership of their businesses and properties, the parallel programs to nationalize enemy-subject properties ensured that in Russia, internment became part of a broader program of permanent socioeconomic and demographic transformation. As such, the measures gained a great deal of popular support. Even among liberals, the deportation of enemy subjects was not very controversial, in part because for the liberals the Russian community at war was one that was defined and bounded by citizenship. No such consensus existed on the deportation of Russian subjects.

Forced Migrations of Russian-Subject Germans

The War Statute granted the army the authority to deport not only enemy subjects, but any group it saw fit from areas under its control. The early operations to deport and intern enemy subjects introduced mass deportation, and within months, individual army commanders began to apply similar directives to Russian-subject minorities. The two most important Russian-subject groups targeted were Germans and Jews.

By all indications, a relatively low-rank officer was the first to order a large-scale expulsion of Russian-subject Germans. On September 7, 1914, Suvalki Governor Kuprianov reported that a corps commander had ordered the expulsion of all "German colonists" from areas occupied by troops in the province. Kuprianov eagerly requested permission to extend this order to cover the entire province. Although at first he was only allowed to deport Germans from areas where troops were present, on November 30 he was granted permission to expel all Germans, including colonists, urban populations, and Germans in government service from the entire province. This added up to about 34,000 Germans.[32] This initiative quickly gained support from the highest levels of the military command, starting with Grand Duke Nikolai Nikolaevich and his Chief of Staff Ianushkevich.

The evolution of the operations against Russia's Germans reveals that the question of German colonist landholdings quickly became the most important factor. While the deportation of enemy subjects expanded from a targeted security operation focused on males of service age to the entire population of enemy subjects in the empire, orders to remove all Germans from given territories narrowed into a more targeted program to remove all rural German landowners.

The policy took shape during one of the largest forced migration operations of the war. On December 23, 1914, Danilov ordered three armies and the commander of the Dvinsk military district to deport "all male German colonists" over fifteen years old from the left bank of the Wistula to internal provinces. Three days later, Ianushkevich wrote to one of his generals that German colonists on the right bank of the Wistula had been "signaling the enemy to reveal Russian army positions." He ordered him to hang any caught on the spot without investigation and deport all male colonists from the entire Wistula region.[33] By the end of 1914, orders had been issued for the deportation of German colonist males from all ten Polish provinces. The governor general of Warsaw, Engalychev, estimated that the deportation orders would affect over 200,000 German men owning 20,000 landed properties.[34]

On January 5, 1915, Ianushkevich explicitly ruled that not only colonists, but also urban German populations should be deported.[35] The initial deportation orders applied only to males over fifteen years of age, but Engalychev, in a circular to the governors of Poland, clarified that officials should "facilitate" the departure of the families of deportees "since this is desirable for state interests."[36] Even without such encouragement, most families decided to leave with the men. In the words of one wife of a German farmer about to be deported, "we women would not think of being left here, defenseless against all manner of outrages about which we have heard."[37] If we count families, then more than 420,000 rural Germans in the Polish provinces faced deportation along with at least a hundred thousand urban residents of German descent.[38]

The deportations immediately precipitated a flood of petitions for exemption from individuals and groups affected, which raised questions regarding the definition of "German," "colonist," and categories to be included or exempted. Suvalki Governor Kuprianov had begun to realize the complexities of the task already in November. He had sent a long telegram to the commander of the Dvinsk Military District, pointing out that all colonists in the province were Russian subjects, that they mostly lived in individual farmsteads, and that they included not only Germans, but also many Poles, Lithuanians, and Russians. In light of this, he asked for clarification on whom to consider a "colonist" and whom a "German." Furthermore, he asked whether women, children, elderly, state employees, army reserves, families of active soldiers, pastors, the ill and infirm should be deported. He received only indeterminate replies, and it appears likely that he and other governors were left to define their own deportation policies.[39] As a result, two weeks after civilian and military officials began to deport colonists from Poland, Engalychev complained to Ianushkevich that the deportations were taking place in a haphazard manner. Some army commanders and governors saw fit to deport the entire German colonist population without exceptions, while others limited the deportations to males over fifteen.[40] Some granted exemptions for a wide variety of reasons, while others granted almost no exemptions.

Pointing out this "lack of leading principles" for the deportations, in early January 1915 Engalychev proposed holding a special conference to work out a set of guidelines. Ianushkevich approved this idea and the conference was held from January 25 to February 2, 1915, under the chairmanship of Engalychev, who had made his own views clear in a letter to Ianushkevich: "For my part, I consider it urgently necessary to take the most severe measures of struggle against Germanism through the deportation of the greatest possible number of German colonists, regardless of their age or sex."[41]

In this spirit, representatives of the Northwest and Southwest Front headquarters and the governor of Petrokov met with the governor general of Warsaw to work out general principles to achieve their declared main goal of the "full cleansing of the element harmful to the war from the region of military activity ." Lacking a clear definition in the law as to the meaning of "German colonist," the conference came up with its own definition and resolved that those to be deported should include the following three categories:

1. Individuals of German descent (*proiskhozhdenie*), owning land or other property outside urban settlements (including temporary residents in towns as seasonal workers).

2. Farm laborers [of German descent].
3. Individuals of German descent engaged in trade and cottage industry in rural areas.

The conference report unanimously concluded that no exceptions
based on age or gender should be made, because "the experience of the
last six months has shown that suspicions of spying do not fall only on
men 15–60 years of age." It also concluded that all who belong in these
categories must leave the Polish provinces with a travel document indicating their destination, which must be outside the area under military
rule, no more than three days after the governor's declaration. If they
had not left by the end of the three days, then they had to be deported
under guard. The conference granted the governor general of Warsaw
the sole power in exceptional cases to grant postponements if "doubts
as to the German nationality of the colonist" arose.[42]

Engalychev, who thenceforth coordinated the operation in Poland,
issued a circular on February 11, 1915, which incorporated the conclu-
sions of the conference and set a deadline of February 20, 1915, for the
deportation of all German colonists from the region.[43]

General Iu. N. Ivanov immediately protested the exclusion of
noncolonist urban German populations from the deportation program,
claiming that "since these Germans were in closer contact with each
other and with Jews, they could spy far more easily than the rural colonists."[44] The issue was crucial, for over 100,000 German-speakers who
were not colonists lived in towns and cities in the ten Polish provinces.
Ianushkevich did not send Ivanov a clear response. He wrote that
Ivanov could deport *colonists* regardless of whether they lived in towns
or rural areas and left the option open of deporting noncolonist Germans residing in towns.[45] In practice, many noncolonist Germans were
deported in the early stages.[46]

With time, however, the general intent of the major orders became
far more directed against "colonists" than "Germans." This reflected
the continuing importance of old *soslovie* (estate) categories. It also reflected the widespread impression that the colonists were less assimilated into Russian culture and life than the urban Germans. Colonist
communities tended to be compact and more easily distinguished; by
appearance alone, colonists were more "other" than the urban Germans. While many of the rural German communities in Poland had

existed for hundreds of years, there had also been a large-scale immigration from Germany and Austria-Hungary in the decades prior to the war. Army commanders and officials tended to see all colonists as unassimilated aliens, no matter how long ago they had become Russian subjects. Ianushkevich expressed his view of the colonists as unassimilated aliens in a letter to N. V. Ivanov:

> The securing of our military interests from the harmful existence of hostile foreigners in the Wistula Region, in the very theater of war, is very much complicated by the excessive number of German colonists [living there]; as current experience is showing, although they have taken Russian subjecthood, [they] are only hiding their often criminal attraction toward their German fatherland.[47]

But the most important explanation for singling out rural Germans was the government's desire to expropriate German landholdings permanently. These laws—well on the way to final drafting when the first deportations occurred—definitively transformed mass deportations from a temporary security measure into a program to alter the demography of landholding and nationality along the western and southern borders far to the interior of the front lines.

Engalychev's February expulsion order ran into problems with the railroads and personnel, and the sheer enormity of the task caused the process to continue into the summer, when the pace of the expulsions picked up considerably. The great retreat of Russian armies through the Polish provinces from April to September added a new urgency to the army's operation; now the fear was that German colonists would fall under enemy occupation, where they could be pressed into army service, betray details about the Russian army, join the espionage service, or simply contribute to the enemy war effort through their farm production. In fact, in June and July, the army turned briefly toward a policy of "scorched earth," forcibly expelling not only colonists, Jews, and other target groups, but also in some instances the entire population.[48] Mass deportations of specific groups were already well under way before the Great Retreat, however, and it would be a mistake to assume that they were merely an appendage to a scorched earth policy, which was only sporadically applied for a short period and in limited areas during the summer of 1915.[49] In fact, already by late June 1915,

Army Headquarters asserted that the army was abandoning policies of forced removal of the entire population, "except for German colonists, who cannot be allowed in the area of army activity."[50]

Despite many logistic difficulties caused by the mass deportations, the army command pressed the operations to further extremes. On June 12, 1915, Ianushkevich informed the commander of the Kiev Military District of a new expansion of the deportation program:

> According to information which has come to the Headquarters of the Supreme Commander, [areas within] the borders of Volynia and other provinces bordering on Austria-Hungary in your military district [Podolia, Kholm, and part of Bessarabia], to this point have still not moved to the final deportation of German colonists living in these regions. These colonies, despite their fairly long existence, differ so much from the core Russian population, that throughout the territory of these provinces, they serve as a prepared base for German conquest. Therefore, now that the enemy is nearing our borders, continuing to allow individuals who are hostile toward our statehood (*gosudarstvennost'*) [to remain there] is particularly undesirable.
>
> In view of this, the supreme commander [Grand Duke Nikolai Nikolaevich] has ordered the deportation of German colonists living in border provinces within the jurisdiction of the Kiev Military District in the shortest period, observing established rules.
>
> Chief of Headquarters Staff, Infantry General Ianushkevich[51]

Ianushkevich issued similar orders to deport all German colonists from border provinces in the Odessa Military District and from the entire Kiev Military District.[52] The commander of the Southwest Front extended the deportation program to the whole of Bessarabia, setting a deadline of July 1, 1915, to complete the operation.[53] Not including the significant numbers of deported and expelled colonists from Poland who had taken refuge in these provinces, the major rural German populations of the additional provinces now to be cleared are set out in Table 4.

During this flurry of mass deportation orders, all the leading army officials responsible for the operation met on June 24, 1915, to unify

Table 4 German colonists deported from Volynia province up to June 22,
1916

July 1915	67,367
October 1915	6,409
December 1915	8,000
1916	34,113*
Total	115,889*

Source: RGIA, f. 1483, op. 1, d. 32, l. 20 (Report compiled by the head of the chancery of the Volynia governor, 22 June 1916).

*Does not include approximately 13,000 colonists known to have been deported from Volynia under Brusilov's orders of June 23, 1916.

and codify deportation practices. The meeting resulted in a set of harsh guidelines. It resolved that all German colonists were to be deported at their own expense, that the deportees could no longer choose their destination but were to be sent to provinces chosen by army and MVD officials, and that no exceptions could be made from the deportations except for the wives and children of soldiers in active duty at the front.[54]

Because some regions were lost to the enemy during the summer retreat and given the massive scale of the operation, implementation was far from complete. Yet military and civilian officials showed remarkable persistence, even after the replacement of Ianushkevich with M. V. Alekseev as Chief of the General Staff in August 1915. Some scholars have blamed most of the excesses against civilians on Ianushkevich personally. While his attitude was undoubtedly important, Alekseev, who has often been portrayed as far more reasonable, actually differed little in his approach to German and Jewish Russian subjects. In fact, the deportations of Germans continued well after the end of the Russian Great Retreat and after Alekseev took charge. Mikhail Lemke, who was at army headquarters during the period, reported that from 9 November 1915 to 8 March 1916, 40,833 German colonists were deported from the Southwest Front alone.[55] Other commanders were equally diligent. In October 1915, the hero of the summer 1916 offensive, Brusilov, complained to Alekseev that during the July deportations from Volynia, wives and mothers of Germans fighting in the army or killed in active duty, fathers over sixty years of age, veterans of previous wars who had received medals of distinction, invalids, the deaf and blind, had all received exemption. Brusilov petitioned to deport all remaining German colonists from Volynia west of a line through

Table 5 Major areas of German colonist settlement

Province	Rural German population		Percent of total population	
	1897	1912	1897	1912
Volynia	171,331	211,000	5.7	5.7
Bessarabia	60,206	62,875	3.1	2.5
Taurida	78,305	135,875	5.4	6.9
Ekaterinoslav	80,979	124,805	3.8	3.9
Kherson	123,453	169,313	4.5	4.8
Other	20,000	30,000		
Total (estimate)	534,272	733,868		

Sources: Dietmar Neutatz, *Die "deutsche Frage" im Schwarzmeergebiet und in Wolhynien: Politik, Wirtschaft, Mentalitäten und Alltag im Spannungsfeld von Nationalismus und Modernisierung (1856–1914)* (Stuttgart: Franz Steiner Verlag, 1993), 254, 259; V. M. Kabuzan, "Nemetskoe naselenie v Rossii v XVIII—Nachale XX veka (Chislennost' i razmeshchenie)," *Voprosy istorii* 12 (1989): 18–29; Henning Bauer, Andreas Kappeler, Brigitte Roth, eds., *Die Nationalitäten des Russischen Reiches in der Volkszählung von 1897, Quellen und Studien zur Geschichte des östlichen Europa* 32, vol. A (Stuttgart: Franz Steiner Verlag, 1991), 184.

Sarno, Rovno, Ostrog, and Iziaslavl', without exception. He claimed this would affect approximately 20,000 individuals, and could be completed within three weeks. The next day Alekseev replied that he had no objections, and Brusilov went ahead with the operation.[56]

As in the deportations of German farmers from Poland, summary statistics of the results of deportations from the western and southwestern parts of the empire are difficult to estimate. Published figures include 10,000 from Kiev province; 20,000 from Podolia; 11,540 from Chernigov; and 20,000 from Bessarabia by the end of 1915.[57] The best statistics available were compiled in June 1916 for Volynia province (see Table 5).

Deportations of rural Germans continued—from new areas and as mopping-up exercises in regions affected by earlier orders—right up to the February Revolution. In August 1916, for example, the last members of 11,965 residents of the Girshengof farming community in Eastern Lifland were deported to Perm.[58] Officials strove to track down and deport every last member of the community, including all women, children, and even workers in Riga and other nearby cities who had permanently left the community long before the war.[59]

This persistence and effort to bring about the total clearing of colonist areas were evident as well when incompletely cleared territories were reconquered. After Brusilov's triumphant offensive in the summer of 1916, several areas of Volynia fell again under Russian rule. Rural Germans and their families had not yet been completely removed from these areas before the enemy moved in a year earlier. On June 23, 1916, Brusilov sent a telegram to Alekseev informing him of his plan to deport these individuals. The plan and its execution revealed a chilling efficiency and striving for totality that had become part of mass deportation practices. Brusilov noted that there were still 13,000 colonists in the districts of Lutsk, Dubna, and Kremenets. He outlined the procedures in minute detail, plotting every step of the operation. The operation was completed with remarkable efficiency from June 27 to July 3, 1916.[60]

If the mass deportation of foreign-subject males who owed military service in enemy states marked an extension of warfare to civilians unprecedented in a century of Russian warfare, the methodical deportation of every last Russian-subject German colonist from some regions—including families of soldiers active at the front, invalids, and the blind—illustrates how far Russia had come in two years of total war toward a radical new approach to nationality.

The Forced Migration of Russian-Subject Jews

The campaign against enemy aliens drew heavily on established patterns of official discrimination and popular mobilization against Jews in the Russian Empire. Thus it is hardly surprising that once forced migration had been established as a legitimate practice, Russian authorities would apply it to Jews.

The army command convinced itself that Russia's Jews were unreliable, that they had close ties to their kin abroad, that they were more attracted to the Austrian and German cultures than to the Russian, and that Jews shirked military service and engaged in spying and espionage on a broad scale. Ianushkevich expressed an intense personal dislike of Jews and "became obsessed with the idea of spies and spying" by Germans, foreigners, and especially by Jews.[61] Ianushkevich's proclivities were not extraordinary among leading generals. A survey sent to leading army officials found that nearly all of them shared a presumption that Jews were disloyal and should be treated as spies.[62] The war statute gave the army a sphere of authority where it could play out these obsessions upon Russia's Jews without hindrance from civilian authorities.

The forced migration of Jews differed from that of other groups in a number of ways. First, mass deportations using trains were only attempted for a brief period. Second, most expulsions occurred only from areas where troops were present, and troops played a much larger role than was typical for other groups. Third, the expulsions were accompanied by violence and looting by soldiers and locals unmatched in the forced migrations of other groups. Given the decentralized nature of the expulsions and the extensive terror-induced mass refugee movements that accompanied them, it is hard to estimate the number of Russian-subject Jews singled out and forced from their homes. Estimates range from half a million to a million.[63]

The first phase of army policy—from the outbreak of the war in July 1914 to January 1915—saw sporadic forcible expulsions of Jews from the immediate front zone toward the interior and the first incidents of hostage-taking. There is little evidence that these scattered and uncoordinated actions were part of an official policy formulated at the highest levels of the military command, and by all indications, they occurred under the orders of individual officers in the field. On the other hand, the army command only very rarely took action to prevent forcible expulsions of Jews from towns along the front lines, or to punish low-level commanders for violence and hostage-taking in this early period.[64]

A more coordinated army policy concerning Jews began in earnest in early 1915. On January 25, 1915, Ianushkevich took the first major step to force the expulsion of Jews from towns near the front, sending a circular to army commanders throughout the front zone authorizing the expulsion (*vyselenie*) of "all Jews and suspect individuals" from the entire region of military activity where troops were present. In follow-up communications, Ianushkevich made clear that he wanted his commanders to expel entire Jewish communities when they suspected any individual Jew of spying.[65] Army Headquarters reiterated this blanket approval at several junctures and did not retract it until 1917. As the Russian army retreated and advanced, it passed through much of the Pale, so it had broad scope to use (and abuse) its extensive powers over the Jewish communities it encountered. Because the front lines shifted most dramatically during the Great Retreat from April to October

1915, the army's encounters with Jewish civilians were the most extensive during that period.

Military commanders in the field energetically applied the powers granted by the War Statute and specified by Ianushkevich. Shortly after Ianushkevich's circular, General N. V. Ruzskii ordered the expulsion of "all Jews and suspect individuals" from points near the front lines under his jurisdiction where troops were deployed. In the order, he stated that the goal was to prevent Jews from acquiring knowledge of military operations (which he assumed they would relay to the enemy).[66] This order, potentially affecting up to 50,000 individuals, was only partially implemented because most of the territory was soon lost to the Germans.[67] During the last week of January, however, Army Headquarters and the governor general of Warsaw coordinated the mass expulsion of all Jews from forty towns in the vicinity of Warsaw, affecting roughly 100,000 individuals. As a result, over 80,000 Jewish refugees appeared in the city of Warsaw within days.[68]

In April and May 1915, the army briefly attempted to move to a third phase in its policy—toward much larger-scale mass deportations more like the operations against enemy subjects and German colonists. These projects differed from the forced expulsions in two ways. First, they intended systematically to clear all Jews from large territories—on the scale of entire provinces—well beyond the narrow zones of troop deployment. Second, unlike the expulsions, deportees were assigned destinations in advance, trains were used, and civilian officials undertook most of the work in implementing the orders.

The commander of the Dvinsk Military District took a step toward such mass deportation on March 17, 1915, when he set a line of Jewish deportation extending well to the interior of the area where troops were present in Vilna province.[69] But the Chief of Army Operations, Iu. N. Danilov, halted this deportation three weeks later due to bottlenecks on the railways.[70] The real deluge of mass deportation orders began shortly after the Austrian and German armies routed the Third Russian Army and broke through at Gorlitse on April 19, 1915. Four days later, the Kurland governor received orders from Army Headquarters to deport the entire Jewish population from areas where troops were present in his province.[71] Days later, Army Headquarters expanded this order to cover a much larger area, covering all points to the west of the line: Riga, Bausk, Ponevezh, Vilkomir, Kovno. The de-

portations were remarkably thorough. The Kurland governor reported
in early June that in seven districts of his province, 26,338 Jews had
been deported and only 519 (less than two percent) allowed to stay.[72]

On May 3, 1915, an even larger operation began—the mass deportation of Jews from Kovno province.[73] According to D. O. Zaslavskii, approximately 150,000 Jews were deported from the province within two
weeks.[74] Additional orders extended the mass operations to other areas
in the northwest, and by May 15, Chairman of the Council of Ministers
Goremykin told his colleagues that recent deportation orders would
apply to 300,000 Jews.[75]

The implementation of this massive operation quickly proved to be
problematic. Shortages of railroad cars and personnel were among the
key practical barriers, but the most serious problem proved to be the
destination of the deportees.[76] The problem was that the military re-
sisted allowing Jewish deportees to resettle in any area under military
rule. Since most of the Pale was under military rule, this left only half
of Poltava province and a small part of Ekaterinoslav province as valid
destinations. Under pressure from the MVD, the army reluctantly allowed some additional areas under military rule to be designated as
valid destinations for deported Jews. But the total area approved for
Jewish resettlement remained quite small, incorporating only areas east
of the Dniepr River in Ekaterinoslav, Mogilev, Chernigov, Poltava, and
Taurida (not including the Crimean Peninsula).[77] Thus, according to
the orders of April-May 1915, the cities and towns of this narrow band
of territory (rural areas remained off limits) would have to absorb the
entire mass of Jewish deportees.

In early May some of the first trains of Jews from Kovno and
Kurland provinces began to arrive in these provinces. On May 8, the
Poltava governor wired the head of the Dvinsk Military District that
eleven trains with 10,738 Jews had arrived in Poltava, and that more
were on the way. The Poltava governor and others protested that there
was no way they could house and feed such a mass of impoverished
Jews. Governors of the five internal provinces allowed for resettlement
frantically appealed to the minister of internal affairs to halt the deportations.[78]

Civilian authorities objected strongly to the army's policies.
Goremykin wrote an important memo to the tsar expressing the government's opposition to further mass deportations of Jews. He asserted

Figure 10. The mass expulsions of Jews and the Pale of Jewish settlement until its abolition on August 4, 1915.

that the "punishment of an entire population for the previous actions of individuals was clearly unfair," and added that it carried many undesirable consequences. The concentration of masses of deportees in the cities of a few provinces would worsen the impoverishment of Jewish communities, cause epidemics, depress wages in cities to which the Jews were sent, exacerbate Christian-Jewish tensions, and lead to pogroms. Most important, Goremykin continued, was the reaction the deportations were already creating in allied countries and West European financial circles, which, "as is well-known, are under strong Jewish influence."[79]

Goremykin's memo was only the highest-level example of a flood of complaints from civilian officials. Many, like the Vilna governor, complained that the deportations were devastating local economies with dire consequences not only for the local populations, but also for the army. He particularly complained that all drugstore owners had been removed, causing a crisis in the supply of medicines, and that firms producing for defense were closing down due to the deportation of crucial skilled workers.[80] The opposition of the civilian government to the army's Jewish policies likely helped prevent even worse atrocities and played an important part in stopping the mass deportations.[81]

More persuasive for the army leadership was the dawning realization that the mass deportation of Jews was creating pressure on the MVD to abolish the restrictions on Jewish residence in order to find room for Jewish deportees. Faced with such pressures, on May 8 the commander of the Northwest Front, M. V. Alekseev, partially acquiesced to pragmatism and the arguments of the Council of Ministers. He sent an important circular to all the leading army authorities in his jurisdiction that shifted army policies into their fourth phase, ordering that deportation be replaced with hostage-taking in areas behind the front, using mass deportation only as a threat and selective measure of punishment.[82] The next day, Danilov informed military authorities throughout the Northwest Front that not only had the policy of mass deportation of Jews been abandoned, but that Jews already deported were to be allowed to return to their homes. But their return was only to be allowed under the condition that hostages be taken from each community.[83] Already on May 10, the commander of the Dvinsk Military District, N. E. Tumanov, informed governors in his jurisdiction of the procedures to be used for hostage-taking. He requested that they draw up lists of potential hostages, choosing the most influential members of the community, including rabbis. Tumanov stressed that governors should ensure that the Jewish populations were well informed that hostages would be hanged in the event of "even the smallest act hostile to the fatherland or, generally, any assistance rendered to the enemy by any members of the Jewish population."[84] In Kovno, the governor and commander of the Tenth Army divided the province into three regions: one to be completely cleansed of Jews, one from which Jewish hostages were to be taken, and one in which no repressive measures were to be taken.[85] Within weeks, Army Headquarters was consistently denying requests from lower-level commanders for permission to deport Jews from their regions, ordering them to take hostages instead. This was the response to General Grigor'ev, a commander of a fortified region, when he wrote to Tumanov that his region contained important railroad lines, and thus he found it necessary to "clear out the unreliable element (*ochistit' ot nenadezhnogo elementa*)" by deporting all Jews without exception. Tumanov responded that mass deportation was no longer allowed (except from areas of troop deployment), and instructed him instead to take five or six hostages from each settlement, including *all* nonstate rabbis, as well as rich and influential Jews.[86]

In a remarkable but brief switch of strategy, Ianushkevich initiated a scorched-earth policy in selected areas of retreat, ordering the destruction of all seed grain and buildings and the deportation of the entire population to the interior *except Jews*. He explained that the Jews were so corrupting and such a burden that it would be better to leave them for the Germans. The policy was reversed three weeks later by Grand Duke Nikolai Nikolaevich. In a similar decision about the same time, Ianushkevich briefly ordered that Jews from occupied Galicia be driven across the front to the enemy side rather than sent to the interior of Russia. This policy was only applied in occupied Galicia, and only for a few weeks at most.[87] But these episodes trenchantly reveal the army's belief that whether deported to the interior, left in their homes, driven toward the enemy, or taken hostage, Jews had to be singled out and treated as dangerous internal enemies.

The above measures were soon abandoned, but hostage-taking continued for months. This practice was not completely unprecedented in Russian history. It was used at times in pre-modern Muscovite warfare and sporadically during the wars of conquest in the Caucasus in the nineteenth century but was widely seen as anachronistic by 1914. The army first took hostages in occupied Galicia in September 1914. According to Governor General of Galicia Bobrinskii, "the policy was [then] extended to become a general measure [within Galicia] during retreat as an insurance against Jewish denunciation and spying."[88] Just over 400 Jews were taken hostage in occupied Galicia—hardly comparable to the systematic Jewish hostage-taking policy put into effect in May 1915 along the front within Russian territory. No summary statistics are available, but the First and Tenth Armies alone reported taking 4,749 hostages—nearly all Jews—by the end of May 1915.[89]

The hostage policy was largely implemented by local civilian officials, usually in response to military requests. The staffs of provincial governors compiled lists of potential hostages, and when hostages were taken, they were required to sign documents officially recognizing that they were to be executed if any acts of spying or aid to the enemy were uncovered among members of their communities.[90]

One of the most remarkable army documents of the war was signed by Alekseev on June 30, 1915. This document, the "Rules on the Deportation of Jews from Military Districts of the Northwest Front," laid out a comprehensive army policy toward Jews. It officially confirmed the right of commanders to order governors to deport Jewish populations from regions of troop deployment and outlined hostage-taking procedures in detail.[91] Any Jewish communities allowed to remain in areas of troop deployment had to have hostages taken from their communities as insurance against their hostile behavior. The document confirmed that hostages were normally to be held under police oversight in their own communities. But if the enemy was advancing and the army was in retreat from an area, the hostages were to be arrested and deported under guard by civilian authorities. Subsequent deportation and hostage-taking orders often cited these rules, which remained on the books until February 1917.

Hostage-taking continued through the summer of 1915. Many of the hostages were sent under guard to prisons in Poltava, Kiev, Vilna, and other internal provinces. In August, under intense criticism from the Duma, the Council of Ministers convinced the army—now under the somewhat more reasonable Chief of Staff Alekseev—to draw back from this draconian policy. It allowed Jewish hostages to return to their original residences (unless they were under enemy occupation). However, although allowed to return, the hostages remained under police oversight, and retained their designation as hostages to be executed if any army official suspected a member of their community of "hostility toward Russian troops or spying."[92]

The total number of hostages taken during the war is difficult to determine. If nearly 5,000 were taken by only two armies already in May 1915, the total number taken during the war probably should be estimated in the tens of thousands. After an August 1915 decision that hostages were to sign documents and remain in their communities, the practice took on a localized character.[93] The degree of decentralization was revealed in 1917, when the Provisional Government had great difficulty discovering the whereabouts and identities of all individuals who had been designated as hostages. The Provisional Government did not grant universal amnesty to Jewish hostages, even if they were Russian subjects, and the army successfully blocked the release of individual hostages for months after the February Revolution.[94] Although the total number of hostages taken remains unclear, the number of Jewish communities threatened with having their prominent community leaders executed at the whim of a local official or army commander was large. Both deportations and hostage-taking declined by the end of 1915. They did not end, however, and this was less a policy shift than a result of the stabilization of the front lines; army commanders retained the power to expel Jews from the immediate front area and take hostages, and when the front lines moved, expulsions sporadically recurred until the February 1917 Revolution.[95]

Violence and Pogroms

One of the most important and least known consequences of the mass deportations was a wave of pogroms and violence, which peaked in the period of the Russian retreat from April to October 1915 but accompanied deportations before and after this period as well. The anti-Jewish violence can be distinguished from prewar pogroms by one fundamental feature: the role of the army. Several scholars have recently asserted that prewar pogroms were not approved at the highest levels of the government.[96] This remained largely true during the war. The Council of Ministers and most other leading civilian authorities opposed pogroms. In fact, already on August 15, 1914, the governor general of Warsaw, describing an attack on Jews within his jurisdiction, predicted in a letter to the Council of Ministers that the war could result in massive pogroms.[97] He warned that despite taking all possible preventive measures, if soldiers instigated violence against Jews, he feared that things could get out of control. With nearly the entire area of Jewish settlement under military rule, the civilian authorities in fact could do little to stop army violence.[98]

One reason for the volatile situation was the role that economic motives played an important role from the very earliest wartime expulsions. For example, already on October 14, 1914, 4,000 Jews were driven from their homes in Grozin (Warsaw province), and forced to make their way by foot to the city of Warsaw. They were denied carts for their belongings, and shortly after their departure, local Poles took over their vacated businesses and properties. When a few of the expellees were allowed to return a week later, local authorities refused to intervene to return properties and apartments to their previous owners.[99] As the expulsions increased in frequency in early 1915, the looting and takeover of Jewish property became increasingly common. The Council of Ministers expressed its concern at the blatant disregard for the most basic norms of private property and imposed strict rules requiring *all* deportee properties (primarily German, enemy subject, and Jewish) to be sequestered by the Ministry of State Properties and protected by local authorities.[100] But though local authorities did manage to bring looting and uncontrolled takeover of deported Russian-subject German and enemy-subject properties somewhat under control, they were unable or unwilling to do the same for Jewish property.

When the deportation of Jews reached mass scale in April and May 1915, the looting and spontaneous takeovers of vacant properties shifted rapidly to violence against Jews and their properties both during and before the actual expulsions or deportations. In some areas, Jews were rounded up, loaded onto railroad cars, and deported in brutal but orderly fashion; in many others, the process was extremely violent and chaotic. The experience of the town Shadovo in Kovno province typified the latter. This town had a population of 5,000, half of whom were Jews. The other half was mostly Polish and Lithuanian, with some Russian civil servants and railroad workers. In late April 1915, the Germans took the town for a week, retreating on May 2. After their departure, Russian scouts and Cossack units entered the town and, according to the testimony of a Jewish resident, immediately began assaulting local Jews and looting their homes and stores. Several women were raped. One Jewish man's eyes were gouged out when he could not pay what some Cossacks demanded. Cossacks turned over part of the loot to the local peasants and encouraged their participation in the pogrom. On the next day, the entire Jewish population abandoned Shadovo and made its way to Boik, another town. There, another group of Cossacks arrived and began another round of violence.

The Jews were again driven out and forced to leave the few belongings they had been able to cart out of Shadovo. The next day, May 5, the group, already driven from their homes and their first place of refuge, received notice that they were all to be expelled within six hours further from the front. As no trains were provided, most went by foot to Ponevezh.[101] Jewish residents of dozens of towns in Kurland and Kovno provinces suffered similar ordeals in April and May. Indeed, for the rest of the war, such violent episodes recurred in areas where troops were present, especially during the Russian retreat, which lasted until October 1915.[102]

The best available records of the pogroms were collected by a Jewish committee, which received reports from its representatives in the communities affected and among the displaced. Its collection of reports has not survived in full, but its published and unpublished records provide a large enough sample to allow for some generalization about the wave of pogroms from April through October 1915.[103] The following discussion is based on reports of 19 pogroms in Vilna, 13 in Kovno, seven in Volynia, and 15 in Minsk. In this sample of 54 cases, pogroms began only three times without soldiers present. The army clearly initiated the violence in nearly every case. More specifically, Cossack units appear to have instigated nearly all the pogroms. Over 80 percent of the reports identify the appearance of Cossacks in the area as the key event spurring the pogrom. In several instances, regular army units appeared in towns and nothing happened, often for several days. But when a Cossack unit entered the town, the looting and violence began. The pattern became widely known throughout the front zones, and by August peasants would often appear on the edge of Jewish settlements when Cossacks were reported in the area, even if they had not yet begun a pogrom. The violence was predominantly linked to attempts to extort payments from the Jews. Rape was mentioned in a third of the reports.

The pogroms described in these reports were not always linked to explicit orders to expel or deport Jews from the areas affected. But Cossack officers often used their power to order expulsions of Jews as a means to loot. In some cases, officers ordered Jews to leave their homes within hours or minutes, denied them access to carts, and beat and robbed them as they departed. The shift from official security-based policies to outright looting and extortion was particularly apparent in the practice of hostage-taking. Initiated as a policy of collective responsibility ostensibly to prevent Jewish spying, hostage-taking often simply legitimated extortion. According to the reports, officers (primarily Cossacks) would take prominent Jews "hostage" and would threaten to kill them unless relatives or the community paid a ransom. In one case, a Cossack officer systematically went through a town's residents, taking nearly every adult male hostage until he received ransom payments for the release of each.[104]

Where local populations joined in the violence and looting, nearly a fifth of the reports indicate that rumors of Jewish coin hoarding stimulated the outbreak of violence. The perception that Jews were hoarding coins was based in small part on reality. Given growing inflation, both Jews and Christians had strong incentive to hold onto their precious metal currency and not exchange it for more rapidly depreciating paper banknotes.[105] Local officials and newspapers spread rumors of Jewish hoarding, and a number of pogroms began when a Cossack, soldier or local, went to a Jewish store and was turned down when demanding to change paper currency for precious metal coins.[106] Thus, throughout the front zones, wartime inflation sharply exacerbated Christian-Jewish relations, which had already been tense in the immediate prewar period. This was especially true in Poland, which had seen an intense prewar boycott of Jewish businesses by Poles, led by the Polish National Democratic Party. Similar developments were evident in the Baltics, Ukraine, and Russian areas as well.[107]

In a number of instances, local peasants and townspeople, soldiers and even Cossacks protected Jews from attacks. In cases when army officials made it clear that violence against Jews and their property would not be tolerated, pogroms did not occur—even if the coin hoarding issue flared up and tensions between Jews and Christians were quite high. An excellent example was in Riga, where General Rodkevich successfully prevented the outbreak of a pogrom, despite a charged anti-Jewish atmosphere and many pogroms in the area immediately outside his control.[108] Only when the framework for the violence was in place and, almost without exception, only when Cossacks or regular troops instigated violence, did the attitudes of the local population come into play. Even so, the army's policies encouraged popular participation in looting and violence, and thereby contributed to the increasingly violent tenor of politics throughout the affected areas.

While violence accompanying deportations was greatest against Jews, deportations of Germans, foreigners, and others at times followed similarly violent patterns.[109] Toward the end of 1916 police received mounting numbers of reports that peasants were cutting down forests on estates owned by enemy subjects and Germans, looting estates of deportees, and spreading rumors of "big riots" to come against German farmers.[110] The problem of popular violence did not end with the February Revolution, and in fact grew in scale as thousands of deported Russian subjects tried to return to their homes. While the Provisional Government lifted all restrictions on Russian subjects, the army prevented the return of deported Russian-subject Jews, Germans, Tatars, and others to their homes, and blocked the government's attempts to shape a policy on the restitution of deportee properties. Although the army did what it could to prevent a return of deported Russian subjects and never officially allowed them to return to their homes, it could not prevent a spontaneous movement of this kind on a fairly large scale.[111] Governors reported that when parties of previously deported German farmers, Jews, and others returned to their homes, violent conflicts frequently erupted between the returning deportees and the new occupants of their homes, lands, and businesses.[112] For example, from April to September 1917, the Ministry of Internal Affairs received several reports that large numbers of German deportees were "spontaneously" returning to their homes in the southwest. In some cases they chased away the Ukrainian refugees whom Russian officials had settled on their lands in 1916. In other cases, the new owners successfully defended their properties from the returning former owners. Local authorities were unsure how to deal with the situation. They were caught between the laws of the Provisional Government, which restored full rights to the deportees, and the orders of the military. As a result, no clear policy emerged and acrimonious—at times violent—conflict continued.[113] These conflicts involved the Ukrainian Rada and German organizations, both of which bitterly condemned the government for its failure to take a clear stand on the issue.[114] Violence broke out too in areas to which enemy aliens had been deported; one of the more dramatic cases was a large pogrom against civilian enemy subjects in Viatka on April 24, 1917.[115]

The army's policies and the violence they evoked had serious consequences affecting the larger context of the war and revolution. First, they undermined Russia's war effort. Not only did they cause enormous economic damage to local economies, but they also tied up the railroads and created expensive and chaotic conditions in the internal provinces which had to deal with rapid influx of forced migrants. The destruction and plundering of local businesses also adversely affected the army, making it more difficult for soldiers to acquire supplies, including medicines.[116] The scale of the damages is suggested by a survey conducted by Jewish aid workers of about 2,300 Jews expelled to Poltava. According to the survey, the destroyed or stolen property of this small group alone exceeded a million rubles in value.[117] Second, the mass expulsions forced the regime to cut the gordian knot of restrictions on Jewish settlement (the Pale) that it had built up and painstakingly enforced over the previous century and to allow Jews to settle in provinces throughout the country. Although in some ways the breakup of the Pale was a historic liberation that Jews had sought for generations, it had a dark side as well. The army and right-wing press encouraged the idea that Jews had been expelled from the front areas as suspected spies, and tensions between locals and the arriving Jews ran high. In fact, the massive pogroms in 1918–19, conducted by all sides in the Civil War and leaving an estimated 100,000 fatalities, cannot be divorced from the conditions under which the Pale was broken. As Hans Rogger has pointed out, the geography of race riots and pogroms in several national and historical contexts reveals that violence tends to be concentrated in areas of large-scale and rapid minority in-migration. It is likely no coincidence that some of the worst excesses of the 1919 pogroms occurred in provinces where the Jewish influx during the war had been the greatest.[118]

Other Mass Operations

While enemy subjects, Russian-German farmers, and Jews together comprised most of the populations singled out, deported, or forcibly expelled from their homes during the war, other categories of Russian subjects were affected as well. On June 27, 1915, the commander of the Dvinsk Military District ordered the arrest and deportation of all "migrant gypsies" to provinces outside military rule.[119] There is also some evidence that several thousand Russian-subject Crimean Tatars were deported to the interior during the war by order of the head of the Odessa Military District.[120]

One of the larger operations was the deportation of Muslims from Kars and Batumi provinces. The Russian Empire granted Russian subjecthood to the entire population of these provinces shortly after acquiring them from the Ottoman Empire in 1878. During World War I, this group was first condemned on religious grounds and then eventually exonerated on ethnic criteria, showing the general shift from old markers of identity to new ones under the pressure of war. The case illustrates well how the practice of deportation could begin with security concerns and quickly become linked to larger attempts to colonize and nationalize regions through transfers of unwanted people and grants of their land to favored groups.

On January 15, 1915, the Viceroy of the Caucasus, Vorontsov-Dashkov, deported about 1,000 "refractory" (*nepokornye*) Russian-subject Muslims from Kars and Batumi to interior Russian provinces.[121] In the next three weeks he ordered the deportation of another 5,000.[122] He accused them of aiding Turkish troops during the brief Ottoman occupation of the provinces in December 1914. According to the head of the Evacuation Administration, Oldenburgskii, they arrived by train in Khar'kov, Kursk, Orlov, Tula, and Nizhnii Novgorod provinces in a state of exhaustion, with major epidemics of typhus breaking out among them.[123] Concerned that epidemics would spread to the Russian population, he immediately issued a decree that all Muslim deportees were to be considered contagious and should be isolated for a minimum of three weeks.[124] The governors of the provinces to which the Kars and Batumi Muslims had been sent complained that they had received no warning of the arrival of the deportees, and the Nizhnii Novgorod governor reported that he feared violence against the Muslims, but would also not settle them with local Tatars because he feared spreading Pan-Turkic ideas.[125] In response to these concerns, the uninhabited Nargen Island in the Caspian Sea was designated as the destination for further Russian-subject Muslim deportees. Within weeks, it had over 5,000 internees.[126] Up to 3,000 Muslims were put on lists of those to be executed for treason.[127]

Meanwhile, Vorontsov-Dashkov's assistant for civilian affairs, Pederson, sent a proposal to the Council of Ministers to deport the entire Muslim population of the two provinces to the Russian interior and permanently revoke their Russian subjecthood. He claimed that these Muslims had failed to assimilate into Russian culture, and despite the greater freedoms they enjoyed under Russian rule, remained loyal to Turkey. According to the proposal, they would be deported *en masse* to the Ottoman Empire at the end of the war. The minister of agriculture voiced strong support, stating that their lands could be given to Russian peasants, and most of the other ministers stated their approval.[128]

Soon thereafter, Georgian Duma deputies declared that the Muslims being deported were not Turks but Adzhars, who were "Georgian despite their Muslim religion, and therefore loyal Russians."[129] As a result of their protests, Grand Duke Georgii Mikhailovich presided over an investigation which ended its twenty-volume report with the conclusion that there had been "absolutely no hostile relationship to the troops or administration on the part of the Adzhars." It blamed Cossacks and Armenians for the allegations of Adzhar disloyalty and accused them of instigating violent confrontations with local Muslims. In the end, the Grand Duke Nikolai Nikolaevich was persuaded to meet with Adzhar leaders, and he even granted them a medal for their loyalty and contribution to the war effort![130] Following this, the Council of Ministers rejected Pederson's proposal. But in the six months the proposal was under consideration, over 10,000 Russian-subject Muslims were deported from the two provinces. They were not allowed to return until June 1917, when the Provisional Government finally reviewed their case. Under army orders, local authorities forced the sale or lease of many of the deportees' land and properties. While officials were motivated at least in part by broader plans to transfer Muslim lands to Russian peasants and Cossacks, in practice they mostly went to Armenian refugees.[131]

Deportation of Individuals

Mass operations against entire population categories accounted for the vast majority of people deported during the war, but they also served to legitimize the use of this radical tool in domestic politics on a case-by-case basis. The army played a particularly important role in extending the practice to individuals who did not fall under categoric mass deportation or expulsion orders, but who were identified as "undesirable" for one reason or another. In areas under direct military rule, military officials at times ordered the police to deport all individuals who had been under police surveillance or who had been identified as "suspect" for any reason, as in a blanket order in September 1914 to deport all *podnadzornye* (individuals under police oversight) from Libava and Vindava on the Lifland coast.[132] *Podnadzornye* included those suspected of criminal or politically unreliable activity, many foreigners (both from enemy and neutral countries), and individuals under police oversight for suspected spy activities.

Each military district expended considerable energy on counterespionage efforts. In May 1915, the commander in chief, Grand Duke Nikolai Nikolaevich, secretly gave the head of the Petrograd military district, M. D. Bonch-Bruevich, the task of coordinating a major campaign to identify and deport potential spies from all areas under military rule.[133] The military solicited denunciations from the public, and the military district offices were quickly swamped with thousands of them.[134] Ianushkevich encouraged a xenophobic tone for the campaign with decrees like his order that all individuals with family or business ties abroad should be placed under the "strictest oversight" and immediately deported if even the slightest suspicion of their loyalty were to arise.[135] Not surprisingly, foreigners, Germans, and Jews appeared most frequently in these denunciations.

Deportation on a case-by-case basis was particularly important for Protestant and non-Orthodox religious groups. The war gave opponents of these groups an emotional new argument—that they were part of a German plot to subvert Russia.[136] The head of the Odessa Military District closed twenty Evangelical congregations on the first day of the war and launched a wide repression of Evangelical and Stundist activities, including the deportation of dozens of pastors.[137] Three months later, the minister of internal affairs, shortly after the outbreak of the war, explicitly accused Evangelicals, Baptists, and Adventists of "being infused with Germanism," ordered the closure of many of their congregations and organizations, and called on governors to act decisively against their activities.[138] The campaign against organized non-Orthodox faiths was particularly intense in the Baltic provinces, where it most clearly overlapped with ethnic tensions. For example, the Kurland governor deported large numbers of German pastors in a thinly veiled attempt to weaken German influence in the Protestant church (*de facto* increasing Latvian influence).[139]

The religious repression also affected many of the nationalities designated as allies in the war effort. This was particularly true in the western provinces, where Protestant, Baptist, and Evangelical congregations complained that authorities were deporting Polish, Latvian, and Lithuanian members in large numbers. The head of a Polish Evangelical community pointed out that there were approximately 40,000 Polish Evangelicals, many of whom had German names but were fully assimilated into Polish culture. He claimed that thousands of them were being deported merely because of their religion and ethnic origins.[140]

Repression, including selective deportation, of national intelligentsias also became common during the war. Ukrainian, Polish, and Baltic political leaders in particular drew the attention of the police. Such repressions were most thoroughly applied in occupied regions, particularly in Galicia, where the Ukrainian and Polish movements were intensely anti-Russian, some of the leadership collaborated with German and Austrian governments in attempts to raise rebellions against Russia, and all were subjects of enemy states.[141] The selective deportation of national leaders, for example, activist Catholic priests from the Polish provinces, deeply exacerbated national tensions.[142] The deportations of prominent individuals and national community leaders such as the Baltic German leader Baron Stackelberg-Sutlem, the Ukrainian national leader Mikhailo Hrushevsky, or the German colonist political and religious leader Jakob Stach generated great public acrimony, both in the communities affected and in the Russian press.[143]

Forced Migration and Nationality

A striking aspect of the mass operations is their similarity to modern "ethnic cleansing." In fact, deportation orders often used the term *polnoe ochishchenie*, which can be translated as "full cleansing."[144] In a structural sense, the operations did have much in common with modern ethnic cleansing, which almost invariably includes security concerns about ethnic groups with kin outside the boundaries of the state, an ideological component, and emancipatory nationalistic rhetoric of removing one group to promote another. There was a similarity too in the shift of concern from nationalizing the individual through assimilation to nationalizing "the economy," "the land," or the population. But if the intent can be read as an attempt to remove unwanted groups from the body politic, the social body, or the wartime nation, the effects were quite contradictory. Commander of the Petrograd Military

District M.D. Bonch-Bruevich expressed both an extreme variant of these intentions and their contradictory results in a June 1915 letter to Ianushkevich: "Purely Russian provinces are being completely defiled by elements hostile to us, and therefore the question arises of the exact registration of all deported enemy subjects, in order to liquidate without a trace this entire alien element at the end of the war."[145]

As Bonch-Bruevich suggests, one important result of the forced migrations was to bring new national and social conflicts to scores of internal Russian provinces. Of all the deportees and expellees, only a fraction were actually imprisoned or kept in camps. Most were simply registered in interior or Siberian provinces. Nearly every province in Russia received forced migrants and refugees in significant numbers. Petitions and letters from enemy aliens of all types often mention that the fact of their deportation alone created a strong stigma and assumption among locals that they were a dangerous element, guilty of spying or criminal activity.[146] The high incidence of epidemics among deportees, who often arrived after weeks in cramped, sealed, infectious boxcars added to the stigma of the deportees and fears of the local populations.[147] After an investigative tour of the places where deportees were settled, Prince Dashkov reported serious tensions, especially with newcomers who were allowed to live in apartments and work in the area.[148] Locals blamed incoming deportees for driving up prices and creating new competition for local business, and the Department of Police received numerous reports of boycotts and violence against deportees. As a result, a dynamic of denunciations, boycotts, riots, and pressure from local officials to deport the deportees elsewhere spread through the country.[149]

Another unintended result of the forced migrations was the mobilization of a new, stronger sense of national unity among the targeted categories. Except for male enemy subjects, who were interned in camps and treated like prisoners of war, most of the deported enemy aliens were left to fend for themselves in their places of exile. Impoverished and unable to make a living in a new environment without assistance, many turned to members of their own ethnicity for help.

This was particularly true for the Germans, many of whom resettled among German communities in the Volga region. If the mass deportations of German farmers reveals one way in which official Russia moved toward nationalizing large territories by striving to make them more "Russian," it also catalyzed the rapid development of a much more unified German national community within Russia. The imperial "German minority" had migrated to Russia in widely different periods from the mid-seventeenth century to 1914, from different parts of Germany, Austria, Poland, and Holland. Although German settlers' political activity on a national level expanded through the Duma after 1905, the far-flung communities had only a weak sense that they were a part of a larger German colonist group—much less that that they were part of the same national community as the urban and Baltic Germans.[150] Even in the early days of the war, many of the older German communities expressed resentment that government and society treated all the varied rural German groups the same, as if they were recent immigrants.[151]

The mass displacements of the war sent Germans from Poland, Volynia, the Baltic region, Ukraine, and Bessarabia to the Volga and other interior provinces. This spurred a mobilization of Germans throughout the empire in order to provide housing and financial support.[152] Community mobilization to provide aid was essential: by the end of 1915, the government had officially cut off all state aid to colonist deportees.[153] Moreover, in some regions local authorities refused to allow deportees to work, and even forced employers to fire those deportees they had hired.[154]

The closer communal contact also spurred a more general interest in German communities throughout the empire. By 1915, *Volkszeitung*, the main Volga German paper, began to include for the first time a large daily section with news from the other German colonies and the Baltic region. Under the pressures of war and the mass deportations, individuals and disparate groups came together into a larger community.[155] Once bans on political organization were lifted in March 1917, German community leaders quickly formed the first successful national organizations of the Russian-German minority.[156] On the communal level, leaders of the relief effort for deportees and refugees during the war became leaders of the movement and sent delegates to national congresses; unlike any prewar meetings, these included representatives from all the disparate Russian-German communities.[157] The first national congress of German settlers was held in April 1917, with 36 of the leading political figures from 15 provinces. Its first order of business was to work to overcome regional and other differences in order to unite behind the common goal of lobbying for relief and compensation for wartime measures. To this end, it created a permanent All-Russian Central Committee of Citizens of German Nationality to resolve potential disagreements between various German groups.[158]

The second German congress in the Volga region held in September 1917 recorded that "there was no more debate over which region we are from, whether we are 'Volga colonists' or other. Rather, at the second congress, the question of unity was entirely 'Are we German'?"[159] Thus the forced migrations unintentionally contributed directly to consolidating the once deeply divided and dispersed German individuals and communities into a single, much more self-conscious German minority in Russia. The regime's actions also contributed to the transformation of the most conservative of all minorities in Russia into a disenfranchised, displaced, and impoverished community which provided many recruits to the revolutionary parties.[160]

A somewhat parallel process was evident among Jews and other groups affected by the deportations. Like the Germans, Jews turned to their own for assistance, and there was a remarkable efflorescence of communal and organizational activity among Jewish populations throughout the empire. The attitudes of the Jewish populations throughout the empire also hardened and radicalized toward the regime, and a sense of a single Jewish community that needed political representation to protect itself noticeably strengthened.[161]

Mobilizing Ethnicity via Exemption Policies

One consequence of the campaign against enemy aliens was that a thousands of enemy subjects immediately appealed for exemption from deportation and other measures on the basis of their Slavic ethnicity, Orthodox religion, or other characteristics. As a result, the regime found itself involved in a massive process of sorting, classifying, and categorizing its population and distilling the complex and multiple identities of its peoples into simpler hierarchies of nationalities ranked by degrees of reliability according to their ethnic origin and correlation to Russia's external enemies during the war. The process itself contributed to the mobilization of ethnicity even for the favored ethnic groups who received exemption.[162]

The most extensive exemptions from categorical deportation orders applied to enemy subjects of Slavic ethnicity.[163] Themes of pan-Slavic unity had undergone a revival in the years prior to the war among both conservatives and some liberals.[164] In the declaration of war, the tsar had proclaimed Russia's role as protector of all Slavs and his support for the unity of all Slavs.[165] Thus it appeared incongruous that thousands of Slavic civilians were being rounded up for deportation and internment as enemy subjects, and each Slavic nationality mobilized to lobby for exemption and better treatment for its ethnic groups.

The first moves toward granting exemptions to Slavic enemy subjects applied to the Czechs. Already on August 3, 1914, Deputy Minister of Interior Dzhunkovskii informed governors in a circular that civilian enemy-subject deportees and prisoners of war of Czech nationality were to be allowed to form military units under the direction of the War Ministry. This of course only applied to able-bodied men, and the numbers actually allowed to form units were insignificant until quite late in the war.[166] Furthermore, most of the men were recruited among prisoners of war rather than among civilian deportees.

More important was an MVD decision of August 14, 1914, to allow exemptions from deportation orders for Ruthenian (Ukrainian), Serb, and Czech enemy-subject males of military age.[167] Even for the most favored Slavic nationalities, exemption from deportation was treated throughout the war as a privilege rather than a right. The MVD decision to exempt Czechs, Ruthenians, and Serbs was not binding on the military, and prior to each major deportation the Slavic aid societies had to petition the army extensively to receive official exemption. On February 27, 1915, Alekseev informed the head of the Minsk Military District that enemy subjects of Slavic origin could not be exempted from deportation orders within the theater of military activity.[168] Likewise, General Trotskii, commander of the Kiev Military District, published a declaration in the local newspapers in February 1915 setting a deadline of March 31 for enemy-subject Slavs, French, Italians, and Ottoman Christians to leave his jurisdiction or face compulsory deportation.[169]

Exemption never became automatic even for the favored Czechs.[170] The first Congress of Czechs in Russia, at its meeting in Kiev on January 13, 1915, spent most of its time on the issue of acquiring exemptions from deportations and wrote to the tsar requesting his aid. In response, Grand Duke Nikolai Nikolaevich demanded easier entry into Russian subjecthood for Czechs, and announced that all previously deported Czechs could petition for permission to return to their homes.[171] After this, deportations of Czechs and Slovaks became less common, but did not completely end. For example, General Savich wrote to Alekseev on September 27, 1915, that Czech enemy subjects would not be allowed to remain in Volynia, a major area of Czech settlement.[172]

In addition to the Czechs and Slovaks, other groups deemed friendly to the Russian state received exemptions from deportation orders during the course of the war. Christians from the Ottoman Empire (Armenians, Greeks, Bulgarians), long a Russian diplomatic concern prior to the war, became an even greater one, both because of Russian projects to annex and colonize parts of the Ottoman Empire, and because of the Ottoman mass deportation and killing of Armenians. Only a small number of Ottoman-subject Armenians lived in the Caucasus prior to the war. But Ottoman repressions catalyzed a massive influx of over 350,000 Armenian refugees from Turkey into the Russian Empire.[173] The Viceroy of the Caucasus, Vorontsov-Dashkov, was sympathetic to the plight of Armenians, and usually exempted them from orders to deport enemy subjects from the Caucasus. Yet recent Armenian scholarship has been quite critical of the Russian high command.[174] Though Armenian and other Christian Ottoman-subjects were exempted from most deportations, their position remained precarious throughout the war, and scattered evidence suggests that many Armenians were included in deportations of enemy subjects from the Caucasus.[175] The Council of Ministers officially exempted Ottoman-subject Armenians and Greeks from deportations and legislation to liquidate enemy-alien properties only on June 11, 1916.[176] Those who had been deported prior to this date were not given the right to return to the Caucasus until August 1917, despite the bitter complaints of the Moscow Armenian Committee and the Armenian Red Cross.[177]

Muslim enemy subjects, even if generally perceived as belonging to a "friendly" nationality, usually did not receive exemptions. For example, 10,000 Muslim Ottoman-subject tobacco workers of Laz nationality from the Sukhumi area were deported during the war to Riazan' and Tambov. They were not allowed to return until the Provisional Government reviewed their case in June 1917 and determined that their "membership in the Georgian nation" was sufficient to grant them permission to return.[178] Likewise, several thousand Tatars with Ottoman passports were deported in early 1915 from Crimea to the Russian interior and Central Asia. Many claimed they were long-term Crimean residents who had lost their citizenship when they temporarily migrated to Turkey to find work, a quite common practice among Crimean Tatars in the second half of the nineteenth century. Their appeals were ignored until the Provisional Government finally heard their case in July 1917 and allowed them to return.[179]

Many members of favored minority groups received a chance for exemption from deportation. Although exemption never became automatic, the conviction prevailed among most officials that these groups were friendly, and that a serious effort should be made to review their cases. There was no such consensus on the issue of enemy subjects of Polish background.

The strength and maturity of the Polish national movement, its closeness to socialist movements, and the clear preference of most politically active Poles for the creation of an independent state extending far east of the Wistula provinces to the Polish-Russian boundaries of 1772—all convinced Russian officials that Poles were not to be trusted. Just as important was the continuing social, cultural, and economic dominance of Polish gentry in many of the provinces of the western borderlands over "Russian" (Ukrainian, Belarusian, and Lithuanian) peasants.

The Grand Duke's declaration in August 1914 that Russia would create a unified autonomous Poland in its historical boundaries under the scepter of the tsar at war's end nominally transformed the official position of Poles. As a memo from the Warsaw Polish Committee expressed it, the declaration "in effect naturalized enemy-subject Poles."[180] Nonetheless, prewar attitudes toward Poles lingered among Russian officials. As a result, enemy-subject Poles received exemptions later and less completely than other Slavs and favored minorities, despite a stream of memos from the Ministry of Foreign Affairs arguing that it was in Russian diplomatic interests to exempt Poles from all deportation orders.[181]

Several of the first orders to deport enemy subjects explicitly included those of Polish nationality. Even when orders did not specify the inclusion of Poles, the general framework created by the army discouraged exemption. For example, General Zhilinskii, on August 3,

1914, ordered that enemy subjects of Slavic nationality, if not of service age, could be exempted from deportations only "if their loyalty and national origin were known to the local police or confirmed by fully reliable individuals."[182] Given the biases of local Russian officials against Poles, this ensured that few Poles would be exempted. Throughout the fall of 1914, Polish organizations appealed to the authorities for a general rule of exemption from deportation orders. The Polish Duma member Sventitskii was particularly active. In December 1915, one of his appeals finally received a favorable reply from the commander of the Southwest Front, Ivanov, who granted permission to exempt enemy-subject Poles if they received a document from a Polish organization certifying their nationality, and if the army and police had no unfavorable records on the individual. But Ianushkevich made the process extremely difficult by requiring the permission of the Grand Duke in each individual case.[183]

Hence many Poles were included in the mass deportations of enemy subjects early in the war. Already by January 1915, a Polish aid committee claimed to have records of 20,000 civilian enemy subjects of Polish, Czech, and Slovak ethnicity deported to the Volga provinces alone. Many more were deported to other Russian provinces, especially Kiev.[184]

The deportations of Polish enemy subjects to the Volga provinces were particularly brutal. According to the Polish committee, the Poles were settled mostly in rural areas, in Tatar and Chuvash farmsteads, where they were often housed with the cattle. Many arrived just with summer clothes and had no money. There were stories of groups being forced to complete their journeys by foot in terrible conditions. One party of 250 Polish deportees was sent on a 475-kilometer march in which 30 died. Locals often considered the newcomers to be *katorzhane* (convicts) and refused to give them work or aid. Theft of their meager possessions was common, and local hostility intensified as the newcomers were blamed for causing inflation in local markets.[185]

The position of deported Poles was alleviated somewhat by the March 5, 1915, decision to allow Polish deportees to live anywhere in the empire outside the huge area under military rule. By spring 1915, deportation orders increasingly exempted *all* Slavs rather than just Czechs, Slovaks, and Serbs. Yet Polish enemy subjects never received categorical exemption from orders to deport enemy subjects in areas under military rule, or from the network of security zones set up throughout the country around factories, rivers, and railroads. Moreover, on October 25, 1916, an imperial decree prohibited Polish deportees and refugees from returning to their homelands in the Wistula provinces until the end of the war.[186] The Provisional Government opposed the law but did not repeal it until July 1917 owing to strong army resistance.[187] This late repeal merely recognized a *fait accompli*, as many of the deportees had simply begun to use collapsing state authority to make their way home.[188]

Although exemption was often arbitrary, ethnic origin most often proved more important than formal citizenship when deportation categories were chosen. This can be seen as part of the general mobilization of ethnicity which occurred under the pressures of total war. Yet Slavic ethnicity did not prove sufficient to gain exemption from deportation for all groups. For Bulgarians, citizenship and the stance of their external national homeland in the war proved more important than nationality.

When it began to look probable that Bulgaria would enter the war against Russia in September 1915, Russian officials prepared to be lenient with Bulgarian subjects in Russia. Chief of the General Staff Alekseev wrote to his subordinates that if Bulgaria entered the war, they should not plan to deport Bulgarian subjects *en masse*.[189] The government acted to curb rising popular anti-Bulgarian sentiments in September 1915, instructing Russian industrialists to stop firing Bulgarian subjects from their businesses in Odessa and throughout South Russia.[190] When Bulgaria finally entered the war against Russia on October 5, 1915, Bulgarians were added to the list of those to be deported from front areas and exclusion zones, but Christians were exempted. Since nearly all Bulgarian subjects were Orthodox Christians, this *de facto* exempted almost all Bulgarians.

But news soon came in that Russian subjects were not treated well in Bulgaria, and military counterintelligence reports contended that Bulgarians were particularly dangerous as potential spies given the closeness of Bulgarian language and culture to Russian. As a result, the Council of Ministers worked out a new law which removed all previous privileges and exemptions for Bulgarian subjects. It required the deportation of *all* Bulgarian subjects from areas under military rule, from regions with factories working for defense, and from all other exclusion zones throughout the country without exception.[191] Thus, in the space of less than a year, Bulgarians in the Russian Empire quickly turned from favored friends to enemy aliens.

The forced migrations, like other wartime practices, made ethnicity newly important on the macro-level as well as in thousands of individual cases. One of the reasons the regime chose to treat ethnic origins more seriously than formal citizenship was the weakness of citizenship in the imperial Russian tradition. After a century of the great internationalizing era of the European long peace, World War I brought a sharp shift toward passports, visas, border controls, and surveillance of foreigners throughout the world.[192] Russia was no exception.[193] But by including Russian subjects of German and Jewish background in its sanctions and by exempting enemy-subject Slavs, the regime showed that citizenship had not become the fundamental defining boundary between the national self and enemy others. The basic problems were several. The tsar and regime pushed to retain the notion of loyalty to the tsar and God as the keys to membership and subjecthood in the naturalization laws. Liberals fought instead for a European-style citizenship and naturalization where the individual would declare loyalty to the state, to the nation, and to the Fundamental Laws rather than to the person of the tsar. Not even the wartime imperative of finding a consensus on something so fundamental as the focal point of the country's patriotism could overcome these disputes. As a result, Russia lacked citizenship and naturalization laws right up to February 1917.[194] In fact, by July 1915 Russia alone had banned all naturalization for the course of the war.[195] It was in part because citizenship had not become a consensus criterion for defining insiders and outsiders that the regime relied so heavily upon ethnicity.

The choice of Germans, Jews, and foreigners as the primary targets of mass deportations transformed traditional patterns of imperial nationality policy in several ways. First, it suddenly reshaped the configuration of perceived friends and foes within the empire. The old Polish enemy suddenly became an ally, while previously favored ethnic Germans became the main enemy.[196] The Latvians, Lithuanians, and Estonians, seen since 1905 as dangerous revolutionaries,[197] became partners of the state in struggles against the Baltic Germans, through whom the imperial regime had ruled the region for two centuries. These sudden shifts illustrate the importance of the war and more generally of the state's power to arbitrarily define and redefine its internal enemies. It is therefore misleading to present the wartime repressions of the German and Jewish diasporas as a natural result of a long-brewing conflict with the imperial center.[198] The choice of domestic enemies, with the possible exception of the Jews, was by no means so predetermined by prewar patterns. The examples of the Bulgarians in Russia and the Muslims of Kars and Batumi above provide cases in point of how the state could and did switch entire groups from friend to foe at its discretion. This point is important when considering issues of continuity in "internal enemy politics" across the divide of 1917. Like the tsarist regime, the Bolsheviks were able to construct their own categories of internal enemies and change them quite radically and suddenly from above.

The choices of primary targets were not, however, arbitrary or explained solely by wartime security considerations. The enemy alien and Jewish diasporas were generally more successful in their trades, professions, and farming than Russians and other groups in the empire, so they provided a means for Russian nationalists—typically seen as members of the dominant imperial nationality—to portray themselves as the underdogs. So there was a powerful socio-economic grounding and logic to the wartime campaign, which was firmly rooted in a program to assert and promote "Russians" and "Russia" against alien others who held desired "dominant" positions in the imperial economy and society.

The process extends to the territorial nationalities' own spaces. In nearly all regions of mass forced migration, Russians were a minority and so were the groups affected. And in each of these regions enemy aliens stood in the way of upward social mobility for other nationalities. For example, many Lithuanians, Latvians, and Estonians could find common ground with the Russian nationalists in an attempt to remove Germans and Jews, who represented socially dominant diasporas standing in the way of the nationalization of their own societies. In Poland, such views were quite developed and competition between Poles, Jews, Germans, and foreigners had been intense before the war. A rapidly growing Polish middle class came into ever sharper conflict and competition with Jews, Germans, and foreigners in the towns, leading to an intense anti-Jewish boycott in Poland in 1913.[199] As a Polish leader quite openly expressed it, the "deportation of Germans is entirely appropriate if these individuals have not assimilated into Polish culture."[200]

This implicit partnership between Russian nationalizing agendas and those of borderland nationalities caused many Russian leaders to pause. For example, when a prominent Pole wrote a letter to Ianushkevich petitioning for the exemption of an enemy alien from deportation on the grounds that "he was among the best carriers of the Polish national ideal," Ianushkevich wrote in the margin: "but the Russian?"[201] Governors from Poland and Volynia wrote that the real long-term internal enemy remained the Poles. The deportations of Germans and aliens could only help them and thus could be detrimental in the long run. Baltic governors pointed out that Russia had long pursued a policy of strict neutrality in nationality disputes, acting as an impartial imperial arbitrator above the fray.[202] Mass deportations and other repression of one group to the benefit of another, the governors of Kurland and Lifland both argued in early 1915, could only exacerbate national tensions, lead to social unrest, and undo the long-established foundations of Russian rule. To a certain degree, the forced migrations and other enemy-alien policies targeted precisely the type of individuals that were most suited to the maintenance of the imperial system.[203]

The purging of alien diasporas along the western and southern borderlands thus had the certainly unintended effect of making the Baltic provinces more Latvian and Estonian, Poland more Polish, Ukraine more Ukrainian, Georgia more Georgian, and so on. In the process, it was also contributing to new problems and tensions in its Russian areas by importing masses of aliens, and contributing to the rise of a new consciousness among the diasporas of their own distinct identities as national minorities.

The regime and army found themselves literally clearing the way for the national assertion of territorially concentrated national groups, including the Russian. While the mass deportations may have begun as temporary operations in the interests of state security, once the transfer of lands, properties, and social positions of the deported individuals to the benefit of core and favored nationalities became part of the program, it became a program for radical nationalizing change.

Conclusion

THE OLD REGIME'S embrace of the campaign against enemy aliens can be seen in part as an attempt to rally popular patriotic support, to make the imperial state more "national" in order to mobilize better for war. The attempt foundered for several reasons. First, radical as the campaign was, it did not satisfy many of its most active supporters because of its leniency toward Baltic Germans and its exclusion of prominent figures at court and in the bureaucracy with German or foreign names. The leaders of right-wing organizations filled the press with polemics against the government and hinted openly that a cabal of traitors at court was protecting the Baltic Germans. Leading generals Ruzskii, Bonch-Bruevich, and Brusilov all expressed their bitterness over government and army unwillingness to implement the campaign wholeheartedly against the Baltic Germans.[1] Moderate proponents of the campaign became frustrated as well. One of the most prominent among them was Serafim Mansyrev, the Progressist Duma deputy from Riga. In June 1916, he dramatically resigned from his post as chairman of the Duma Committee for the Fight against German Dominance, bitterly denouncing the government for focusing its sanctions against small German landholders, while leaving the properties and social primacy of the Baltic Germans largely untouched.[2]

To read the fulmination in the press about favoritism toward the Baltic Germans, one could be led to believe that they were entirely unaf-

166

fected by the war. This was far from the case. In August 1916, the tsar signed into law a historic decree which eliminated all Baltic German privileges in town and countryside, essentially abolishing distinctions between imperial and local Baltic law.[3] Purges of the Baltic administration removed German governors and officials and strove to replace them with ethnic Russians, Estonians, Latvians, and Lithuanians.[4] Nonetheless, Baltic German elites did escape the harsher treatment meted out to other enemy-alien categories, and the official measures were too late and too lenient to mollify the most aggressive proponents of the campaign.

If the regime was hesitant to endorse a full-scale campaign against German elites in the Baltics, it was even more reluctant to purge ethnic Germans from the imperial court, bureaucracy, and army command. Not only did over fifteen percent of the officer corps have Germanic last names, but nearly all the leading branches of government, civil service, and economy were staffed by individuals with German and foreign names. For example, nearly thirty percent of the members of the State Council, and over half the members of the court chancery had names of Germanic derivation.[5] Elite Russians with German and foreign names felt the pressure. The Procurator of the Holy Synod, Vladimir K. Sabler, who in May 1915 officially changed his name to Vladimir K. Dessiatovsky, was one of dozens of officials to Russify their name during the war.[6] Bureaucrats played the "German traitor" card at times to destroy their rivals, just as some businessmen used it to eliminate competitors.[7] But although the campaign against enemy aliens resulted in the removal of some of these most visible "Germans" in Russian society, most retained their posts and increasingly became a focal point for popular discontent.

By early 1917, gendarme reports on the mood of the population noted widespread rumors among all social classes that treason was rampant within the imperial elite. Many of the rumors centered on the allegedly German Empress Aleksandra, the chairman of the Imperial Court, Count Vladimir Frederiks, and the chairman of the Council of Ministers, Boris Shtiurmer.[8] In the countryside the "great killing-off legend" held that the German clique in the elite was intentionally sending peasant soldiers to their death at the front so they would not claim landlord properties at the end of the war.[9] Soldiers' letters intercepted by the censor often claimed that Russia was being sold out by

German generals in league with the "German party" at court, and memoirs of military commanders with German names often refer to the intense suspicions they felt from the rank and file, and from society as a whole. In many army units it was a major element in the breakdown of trust between soldiers and commanders.[10] The street protests of the February Revolution included considerable violence directed against Germans, foreigners, and others accused by the crowds of treason.[11] The rhetoric of the campaign thus eventually turned against the imperial elite itself.

But the ferment was not simple xenophobia and spy mania. Across the political spectrum, many of those who turned against the old regime did so in the name of patriotism. The Right bitterly denounced the administration as incapable of acting in a more complete fashion against enemy aliens because of "the inability of the bureaucracy to take up truly Russian national ideas."[12] The campaign, which had been seen by some early in the war as a way for the government to unite with the people in a popular patriotic outpouring against enemies within and without, became a bone of contention between the government and its self-proclaimed most patriotic supporters.

The campaign also contributed to the movement of liberals and moderates away from patriotic support for the government to patriotic opposition. The most dramatic example was the leader of the liberal opposition, Pavel Miliukov. Toward the end of 1916, rumors proliferated about Rasputin, Shtiurmer, Aleksandra, and the German clique at the top of government and court, focusing on their purported schemes to conclude a separate peace.[13] On November 1, 1916, Miliukov lent his credibility to the rumors in a dramatic speech in the Duma, in which he openly accused the government of treason. The speech created a sensation. Censors banned its publication, but handwritten copies circulated rapidly throughout the country along with stories that extrapolated wildly from the original.[14] Miliukov quite consciously wanted the speech to undermine the government's viability and succeeded spectacularly, setting the stage for the February Revolution, "in which anger over alleged government treason was initially the single most important motive."[15]

In a broader sense, most liberals saw citizenship as the fundamental division between nations at war. Hence they willingly supported measures against enemy citizens. But this support was offered on the implicit condition that the government would allow the creation of a real "civic nation" based on equal rights for all Russian citizens. After the regime made it clear that it did not intend to grant equal rights to all its subjects, and instead turned on its own subjects of German, Jewish, and other suspect origins, liberals increasingly saw the rulers as standing in the way of the successful mobilization of patriotic energies along the lines of the "nation-in-arms."[16] Moderate Octobrists and even a wing of the Nationalist Party bitterly denounced the government for deporting and expropriating Russian subjects who had family members fighting in the Russian army. The broad coalition that formed the Progressive Bloc in mid-1915 and became the focal point of the opposition was united by the conviction that the old regime needed to be overthrown in order to create a truly united citizenry and inspire a patriotic upsurge to defeat the enemy. In fact, when the liberals came to power in February 1917, among the first acts of the Provisional Government was to halt the implementation of nearly all the decrees affecting Russian subjects.[17]

So the attempt to gain popular support by endorsing a Russian nationalist campaign can hardly be called a success. Just as significantly, the campaign had the unintended effect of radicalizing and mobilizing the groups affected, contributing to their own sense of national grievance, unity, and identity. The displacements and hardships of the war years led Germans, Jews, and others to mobilize to provide aid and assistance to their fellows, creating the infrastructure for a much tighter sense of themselves as national communities. The shift was particularly dramatic among the Germans. Prior to the war, the Germans had been the least radical of all the national minorities in the empire, and the various merchants, townsmen, nobles, civil servants, and farmers in widely disparate communities had relatively little sense of common identity. With many of them suddenly disenfranchised, displaced, and impoverished, these disparate groups came together to form a much more politically united and consciously German minority. The radical measures of the government spurred significant numbers of this minority—formerly led by conservatives and moderates—to join revolutionary parties.[18] The Jewish minority underwent a comparable transformation.[19]

A similar dynamic was evident with favored minority communities as well. Czechs, Poles, Slovaks, and others facing deportation or expropriation as enemy subjects could benefit from a gradually established set of exemption criteria. The practices of deportation and expropriation led to a major project to sort, define, and categorize individuals according to their ethnicity, immigrant status, or citizenship, and to determine whether entire population categories were to be considered members of the wartime community or internal enemies. Through this process, nationality and ethnicity were in a sense constituted and ascribed as a function of wartime practices.

It was not only the state ascribing identities, but a dynamic process that involved the communities themselves. National aid committees distributed and denied food and services based on their own decisions about individuals' ethnicity. In this way minority groups became increasingly united, both around the goal of helping their co-ethnics and in lobbying for more resources and more favorable policies from the center.[20]

For these and other reasons, the World War I experience marks a sharp break in the history of nationality in the Russian Empire. While in the prewar decades even the most aggressive cultural Russification policies had primarily aimed to convert and assimilate minorities into Orthodoxy and Russian culture, the war brought about a qualitative shift. The practices examined in this study are not about assimilating or converting. In fact, the naturalization of foreigners was banned, and the deliberations of the various committees considering appeals for exemption show that evidence of assimilation was much less decisive than ethnic origins or the date of naturalization of immigrants. The intent of the measures was not to assimilate individuals, but rather to nationalize larger abstractions: the economy, the land, and the population.

To a certain degree, this was all part of a major wartime expansion of the state and its claims to control and manage the population and the economy, an expansion widely noted in the historiography of the war in all participating countries, and increasingly recognized as an important precedent for the extensive claims of the Soviet state.[21] The campaign against enemy minorities contributed to strengthening the national state through the expansion of documentary controls over the population, greater police and state oversight of foreigners and immigrants, the creation of a network of inspectors, administrators, and liquidators to oversee and control corporations and economic transactions, and the transfer of many businesses and properties to state institutions. The campaign shows how the old regime introduced these and other state practices that would ultimately become central to the Bolshevik revolutionary repertoire, from the nationalization of private property to the identification, purge, and removal of enemy population categories.

Yet this was not a simple case of a powerful and interventionist state operating upon the population. In part, the government and army used the blunt and extreme tools of mass deportation and expropriation because state power was so brittle and limited. This was particularly true in the multiethnic western borderlands, where the army often acted like an occupying force in hostile foreign lands. As the Moscow riot shows, the authorities' ability to keep social order was shaky even in the second capital—in the Russian core of the country. Russia's rulers and the leaders of the campaign against enemy aliens often acted out of a sense of weakness. One can see it in the paranoid Russian officers who saw security threats in isolated German farming communities and wildly exaggerated the subversive potential of Jews. It was also apparent in the basic slogan of the campaign, which portrayed it as a fight against the *zasil'e* (dominance) of Germans and foreigners over Russians in the economy and society.

This underlying sense of weakness is a key to the role of Russian nationalism during the war. Most national movements draw heavily on the fact or perception that the national group is economically disadvantaged by the existing state structure. The campaign against enemy minorities shows that Russian nationalists were able to see themselves in just such an aggrieved situation and developed a radical emancipatory program that challenged the legitimacy of imperial elites, the internationalized and multiethnic imperial economy, and even the imperial state structure itself. With its emancipatory economic nationalist message, this campaign presented arguably the most dynamic and popular manifestation of Russian nationalism in the late imperial period, and it suggests that Russian nationalism should be taken more seriously as a force toward the end of the old regime.

In this respect, the Ottoman Empire provides the closest point of comparison for the Russian case.[22] In both cases, the imperial regime—at times reluctantly responding to popular pressure—embraced a radical economic nationalist mobilization against foreign and native minority commercial diasporas. In both cases, this dynamic mobilization undermined social order, exacerbated ethnic conflict, and contributed to the fall of the old regime.[23]

In nearly every aspect of the Russian campaign, officials strove to

transfer properties and businesses to Russians. But the results often differed from the intentions. In fact, the mobilization against dispersed
enemy minorities strengthened other territorially based nationalisms.
By targeting primarily German, foreign, and Jewish diasporas—most
actively in the non-Russian borderlands—the regime promoted territorial nationalities at the expense of the dispersed, a nationalizing trend
that continued in the region. This was true in the new states of Eastern
Europe, where nationalization and agrarian reform were facilitated if
elites were not of the core ethnicity.[24] It was also true in the Soviet
Union, which provided substantial support for the territorial nationalities, but in times of international tension in the 1930s, and especially
during World War II, turned to similar attacks on many of the same
groups that had been targeted during the First World War.[25] In all
these cases, nationalizing pressures and agendas mixed in combustible
fashion with international tensions or war to foster radical state actions.

The wartime burst of Russian economic nationalism did not disappear without a trace under the Bolsheviks. World War I did a great
deal to break down the prewar world financial and economic systems,
and contributed quite significantly to a worldwide shift of countries toward greater economic self-sufficiency and isolation. That shift was
most pronounced and remarkable in the Soviet case. With the aban-
donment of the ideal of world revolution and the turn to "socialism
in one country" as its industrializing ideology, the Soviet regime
embraced an extreme form of economic autarky, liquidating the last
foreign enterprises operating on Soviet soil, launching purges of foreigners, technicians, managers, and engineers under accusations of espionage, and generally embarking on a war-like mobilization of native
forces for the industrialization campaign.[26] It has been argued that
Marxism-Leninism completed a dialectical transformation of Marxism
from an ideology that took the international proletariat as the fundamental working unit of history to an ideology primarily concerned with
the emancipation and development of relatively backward nations—in
effect, that "Marxism-Leninism became a variant of nationalism."[27] It is
no anomaly that in the twentieth century communism found its greatest resonance not in the industrially developed world, but rather in the
underdeveloped world, as an ideology of anti-imperial national liberation, a program to mobilize developing countries against the international economy and multinational corporations, and a model for

autarkic economic development. The origins of this fundamental feature of the Soviet system are found more easily in Russian Slavophile and populist traditions, with opposition to the economically advanced and capitalist West at the center of their concerns, than in classic Marxism.[28] If the Soviet system owes more to economic nationalism than scholarship has generally granted, then the emergence of this form of nationalism during World War I becomes an important formative episode as well as a destructive one. In any event, now that the Soviet Union is history and Russia struggles to reconnect itself to the international economy, it is even more apparent that one of the great breaking points of the twentieth century came when those connections were broken.

During the First World War, popular and military pressures pushed Russia's old regime to embrace—at first reluctantly, then with enthusiasm—a radical campaign that had a powerful set of Russian-centered economic nationalist slogans and agendas at its core. In thinking about the end of the old regime and the beginning of the new, it suggests that we reconsider the role of Russian nationalism and the radicalizing and nationalizing effects of the Great War.

Appendix

Wartime Leaders

Adrianov, Aleksandr Aleksandrovich (b. 1861): Moscow City Governor (February 1, 1908–June 4, 1915). When Moscow was placed under a state of "extraordinary safeguard" on July 11, 1914, Adrianov was given extra-judicial powers. Forced to retire on 4 June 1915 as a result of the Moscow riots of May 26–29, 1915.

Alekseev, Mikhail Vasil'evich (1857–1918): Commander of the Southwest Front (1914–1915), Commander of the Northwest, then the West Front (1915); Chief of the Headquarters of the Supreme Commander (August 18, 1915–May 1917).

Bonch-Bruevich, Mikhail Dmitrievich (1870–1956): General Quartermaster of the Third Army (1914); Commander of the Headquarters of the Sixth Army (1914–1915); Commander of the Headquarters of the Northern Front (1915–1916); Chief of the Garrison of Pskov (March 1916). Served as General-Lieutenant in Red Army in 1917.

Brusilov, Aleksei Alekseevich (1853–1926): Commander of the Eighth Army (1914); Commander of the Southwest Front (1916–1917); Commander in Chief (May-June 1917).

Chelnokov, Mikhail Vasil'evich: Member of the Duma (1907–1917). Switched from the Kadet Party to the Progressist Party in Fall 1914. Mayor of Moscow (1914–1917).

Danilov, Iurii Nikoforovich (1866–1937): General Quartermaster of Army Headquarters (1914–September 1915); Commander of the Headquarters of the Northern Front (1916–1917); Commander of the Fifth Army (February–September 1917).

Dzhunkovskii, Vladimir Fedorovich (1865–1938): Assistant Minister of Internal Affairs and Commander of the Corps of Gendarmes (1913–August 1915).

Engalychev, Pavel Nikolaevich: Head of the Imperial Nikolaev Military Academy; Governor General of Warsaw from December 23, 1914; member of the suite of the tsar.

Goremykin, Ivan Logginovich (1839–1917): Chairman of the Council of Ministers (1914–1916).

Ianushkevich, Nikolai Nikolaevich (1868–1918): Chief of Army Headquarters (July 1914–August 18, 1915); Assistant for Military Affairs to the Viceroy of the Caucasus (1915–1917).

Ivanov, Nikolai Iudovich (1851–1919): Commander of the Armies of the Southwest Front (1914–1917); during the Civil War, Commander of the White Cossack Army under F. N. Krasnov.

Karaulov, Mikhail Aleksandrovich (1878–1917): Member of the Fourth Duma and member of the Progressist faction. Co-founder and chair of the Society of 1914.

Khvostov, Aleksei Nikolaevich (1872–1924). Member of the Fourth Duma and chairman of the Right faction; Minister of Internal Affairs (1915–1916).

Kurlov, Pavel Grigor'evich (b. 1860): Special Plenipotentiary for Civilian Affairs in the Baltic provinces (1914–1915).

Lindeman, Karl: Member of the Octobrist faction in the Third Duma and leading figure in German colonist politics. Member of the Moscow City Duma during the war. Chairman of the Association of Russian-Citizen Settlers of German Descent, formed in April 1917.

Maklakov, Nikolai Alekseevich (1871–1918): Minister of Internal Affairs (1912–June 1915).

Mansyrev, Seraphim: Member of the Fourth Duma from Riga. Chairman of the Duma's Committee for the Fight Against German Dominance in All Spheres of Russian Life (August 1915–June 1916); member of the board of directors of the Society of 1914.

Miliukov, Pavel Nikolaevich (1859–1943): Member of Third and Fourth Dumas; leader of the Kadet Party and initiator of the Progressive Bloc in 1915.

Nikolai Nikolaevich (1856–1929): Grand Duke; Commander in Chief (July 20, 1914–August 25, 1915); Commander of the Caucasus Armies (August 1915–March 1917).

Nol'de, Boris Emmanuilovich (1876–1948): Head of the Second Department of the Ministry of Foreign Affairs and juridical counsel for the Ministry of Foreign Affairs.

Polivanov, Aleksei Andreevich (1855–1920): War Minister (1915–1916); chairman of the Special Committee for State Defense 1915–1916).

Ruzskii, Nikolai Vladimirovich (1854–1918): Commander of the Third Army (1914); Commander of the Armies of the Northwest Front (1914–1915); Commander of the Northern Front (1915–1917).

Shtiurmer, Boris Vladimirovich (1848–1917). Member of the State Council; Chairman of the Council of Ministers (March–July 1916)

Stishinskii, Aleksandr Semenovich (1851–1922): Member of the State Council, expert on police and land affairs; head of special committee to draw up legislation limiting the land ownership and rights of enemy aliens during the war.

Notes

Abbreviations Used in the Notes

AVPRI: Arkhiv vneshnei politiki Rossiiskoi Imperii (Archive of the Foreign
           Policy of the Russian Empire).
GARF: Gosudarstvennyi arkhiv Rossiiskoi Federatsii (State Archive of the
           Russian Federation).
MID: Ministerstvo inostrannykh del (Ministry of Foreign Affairs).
MVD: Ministerstvo vnutrennikh del (Ministry of Internal Affairs). In the
           Russian Empire, this ministry included not only the police, but also
           city governors, provincial governors, and other important officials.
MTiP: Ministerstvo torgovli i promyshlennosti (Ministry of Trade and
           Industry).
RGB: Rossiiskaia gosudarstvennaia biblioteka (Russian State Library),
           Manuscript Division.
RGIA: Rossiiskii gosudarstvennyi istoricheskii arkhiv (Russian State Historical
           Archive)
RGVIA: Rossiiskii gosudarstvennyi voenno-istoricheskii arkhiv (Russian State
           Military-Historical Archive).
Stavka: The General Headquarters of the Russian Army.

Introduction

1. There were roughly 600,000 enemy citizens registered as permanent residents of the Russian Empire in 1914, plus over a hundred thousand temporary visitors. Henning Bauer, Andreas Kappeler, and Brigitte Roth, eds., *Die Nationalitäten des Russischen Reiches in der Volkszählung von 1897*, vol. B. (Stuttgart: Franz Steiner Verlag, 1991), 211; V. V. Obolenskii, *Mezhdunarodnye i mezhkontinental'nye migratsii v dovoennoi Rossii i SSSR* (Moscow: Ts.S.U. SSSR, 1928), 108, 110.

2. Some of the better works include: J. C. Bird, *The Control of Enemy Alien Civilians in Great Britain, 1914–1918* (New York: Garland, 1986); Gerhard Fischer, *Enemy Aliens: Internment and the Homefront Experience in Australia: 1914–1920* (St. Lucia, Queensland: University of Queensland Press, 1989); Jean-Claude Farcy, *Les Camps de concentration français de la Première Guerre Mondiale (1914–1920)* (Paris: Anthropos, 1995); J. Spiropulos, *Ausweisung und Internierung Feindlicher Staatsangehöriger* (Leipzig: Rossberg'sche Verlagsbuchhandlung, 1922); Frederick D. Luebke, *Germans in Brazil* (Baton Rouge: Louisiana State University Press, 1987); Panikos Panayi, ed., *Minorities in Wartime: National and Racial Groupings in Europe, North America, and Australia during the Two World Wars* (Oxford: Berg, 1993) and *The Enemy in Our Midst: Germans in Britain during the First World War* (New York: Berg, 1991); Lubomyr Luciuk, *A Time for Atonement: Canada's First National Internment Operations and the Ukrainian Canadians 1914–1920* (Kingston, Ontario: Limestone Press, 1988).

3. V. M. Gessen, *Poddanstvo, ego ustanovlenie i prekrashchenie* (St. Petersburg: Pravda, 1909), 95; E. M. Borchard, "Enemy Private Property," *American Journal of International Law* 18, no. 2 (April, 1924): 523–532; Spiropulos, *Ausweisung*, 1–15; James Wilford Garner, *International Law and the World War*, 2 vols. (London: Longmans, Green, 1920) and "Treatment of Enemy Aliens: Measures in Respect to Personal Liberty," *American Journal of International Law* 12, no. 1 (1918): 27–55; "Die Zivilgefangenen," in *Völkerrecht im Weltkrieg* 3, pt. 2 (Berlin: Deutsche Verlagsgesellschaft für Politik, 1927), 719–826.

4. In the course of the war, France interned roughly 60,000 civilian enemy aliens; Britain, 30,000; Germany, 110,000; the United States, 2,300; Australia, 4,500. Unfortunately, figures for the Hapsburg and Ottoman empires are not available. Wilhelm Doegen, *Kriegsgefangene Volker: Der Kriegsgefangenen Haltung und Schicksal in Deutschland* (Berlin: Dietrich Reimer, 1919), Table G; Spiropulos, *Ausweisung*, 67, 78, 90–92; Richard B. Speed, III, *Prisoners, Diplomats, and the Great War: A Study in the Diplomacy of Captivity* (London: Greenwood Press, 1990), 146; Farcy, *Les Camps de concentration*, 129; Jörg Nagler, "Victims of the Home Front: Enemy Aliens in the United States during the First World War," in Panayi, ed., *Minorities in Wartime*, 191–215.

5. Joshua Sanborn, "Military Reform, Moral Reform, and the End of the Old Regime," in Marshall Poe and Eric Lohr, eds., *Military and Society in Russian History, 1450–1917* (Leiden, The Netherlands: Brill, 2002), 507–524. Sanborn shows that Russia's military reformers from the 1870s onward were very explicitly aware of this link, and consciously tried to promote a greater sense of nation among soldiers and the populace as a whole.

6. Michael Howard, *War in European History* (New York: Oxford University Press, 1976), 93.

7. The most comprehensive roundup of enemy citizens in the nineteenth century was in France, which interned 30,000 Germans in 1870. After three weeks, France acceded to international outrage and pressure and allowed their release. Spiropulos, *Ausweisung*, 46; V. N. Aleksandrenko, "O vysylke inostrantsev," *Zhurnal Ministerstva iustitsii* 5, pt. 2 (1905): 35–69.

8. Bernard Gainer, *The Alien Invasion: The Origins of the Aliens Act of 1905* (London: Heinemann, 1972); John Torpey, *The Invention of the Passport: Surveillance, Citizenship and the State* (Cambridge: Cambridge University Press, 2000).

9. On the changing definition of the term *inorodets* (alien), see John W. Slocum, "Who, and When, Were the *Inorodtsy?* The Evolution of the Category of 'Aliens' in Imperial Russia," *The Russian Review* 57 (April 1998): 173–190. For an explanation of the term's use on the eve of the war, see L. Shternberg, "Inorodtsy: Obshchii obzor," in A. I. Kastelianskii, ed., *Formy natsional'nogo dvizheniia v sovremennykh gosudarstvakh* (St. Petersburg, 1910), 531. The term *inorodets* rarely appeared in the wartime campaign, perhaps because Russian-subject Germans, who were not technically *inorodtsy*, were so central to the campaign.

10. Andreas Kappeler, *Russland als Vielvölkerreich: Entstehung, Geschichte, Zerfall* (Munich: C. H. Beck, 1992); Andreas Kappeler, ed., *The Formation of National Elites* (New York: New York University Press, 1992); David Saunders, *The Ukrainian Impact on Russian Culture, 1750–1850* (Edmonton: Canadian Institute of Ukrainian Studies, University of Alberta, 1985); Zenon E. Kohut, *Russian Centralism and Ukrainian Autonomy: Imperial Absorption of the Hetmanate, 1760s–1830s* (Cambridge, Mass.: Harvard University Press, 1988); Daniel Stone, *Polish Politics and National Reform, 1775–1788* (New York: Columbia University Press, 1976).

11. Roger Bartlett, *Human Capital: The Settlement of Foreigners in Russia, 1762–1804* (Cambridge: Cambridge University Press, 1979); Detlef Brandes, *Von den Zaren Adoptiert: Die Deutschen Kolonisten und die Balkansiedler in Neurussland und Bessarabien 1751–1914* (Munich: R. Oldenbourg Verlag, 1993); Zhanna Mikolaivna Kovba, "Ches'ka emigratsiia na ukraini v drugii polovini XIX—na pochatku XX storichnia" (Ph.D. diss., L'viv, 1974); Karl Stumpp, *Die Auswanderung aus Deutschland nach Russland in den Jahren 1763 bis 1862* (Tubingen, 1972). By 1914, the number of individuals claiming German as their first language was about 2.5 million. See Vladimir Maksimovich Kabuzan, "Nemetskoe naselenie v Rossii v XVIII—nachale XX veka (Chislennost' i razmeshchenie)," *Voprosy istorii* 12 (1989): 18–29.

12. Barbara Anderson, *Internal Migration during Modernization in Late Nineteenth Century Russia* (Princeton: Princeton University Press, 1980); Obolenskii, *Mezhdunarodnye i mezhkontinental'nye migratsii;* Rogers Brubaker, "Aftermaths of Empire and the Unmixing of Peoples," *Ethnic and Racial Studies* 18, no. 2 (1995): 189–218.

13. On Russia's participation in the internationalization of economic activity, see John McKay, *Pioneers for Profit: Foreign Entrepreneurship and Russian Industrialization, 1885–1913* (Chicago: University of Chicago Press, 1970).

14. Robert Kann, *The Multinational Empire: Nationalism and National Reform in the Habsburg Monarchy, 1848–1918*, vol. 2 (New York: Columbia University Press, 1950). On this aspect of Soviet nationality policy, see Yuri Slezkine, "The USSR as a Communal Apartment, or How a Socialist State Promoted Ethnic Particularism," *Slavic Review* 53, no. 2 (Summer 1994): 414–452.

15. On failed Russian projects to decentralize or create a federal system, see Georg von Rauch, *Russland: Staatliche Einheit und nationale Vielfalt: Föderalistische Kräfte und Ideen in der russischen Geschichte* (Munich: Isar-Verlag, 1953) and Dimitri von Mohrenschildt, *Toward a United States of Russia: Plans and Projects of Federal Reconstruction of Russia in the Nineteenth Century* (Rutherford: Fairleigh Dickinson University Press, 1981).

16. Theodore Weeks, *Nation and State in Late Imperial Russia: Nationalism and Russification on the Western Frontier* (DeKalb: Northern Illinois Press, 1996), 3–18;

Edward C. Thaden, ed., *Russification in the Baltic Provinces and Finland, 1855–1914* (Princeton: Princeton University Press, 1981), 3–9.

17. Hans Rogger, "Nationalism and the State: A Russian Dilemma," *Comparative Studies in Society and History* IV, no. 3 (The Hague, 1961–1962): 253–254.

18. The idea is "classically nationalist" in the sense of Roman Szporluk's interpretation of Friedrich List as a progenitor of nationalism as an ideology. See Roman Szporluk, *Communism and Nationalism: Karl Marx versus Friedrich List* (New York: Oxford University Press, 1988).

19. Donald Quataert, *Social Disintegration and Popular Resistance in the Ottoman Empire, 1881–1908: Reactions to European Economic Penetration* (New York: New York University Press, 1983); Karl Gerth, "Nationalizing Consumption, Consuming Nationalism: The National Products Movement in China, 1905–1937" (Ph.D. diss., Harvard University, 2000); Resat Kasaba, *The Ottoman Empire and the World Economy—The Nineteenth Century* (Albany: State University of New York, 1988), 105–116; Benjamin Braude and Bernard Lewis, eds., *Christians and Jews in the Ottoman Empire: The Functioning of a Plural Society* (New York: Holmes and Meier, 1982), esp. 261–338; Sevket Pamuk, *The Ottoman Empire and European Capitalism, 1820–1913: Trade, Investment, and Production* (Cambridge: Cambridge University Press, 1987); Stanford J. Shaw and Ezel Kural Shaw, *History of the Ottoman Empire and Modern Turkey*, vol. 2, *Reform, Revolution, and Republic: The Rise of Modern Turkey, 1808–1975* (Cambridge: Cambridge University Press, 1977); Nasim Sousa, *The Capitulatory Regime of Turkey: Its History, Origin and Nature* (Baltimore: Johns Hopkins University Press, 1933). The situation also shares many common features with present-day Indonesia and Malaysia, where the Chinese commercial diaspora has been the focus of core nationalist resentments, and in other contexts where commercial diasporas are perceived by a core population as holding a dominant position. See Daniel Chirot and Anthony Reid, eds., *Essential Outsiders: Chinese and Jews in the Modern Transformation of Southeast Asia and Central Europe* (Seattle: University of Washington Press, 1997), 61 .

20. For an overview of historiography on this issue, see the introduction by Geoffrey Jones and Grigorii Gerenstain, introduction to P. V. Ol', *Foreign Capital in Russia* (New York: Garland, 1983) and see Chapter 3 below.

21. Peter Holquist, "To Count, To Extract, To Exterminate: Population Statistics and Population Politics in Late Imperial and Soviet Russia," in Ronald Grigor Suny and Terry Martin, eds., *A State of Nations: Empire and Nation-Making in the Age of Lenin and Stalin* (Oxford: Oxford University Press, 2001): 111–144; "'Information is the Alpha and Omega of Our Work': Bolshevik Surveillance in Its Pan-European Context," *The Journal of Modern History* 69 (September 1997): 415–450; "What's so Revolutionary about the Russian Revolution? State Practices and the New-Style Politics, 1914–21," in David Hoffman and Yanni Kotsonis, eds., *Russian Modernity: Politics, Knowledge, Practices* (New York: St. Martin's Press, 2000), 87–111.

22. John B. Dunlop, *The Rise of Russia and the Fall of the Soviet Union* (Princeton: Princeton University Press, 1995); Yitzhak M. Brudny, *Reinventing Russia: Russian Nationalism and the Soviet State, 1953–1991* (Cambridge, Mass.: Harvard University Press, 1998); David Brandenberger, *National Bolshevism: Stalinist Mass Culture, Russocentrism and the Formation of Modern Russian National Identity, 1931–1956* (Cambridge, Mass.: Harvard University Press, 2002); Shaw and Shaw, *His-*

tory of the Ottoman Empire; Istvan Deak, "The Habsburg Army in the First and Last Days of World War I: A Comparative Analysis," in B. K. Kiraly and N. F. Dreisiger, eds., *War and Society in East Central Europe* (New York: Columbia University Press, 1985); Henry Cord Meyer, *Mitteleuropa in German Thought and Action, 1815–1945* (The Hague: Nijhoff, 1955); Audrey Helfant Budding, "Serb Intellectuals and the National Question, 1961–1991" (Ph.D. diss., Harvard University, 1998).

23. One of the best studies to date on the problem concludes that Russian patriotism and nationalism ultimately played only a negative role in the revolution mainly through the "absence of a commonly recognized national identity." Hubertus Jahn, *Patriotic Culture in Russia during World War I* (Ithaca: Cornell University Press, 1995), 177. Likewise, Geoffrey Hosking's major study of the problem of the Russians within the empire argues that the imperial state structure impeded the formation of a Russian nation, and he is skeptical about the notion of a powerful Russian national challenge to the imperial state. Geoffrey Hosking, *Russia: People and Empire, 1552–1917* (Cambridge, Mass.: Harvard University Press, 1997). For an excellent discussion of the problem of peasant national identity that questions the predominant view on peasants' lack of national and civic identity and argues for the importance of national discourse during the war, see Joshua Sanborn, "The Mobilization of 1914 and the Question of the Russian Nation: A Re-Examination"; Scott J. Seregny, "Zemstvos, Peasants, and Citizenship: The Russian Adult Education Movement and World War I"; "Citizenship and the Russian Nation during World War I: A Comment"; and replies by Sanborn and Seregny in *Slavic Review* 59, no. 2 (Summer 2000): 267–342.

24. Mark von Hagen, "The Great War and the Mobilization of Ethnicity," in Barnett R. Rubin and Jack Snyder, eds., *Post–Soviet Political Order: Conflict and State-Building* (London: Routledge, 1998), 34–57.

25. Anderson, *Imagined Communities*, 83.

26. Rogers Brubaker, *Nationalism Reframed: Nationhood and the National Question in the New Europe* (Cambridge: Cambridge University Press, 1996), 20.

27. Brubaker, *Nationalism Reframed*, 19. See also Denis V. Dragunskii, "Imposed Ethnicity," *Russian Social Science Review* (March–April 1995): 71–75.

28. Sanborn, "The Mobilization of 1914," 267–289. Sanborn focuses on ways in which mobilization occurred within a single national framework that transcended ethnic differences. The mobilization against enemy aliens supports this argument in some ways, as an attempt to mobilize the Russian citizenry as a whole against foreigners and a core set of trusted nationalities against a limited set of enemy minorities. But on balance, I put more stress on the ways that mobilization exacerbated ethnic differences and centered on a narrower, more specifically Russian base.

29. The narratives with the best coverage of the war years for two of the major targets of the enemy alien campaign include: Ingeborg Fleischhauer, *Die Deutschen im Zarenreich: Zwei Jahrhunderte deutsch-russische Kulturgemeinschaft* (Stuttgart: Deutsche Verlags-Anstalt, 1986); Heinz-Dietrich Löwe, *The Tsars and the Jews: Reform, Reaction and Anti-Semitism in Imperial Russia, 1772–1917* (Switzerland: Harwood Academic Publishers, 1993); Simon Dubnow, *History of the Jews in Russia and Poland from the Earliest Times until the Present Day*, vol. 3 (Philadelphia: The Jewish Publication Society of America, 1920).

30. Peter Gatrell, "Refugees in the Russian Empire, 1914–1917: Population Displacement and Social Identity," in Edward Acton, Vladimir Iu. Cherniaev, and William G. Rosenberg, eds., *Critical Companion to the Russian Revolution, 1914–1921* (Bloomington: Indiana University Press, 1997), 554–564 and his *A Whole Empire Walking: Refugees in Russia During World War I* (Bloomington: Indiana University Press, 1999), esp. 195–197.

1. Nationalist Challenges, Imperial Dilemmas

1. Gosudarstvennyi arkhiv Rossiiskoi Federatsii (GARF), f. 215, op. 1, d. 174, l. 180. Unless otherwise noted, all dates are given according to the Julian (O.S.) calendar, which was 13 days behind the Gregorian (N.S.) in 1914.

2. "Russkie poddannye v Germanii i Avstro-vengrii vo vremia voiny," *Russkie vedomosti*, 22 July 1914, 2.

3. Quoted in *Rech'*, 22 July 1914, 1.

4. Gendarme reports on these demonstrations can be found in GARF, f. 270, op. 1, d. 99; Iurii Il'ich Kir'ianov, "Demonstratsii rabochikh v 1914 g.—Feb. 1917 g." in *Rabochii klass kapitalisticheskoi Rossii* (Moscow: RAN, 1992), 72.

5. Rossiiskii gosudarstvennyi istoricheskii arkhiv (RGIA), f. 1282, op. 3, d. 707 (Addresses of various institutions and organizations to Nicholas II, 1914).

6. The German-language press was unanimous in declaring support for Russia in the war and enthusiasm for the "unification of Russian society." See *Volkszeitung*, 27 July 1914, which includes excerpts from other German papers.

7. *Rech'*, 25 July 1914, 2. The tsar changed the name of St. Petersburg to Petrograd on August 18.

8. A. Aleksandrov (State Duma member), "Oni oshiblis . . .," *Rech'*, 23 July 1914.

9. For a good overview, see chapter 2 ("Union Sacrée") in Raymond Pearson, *The Russian Moderates and the Crisis of Tsarism 1914–1917* (London: Macmillan, 1977). See also Jay Winter and Jean-Louis Robert, *Capital Cities at War: Paris, London, Berlin, 1914–1919* (Cambridge: Cambridge University Press, 1997); *Der Geist von 1914: Zerstorung des universalen Humanismus?* (Rehburg-Loccum: Evangelische Akademie Loccum, 1990); Jeffrey Verhey, "The 'Spirit of 1914': The Myth of Enthusiasm and the Rhetoric of Unity in World War I" (Ph.D. diss., University of California, Berkeley, 1992).

10. Joshua Sanborn, "The Mobilization of 1914 and the Question of the Russian Nation: A Re-Examination," *Slavic Review* 59, no. 2 (Summer 2000): 267–289.

11. "Razgrom nemetskogo posol'stva," *Rech'*, 23 July 1914, 3.

12. "Manifestatsii protiv Germanii," *Russkie vedomosti*, 23 July 1914, 3–4; "Anti-German Riots: Fierce Russian Onslaught on the Embassy," *The Times* (London), 5 August 1915. GARF, f. 270, op. 1, d. 99, l. 38 (St. Petersburg gendarme administration chief Popov to Dzhunkovskii, 23 July 1914). One 58-year-old man, a German subject, was found dead and mutilated in the embassy after the riot. "Ubiistvo v germanskom posol'stve," *Rech'*, 24 July 1914, 4.

13. GARF, f. 270, op. 1, d. 99, l. 39 (Popov to Dzhunkovskii, 24 July 1914).

14. "Zapreshchenie manifestatsii," *Rech'*, 24 July 1914, 2.

15. GARF, f. 215, op. 1, d. 174, l. 28 (Minister of Internal Affairs Maklakov's circular to all provincial and city governors, 21 July 1914). This important circular

expressed the dilemma as follows: "In the general rise of healthy popular sentiments, we need to seek the forces to maintain state order and peace in the empire.
We need to preserve this unification of all the population in a common patriotic attitude, and not distance the population from the authorities."

16. Maksim Germanovich Lekomtsev, "Formy bor'by rabochikh tsentral'nogo
promyshlennogo raiona v gody pervoi mirovoi voiny (iiul' 1914–fevral'; 1917)"
(Kand. Diss., RAN Institut Istorii, Moscow, 1991), 165.

17. RGIA, f. 1276, op. 10, d. 132, ll. 1–2ob (Maklakov to Goremykin, 22 November 1914). Most of the damages were suffered by six Danish firms and one
British company. The rioters reportedly mistook them for German.

18. Sanborn, "The Mobilization of 1914," 275–279; Kiromiya, "Donbass
Miners," 141; I. T. Shcherbina, *Rabochee dvizhenie na Ukraine v period pervoi mirovoi
imperialisticheskoi voiny. Iul' 1914–fevral 1917 g.: sbornik dokumentov i materialov*
(Kiev: Naukova Dumka, 1966), 11–17; GARF, f. 270, op. 1, d. 99, l. 24 (Colonel
Pozhoga to Dzhunkovskii, 20 July 1914).

19. GARF, f. 270, op. 1, d. 92, ll. 2–42 (Collection of materials relating to the
mood of the Baltic provinces in relation to military activities). Newspaper accounts
are published in A. P. Tupin, *Pribaltiiskii krai i voina: Materialy iz russkoi pechati za
avgust, sentiabr' i oktiabr' 1914 g.* (Petrograd: A. P. Tupin, 1914).

20. The materials for the mission are contained in GARF, f. 270, op. 1, d. 91
and 92.

21. GARF, f. 270, op. 1, d. 99, ll. 39 ff.

22. Kir'ianov, "Demonstratsii rabochikh," 69. The misrepresentation of these
demonstrations by Soviet scholars as "anti-war protests" is revealed by Kir'ianov.
Many of the "strikes" demanded only the removal of enemy alien personnel. See
his "Byli li antivoennye stachki v Rossii v 1914 godu?" *Voprosy istorii* 2 (1994): 43–
52.

23. "Patrioticheskie manifestatsii," *Moskovskie vedomosti,* 10 October 1914.

24. GARF, 102, Osobyi otdel (hereafter OO), op. 245, d. 246 part 1, l. 57
(Maklakov to Adrianov, 21 October 1914).

25. GARF, f. 102, OO, op. 245, d. 246 part 1, l. 57.

26. RGIA, f. 1483, op. 1, d. 36, l. 18.

27. Ibid.

28. See "Iz chernoi knigi rossiiskogo evreistva," *Evreiskaia starina* 10 (1918):
195–296; Eric Lohr, "The Russian Army and the Jews: Mass Deportations, Hostages, and Violence during World War I," *The Russian Review* 60, no. 3 (July 2001):
404–419.

29. GARF, f. 215, op. 1, d. 524, ll. 2–3 (Acting governor general of Warsaw to
Council of Ministers, 6 September 1914).

30. On military rule, see Daniel Graf, "The Reign of the Generals: Military
Government in Western Russia, 1914–1915," (Ph.D. diss., University of Nebraska,
1972). The introduction to opis 1 in RGVIA, f. 2005 (Voenno-politicheskoe i
grazhdanskoe upravlenie pri verkhovnom glavnokomanduiushchem) contains a description of the delineation of army powers in civilian rule. See also appendix 2
to *Polozhenie o polevom upravlenii voisk v voennoe vremia* (Petrograd: Voennaia Tip.
imperatritsy Ekateriny Velikoi, 1914); Vladimir Rozenberg, *Sovremenye
pravootnosheniia k nepriiatel'skim poddannym: s prilozheniem uzakonenii po etomu
predmetu* (Petrograd, 1915); Iu. N. Danilov, *Rossiia v mirovoi voine 1914–1915 gg.*

(Berlin: Slovo, 1924), 103. Moscow was declared under military rule on 2 October 1915.

31. RGVIA, f. 2005, op. 1 (introduction).

32. RGVIA, f. 1759, op. 3 dop., d. 1433, l. 57. A remarkable 1913 map shows the locations of Russian counterintelligence centers throughout the empire and abroad. There were 57 centers in the Kiev Military District alone, with many concentrated in areas near the border. The map shows eight secret counterintelligence centers on Austrian territory in Galicia. On army concerns over the weakness of its counterintelligence system revealed by the Russo-Japanese War, and its attempts to remedy the situation, see I. V. Derevianko, "Shpionov lovit' bylo nekomu," *Voenno-istoricheskii zhurnal* 12 (1993): 51–53.

33. RGVIA, f. 1343, 8, 107, l. 10–11. In 1909, the Warsaw governor general requested that local officials begin providing yearly reports on the number of foreigners living in the Polish provinces, along with reports on any suspicious activities among them. GARF, f. 215, op. 1, d. 429, l. 14.

34. RGIA, f. 1276, op. 10, d. 106, ll. 1–21.

35. There is a large literature on spy fever in European countries, but little on this important and widespread phenomenon in Russia. See, for example, David French, "Spy Fever in Britain, 1900–1915," *The Historical Journal* 21, no. 2 (1978): 355–370; Aleksandr S. Rezanov, *Nemetskoe shpionstvo (Kniga sostavlena po dannym sudebnoi praktiki i drugim istochnikam* (Petrograd: M. A. Suvorin, 1915).

36. RGVIA, f. 2005, op. 1, d. 20, l. 22–22ob (Ianushkevich to Dvinsk Military District, 14 October 1914).

37. N. D. Polivanov, *O nemetskom zasilii: Broshiura Shtabom verkhovnogo glavnokomanduiushchego otpravlena na peredovye positsii*, 12th ed. (Petrograd, 1917).

38. Already in April 1914, the Council of Ministers worked out a bill on state treason which would deprive foreigners of the right to trial if accused of spying. The bill was discussed in the Duma in June 1914, but was not passed before the war. RGIA, f. 1276, op. 10, d. 106, ll. 1–21.

39. Bakhmetieff Archives, Bark Memoirs, ch. 14, 43; Michael Cherniavsky, *Prologue to Revolution: Notes of A. N. Iakhontov on the Secret Meetings of the Council of Ministers, 1915* (Upper Saddle River, N.J.: Prentice Hall, 1967), 32–40; Sergei Nelipovich, "General ot infanterii N. N. Ianushkevich: 'Nemetskuiu pakost' uvolit' i bez nezhnostei: deportatsii v Rossii 1914–1918 gg." *Voenno-istoricheskii zhurnal* 1 (1997): 42–53.

40. M. D. Bonch-Bruyevich, *From Tsarist General to Red Army Commander* (Moscow: Progress, 1966), 63–65.

41. "Akkermanskaia German-Turetskaia epopeia," *Novoe vremia*, 28 December 1914. The term "colonist" (*kolonist*) refers to a distinct legal category and was the term often used by the German farmers themselves. While the term has its drawbacks, it is more accurate than the alternatives; not all ethnic German farmers were colonists and not all colonists were Germans.

42. RGVIA, f. 2005, op. 1, d. 28, ll. 23–74.

43. For two arguments that he was innocent, see George Katkov, *Russia 1917: The February Revolution* (London: Longman, 1967), 119–131; K. F. Shatsillo, "'Delo' polkovnika Miasoedova," *Voprosy istorii* 42, no. 4 (April 1967): 103–116.

44. Katkov, *Russia 1917*, 119.

45. RGVIA, f. 970, op. 3, d. 1973, ll. 1–7 (Report of General Baranov to the Imperial Court on accusations of treason against Rennenkampf). The secret report

concluded that "he [Rennenkampf] was a talented and brave soldier. However, with the plethora of rumors that he sacrificed his army and ran, he cannot be allowed to return to service."

46. In sharp contrast to its support of the extreme Right, the regime ordered roughly 80 socialist periodicals closed in the first days of the war. A. F. Berezhnoi, *Russkaia legal'naia pechat' v gody pervoi mirovoi voiny* (Leningrad: Izd. Leningradskogo universiteta, 1975), 25.

47. For a bitter extended account of the ways in which censors prevented the Jewish and liberal press from refuting accusations of spying and from criticizing army policies toward Jews during the first year of the war, see RGIA, Pechatnaia zapiska 310, "Voennaia tsenzura i evreiskii vopros, n/d [early 1916]."

48. C. Jay Smith, Jr., "Miljukov and the Russian National Question" in Hugh McLean, ed., *Russian Thought and Politics* (Cambridge, Mass.: Harvard University Press, 1957).

49. Carleton J. H. Hayes, *The Historical Evolution of Modern Nationalism* (New York: Macmillan, 1950), 77–78.

50. See Melissa Stockdale, "Russian Liberals and the Contours of Patriotism in the Great War," in *Russkii liberalizm, istoricheskie sud'by i perspektivy* (Moscow: ROSSPEN, 1999) 283–292.

51. V. V. Shelokhaev, "Teoreticheskie predstavleniia rossiiskikh liberalov o voine i revoliutsii (1914–1917)," in *Pervaia mirovaia voina: Diskussionnye problemy istorii* (Moscow: Nauka, 1994), 190, and V. V. Shelokhaev, "Natsional'nyi vopros v Rossii: liberal'nyi variant resheniia," *Kentavr* 3 (1993): 100–115.

52. The leader of the extreme right-wing Union of Russian People, V. M. Purishkevich, even cooperated with the colonists in prewar Duma elections in Bessarabia. Christoph Schmidt, *Russische Presse und Deutsches Reich, 1905–1914* (Cologne: Böhlau Verlag, 1988), 100–108.

53. Baron Rosen, *Forty Years of Diplomacy*, vol. 2 (London: Allen and Unwin, 1922): 83–86; M. V. Murav'ev, *Nemtsy v Rossii (Materialy dlia orientatsii)* (Moscow: Tip. A. I. Mamontova, 1917), 65; Dominic C. B. Lieven, "Pro-Germans and Russian Foreign Policy, 1890–1914," *International History Review* 2 (1980), 34–54.

54. For the document, see F. A. Golder, ed., *Documents of Russian History, 1914–1917* (New York, 1927), 3–23. For its context and significance, see David M. McDonald, "The Durnovo Memorandum in Context: Official Conservativism and the Crisis of Autocracy," *Jahrbücher für Geschichte Osteuropas* 44 (1996): 481–502.

55. RGIA, f. 1282, op. 3, d. 707.

56. See the clear expression of these views by the leader of the Right faction in the State Duma: A. N. Khvostov, "Pis'mo k izdateliu," 30 May 1915, 2.

57. The theme of fighting German dominance was central in attempts of the Right to unify its various organizations during the war. GARF, f. 116, op. 1, d. 38, ll. 28–31.

58. GARF, f. 116, op. 1, d. 632. For a strong argument that prewar anti-Semitism was grounded in such antimodern sentiments, see Heinz Dietrich Löwe, *Antisemitismus und reaktionäre Utopie: Russischer Konservatismus im Kampf gegen den Wandel von Staat und Gesellschaft, 1890–1917* (Hamburg: Hoffmann und Campe Verlag, 1978). For example, see "Nemetskoe zasil'e na Moskovsko-Kazanskoi linii," *Russkoe znamia*, 26 February 1916.

59. Upon his appointment, Khvostov declared the fight against German domi-

nance and against inflation to be two of the three most important issues facing the nation. RGIA, f. 1483, op. 1, d. 29, ll. 12ob-15; M. Suborin, "Iz nedavnego proshlogo: Beseda s ministrom vnutrennikh del A. N. Khvostovym," *Byloe* 1 (July 1917): 62; V. Semennikov, *Romanovy i germanskie vliianiia 1914–1917gg.* (Moscow: Krasnaia gaz., 1929), 80–94; W. Bruce Lincoln, *A Passage Through Armageddon: The Russians in War and Revolution* (New York: Oxford University Press, 1994), 206–207. On the conspiracy theories of bankers and the Jews, see C. C. Aronsfeld, "Jewish Bankers and the Tsar," *Jewish Social Studies* 35 (1973): 87–104. For some comparable wartime rhetoric from the Left, see V. I. Lenin, *Imperialism: The Highest Stage of Capitalism* (New York: International Publishers, 1985), 64.

60. RGIA, f. 970, op. 3, d. 1504, ll. 5–7ob.

61. *Korennik: Monarkhicheskii-patrioticheskii ezhenedel'nik* 1 (1916): 5.

62. See Eric Lohr, "The Russian Press and the 'Internal Peace' at the Beginning of World War I" in Troy Paddock, ed., *A Call to Arms: Propaganda and Public Opinion in Newspapers during the Great War* (Westport, Conn.: Praeger, forthcoming). Iv[an] Tobolin, "Reptil'nyi fond 1914–1916 g.g.," *Krasnyi arkhiv* 105 (1941): 332–338; Berezhnoi, *Russkaia legal'naia pechat'*, 25; RGIA, f. 776, op. 1, d. 44, ll. 40–40ob.

63. The more mainstream conservatives were certainly not sympathetic to Jews, Germans, foreigners and other aliens, and many displayed a strong anti-Semitic and anti-alien set of views in their memoirs and letters. However, it was generally only on the extreme Right that anti-Semitism was prominent and open. For some members of the extreme Right, the Jewish declarations of loyalty and enlistment in the army even engendered short-lived declarations of unity with the Jews in the common struggle. *Volkszeitung* [Saratov], 31 August 1914, claimed that leaders of the ferociously anti-Semitic extreme Right in the Duma, Purishkevich and Zamyslovskii, expressed these sentiments in the first month of the war. In the summer of 1915, Vasilii Shulgin led a break-away group of the Nationalist Party to form the Progressive Nationalist faction, which among other things declared support for Russian-subject Jews and Germans as long as they served loyally in the army. Robert Edelman, *Gentry Politics on the Eve of the Russian Revolution: The Nationalist Party 1907–1917* (New Brunswick, N.J.: Rutgers University Press, 1980), 228–229.

64. Edelman, *Gentry Politics*, 202.

65. *Germanskie i avstriiskie firmy v Moskve na 1914 god.* (Moscow: "Russkaia Pechatnia," 1915), 6.

66. Boris Suvorin, "Zashchitnikam nemetskogo mezhdunarodnogo prava," *Novoe vremia*, 5 July 1914, 5–6.

67. David R. Costello, "Novoe Vremia and the Conservative Dilemma, 1911–1914," *The Russian Review* 37 (1978): 30–50.

68. On the prewar history of the Moscow Merchants and their attempts to promote Russian business, see Thomas C. Owen, *Capitalism and Politics in Russia: A Social History of the Moscow Merchants, 1855–1905* (New York: Cambridge University Press, 1981); Alfred Rieber, *Merchants and Entrepreneurs in Imperial Russia* (Chapel Hill: University of North Carolina Press, 1982).

69. *Germanskie i avstriiskie firmy*, introduction. In Petersburg, a major 1913 anti-Austrian demonstration ended with the crowd breaking windows of German and Austrian shops. GARF, f. 1282, op. 1, d. 1008.

70. RGIAgM (Rossiiskii gosudarstvennyi istoricheskii arkhiv gor. Moskvy), f. 3, op. 4, d. 4355 (Records of the Moscow Merchant Society); "Boikot nemetskikh tovarov," *Golos Moskvy*, 13 September 1914, 5.

71. *Doklad: Kommissii po vyiasneniiu mer bor'by s germanskim i avstro-vengerskim vliianiem v oblasti torgovli i promyshlennosti. Oktiabr' 1914–aprel' 1915* (Moscow, 1915). Free copies of this document were widely distributed to the press, Duma members, local and central government officials, and to over a hundred exchange committees and merchant organizations throughout the country. The document contains long lists of goods to be boycotted along with a detailed explanation of the rationale for the boycott—to create a more "Russian" economy.

72. "Boikot nemetskikh tovarov," *Novoe vremia*, 6 June 1915. The organization received 95 questionnaires from exchange committees throughout the country detailing levels of Austro-German and foreign influence in local economies, and encouraged the committees to initiate their own campaigns of action. RGIAgM, f. 3, op. 4, d. 4268, l. 2.

73. RGIA, f. 23, op. 7, d. 761, l. 57 (Activities of the Moscow Merchant Society relating to the fight against German dominance, n.d.).

74. Chelnokov, along with a handful of other prominent Kadets, switched to the Progressist Party largely over the issue of German dominance. For an overview of the campaign against the Company of 1886, see "Germaniia i Russkaia elektrotekhnicheskaia promyshlennost'," *Golos Moskvy*, 2 September 1914; V. S. Diakin, *Germanskie kapitaly v Rossii: Elektroindustriia i elektricheskii transport* (Leningrad: Nauka, 1971).

75. "Budushchee nemetskogo zasil'e," *Golos Moskvy*, 5 May 1915, 1.

76. The Society of 1914 worked closely with other civic organizations. The Society for the Economic Rebirth of Russia had similar origins and stated goals, but focused more specifically on economic issues and studies of a more academic nature. Economically Independent Russia (*Samodeiatel'naia Rossiia*), founded in February 1915, focused on German dominance in education and culture. RGIA, f. 733, op. 196, d. 982, ll. 2–20; RGIA, f. 1483, op. 1, d. 14, l. 30 (Society of 1914 to F. F. Trepov, 4 June 1916).

77. GARF, f. 102, op. 73, d. 235, l. 13.

78. Obshchestvo 1914 goda, *Otchet Soveta o deiatel'nosti 'Obshchestva 1914 goda' za 1915 god* (Petrograd Rassvet, 1916).

79. See, for example, Obshchestvo 1914 goda, *Otkrytoe pis'mo Soveta Obshchestva g.g. chlenam Gosudarstvennoi dumy 15 iiunia 1916 goda* (Petrograd, n.d.).

80. GARF, f. 102, op. 73, d. 235, l. 18 (Director of the Department of Police to A. A. Katenin, 15 July 1915).

81. Obshchestvo 1914 goda, *Zadachi, programma i deiatel'nosti Torgovopromyshlennogo otdela obshchestva 1914 goda v 1915 godu* (Petrograd: Rassvet, 1916); Obshchestvo 1914 goda, *Ustav obshchestva potrebitelei pri obshchestve 1914 goda* (Petrograd: Rassvet, 1916).

2. The Moscow Riots

1. Actually, the "German" Mandl' firm had long ago been renamed the Mars firm, and was of mixed Russian and Austrian ownership, and the "German" Grand Duchess was from Denmark.

2. RGB, Otdel rukopisei, f. 261, kor. 20, d. 6 (Nikolai Petrovich Kharlamov,

Zapiski biurokrata: Vospominaniia "Bor'ba s nemetskim zasil'em vo vremia russko-germanskoi voiny 1914–1916 gg."), ll. 61ob-62. The main sources for the following account of the pogrom are Kharlamov's memoir and the secret official report of an investigation into the pogrom and its causes led by Senator Nikolai Krasheninnikov: RGIA, f. 1405, op. 533, d. 2536, ll. 1–15ob (Report of Senator Krasheninnikov to the Ruling Senate, 10 September 1915). These sources reinforce each other. Kharlamov, a member of the ministerial council of the MVD, was sent to Moscow by Dzhunkovskii on 29 May to investigate the causes of the pogrom. Two weeks later, he and his team of three were put under Senator Krasheninnikov's authority. Kharlamov interviewed over a hundred officials and individuals during the investigation and gathered dozens of relevant documents. For the most complete press reports, see "Razgrom nemetskikh magazinov," *Russkie vedomosti*, 31 May 1915, 4; K. Arsen'ev, "Na temy dnia," *Vestnik Evropy* (February 1916): 363–368; for a fictionalized discussion of the pogrom, see Aleksandr Solzhenitsyn, *November 1916: The Red Wheel / Knot II* (New York: Farrar, Straus and Giroux, 1999), 92–95.

3. RGB, Otdel rukopisei, f. 261, kor. 20, d. 6, l. 62.

4. French concern over the fate of this category in Russia was a bit hypocritical, given that many Alsatians and Lorrainers in France were treated with great suspicion and some were interned for the course of the war. See "The Kiss of France: The Republic and the Alsatians during the First World War," in Panayi, ed., *Minorities in Wartime*, 27–49.

5. GARF, f. 63, 1915, d. 1325, l. 521.

6. RGB, Otdel rukopisei, f. 261, kor. 20, d. 6, l. 62.

7. Ibid., l. 63ob.

8. RGIA, f. 1405, op. 533, d. 2536, l. 3ob.

9. The Shrader Company was a commercial firm dealing in wool products, founded in 1907 with a founding capital of 3 million rubles in 600 shares, of which only 96 belonged to German subjects. All its managers were Russian subjects, 11 members of the Shrader family were at the front fighting in the Russian army, and the firm had eight large contracts to supply the army with clothing. In October 1917, the Ministry of Trade and Industry forced the liquidation of the 96 enemy-subject shares. RGIA, f. 23, op. 28, d. 2497, ll. 1–10.

10. RGB, Otdel rukopisei, f. 261, kor. 20, d. 6, l. 64.

11. Ibid., l. 64.

12. Ibid., l. 64ob.

13. Ibid., l. 64ob.

14. The following account is based on Kharlamov's version of the meeting. Ibid., l. 65.

15. RGIA, f. 1405, op. 533, d. 2536, l. 9ob.

16. Ivan I. Menitskii, *Rabochee dvizhenie i sotsial-demokraticheskoe podpol'e v voennye gody (1914–1917)* (Moscow, 1923), 123.

17. "Zaiavlenie no. 174" in *Prilozhenie k stenograficheskim otchetam*, no. 27, 1915, 2. This report mentions only three killed and lists their names. The death toll was undoubtedly higher. *Moskovskie vedomosti* reported the discovery of three more unidentified bodies in the Moscow River in the week following the pogrom. Furthermore, the report does not include the two managers killed on the evening of May 27.

18. It is difficult to compare the Moscow riot with major Jewish pogroms,

since none of them had such detailed accounting of the damages as there was for the May riot.

19. GARF, f. 102, OO, op. 245, d. 246 part 1, ll. 71–80.

20. This estimate is arrived at by subtracting the accounted claims of Russian, neutral, and allied subjects from the Moscow City Duma's estimate of 70 million rubles total damages. GARF, f. r-546, op. 1, d. 1, ll. 105–108 (Report based on data collected before the October Revolution by a committee of the Ministry of Finance to calculate losses to the population caused by the war, 1917).

21. Zaiavlenie no. 174 in Gosudarstvennaia Duma, *Prilozhenie ko stenograficheskim otchetam*, no. 27, 1915, 2. These estimates do not include damage to inventories, lost revenue from the period of closure, or personal injury. GARF, F. r-546, op. 1, d. 1, ll. 105–108; GARF, f. r-546, op. 1, d. 8, ll. 2–3 (RFSR Finance committee of the State Treasury. Special section on financial questions in connection with the implementation of the Brest-Litovsk treaty, n. d. [1916]). Newspapers commonly cited the figure of 100 million rubles of damage. See N. Ezhov, "Vnutrennie izvestiia: Moskovskie nastroeniia," *Novoe vremia*, 3 July 1915, 6.

22. Iu I. Kir'ianov, "'Maisie besporiadki' 1915 g. v Moskve," Voprosy istorii 12 (1994): 137–150. See also GARF, f. 63, 1915, d. 1325, ll. 278–280 (Report of the Moscow city governor, 10 June 1915); *Put' k oktabriu* 3 (Moscow: Moskovskii rabochii, 1923), 131–133. For a statement of the Soviet line, see *Istoriia Moskvy* 5 (Moscow, Akademii nauk SSSR, 1955), 316.

23. Jane McDermid and Anna Hillyar, *Women and Work in Russia, 1880–1930: A Study in Continuity through Change* (London: Longman, 1998), 144.

24. P. E. Liubarov, "Torgovye rabochie i sluzhashchie v gody Pervoi mirovoi voiny," in *Rabochii klass kapitalisticheskoi Rossii* (Moscow: RAN, 1992): 110–124.

25. For an account of the complexities of worker-foreman tensions before and during the war, see S. A. Smith, "Workers against Foremen in St. Petersburg, 1905–1917," in Louis H. Siegelbaum and Ronald Grigor Suny, eds., *Making Workers Soviet: Power, Class and Identity* (Ithaca: Cornell University Press, 1994).

26. RGB, Otdel rukopisei, f. 261, kor. 20, d. 6, l. 65.

27. Ibid., l. 65ob.

28. "Zaiavlenie no. 174" in Gosudarstvennaia Duma, *Prilozhenie k stenograficheskim otchetam*, no. 27 (1915): 2.

29. "Miniatiury," *Russkie vedomosti*, 31 May 1915. *Pugachevshchina* refers to the Cossack uprising led by Emelian Pugachev from 1873–74. The extremely violent rebellion spread rapidly through a broad expanse of the country and became the term of choice for anyone raising the specter of popular violence and a collapse of state authority.

30. Most recent scholarship has contested the argument of government complicity in anti–Jewish pogroms—at least at the highest level of power. According to Michael Ochs, "in the minds of Russian officialdom, the state's monopoly on violence was sacrosanct." See his article in John D. Klier and Shlomo Lambroza, eds., *Pogroms: Anti-Jewish Violence in Modern Russian History* (Cambridge: Cambridge University Press, 1992), 185. On the "pogrom paradigm," see John Klier's article in the same volume. Other articles in the volume support Ochs's interpretation that the government did not directly promote or organize pogroms. See also Edward Judge, *Easter in Kishinev: Anatomy of a Pogrom* (New York: New York University Press, 1992).

31. See GARF, f. 102, op. 265 (perliustratsiia), d. 1027, ll. 503, 534 and d. 1042, l. 18.

32. Maurice Paleologue, *An Ambassador's Memoirs*, vol. 1 (London: Hutchinson, 1925), 347.

33. Gosudarstvennaia duma, *Stenograficheskie otchety*, 3 August 1915, col. 414.

34. *Prilozhenie k izvestiiam Moskovskoi Gorodskoi Dumy za 1915 g.*, no. 15, 29 May 1915.

35. K. Arsen'ev, "Na temy dnia," *Vestnik Evropy* (February 1916): 363–368; A. P. Martynov, *Moia sluzhba v otdel'nom korpuse zhandarmov: vospominaniia*, ed. Richard Wraga (Stanford: Hoover Institution, 1972), 271.

36. For a number of speeches addressing the issue, see Gosudarstvennaia Duma, *Stenograficheskie otchety*, 3 August 1915.

37. RGB, Otdel rukopisei, f. 261, kor. 20, d. 6, l. 62ob. The same quote appeared in K. Arsen'ev, "Na temy dnia," *Vestnik Evropy* (February 1916): 365.

38. GARF, f. 102, II, op. 73 part 1, d. 58, l. 7 (Instructions to Senator Krasheninnikov, June 1915).

39. "Ukhod moskovskogo gradonachal'nika," *Russkie vedomosti*, 2 June 1915, 2.

40. Bakhmetieff Archives, Bark Memoirs, chapter 14.

41. RGIA, f. 1405, op. 533, d. 2536, ll. 1–15ob. According to Kharlamov, Krasheninnikov's final report was kept secret and only four copies were made. RGB, Otdel rukopisei, f. 261, kor. 20, d. 6.

42. RGIA, f. 1405, op. 533, d. 2536, l. 15.

43. Ibid., ll. 10–10ob.

44. Iu. I. Kir'ianov, "Demonstratsii rabochikh v 1914 g.–Feb. 1917 g.," in *Rabochii klass*, 67–109.

45. RGIA, f. 1405, op. 533, d. 2536, ll. 11ob–12ob.

46. Ibid., l. 9ob.

47. See GARF, f. 102, op. 265 (perliustratsiia), d. 1027 and d. 1042.

48. "Iz istorii rabochego dvizheniia vo vremia mirovoi voiny (Stachochnoe dvizhenie v Kostromskoi gub.)," *Krasnyi arkhiv* 67 (1934): 5–27; M. G. Fleer, *Rabochee dvizhenie v gody voiny* (Moscow, 1925), 207–214.

49. Diane Koenker and William Rosenberg, *Strikes and Revolution in Russia* (Princeton: Princeton University Press, 1989), 59.

50. Ordering the troops to fire into crowds was a very risky venture. The rebellion of soldiers in the Petrograd garrison during the February 1917 Revolution was a crucial point in the transition from street demonstrations and strikes to a full-scale revolution. Given that the Moscow garrison, like the Petrograd garrison in 1917, had many recent call-ups who were not fully trained and older soldiers of questionable reliability, Adrianov's hesitance to send them in appears more understandable in retrospect.

51. RGB, Otdel rukopisei, f. 261, kor. 20, d. 6, l. 54.

52. The memoir of the Social Democrat activist worker Sh. N. Ibragimov confirms that the assumption that Elizaveta Fedorovna was a protector of Germans was widespread among workers at the time. *Put' k oktiabriu* 5, 140. Irina Kudrina of the Russian Academy of Sciences (Moscow) is currently working on a biography of the Grand Duchess, which includes a section on public antipathy against her as a "German" during the war.

53. The Council of Ministers complained about his demagoguery and

speeches about German spies throughout the summer and plotted for his removal. See Cherniavsky, *Prologue to Revolution*, 32–34, 40.

54. Citing only an indirect source, Kir'ianov claims that a party within the government led by the Grand Duke Nikolai Nikolaevich and Iusupov, with Adrianov's support, allowed or organized the riots as part of their struggle against another influential group which favored a separate peace with Germany to bring the war to a close. Kir'ianov, "Maiskie besporiadki," 137–150.

55. GARF, f. 102, OO, op. 245, d. 246 part 1, ll. 71–80 (MVD Chief of the division for the preservation of public safety and order in Moscow to the Department of Police, 4 June 1915).

56. GARF, f. 102, op. 265 (perliustratsiia), d. 1042, l. 17 (I. Dudchenko to his relative in Odessa, 30 May 1915). These rumors built on established patterns linking cholera outbreaks and labor violence. See Theodore Friedgut, "Labor Violence and Regime Brutality in Tsarist Russia: The Iuzovka Cholera Riots of 1892," *Slavic Review* 46, no. 2 (1987): 245–265.

57. Panikos Panayi, "Anti-German Riots in Britain during the First World War," in Panikos Panayi, ed., *Racial Violence in Britain, 1840–1950* (Leicester: Leicester University Press, 1993), 65–91. The British riots were reported in the Russian press.

58. RGB, Otdel rukopisei, f. 261, kor. 20, d. 6, ll. 65ob-66; RGIA, f. 1405, op. 533, d. 2536, ll. 7ob-8. The firm Robert Kents was owned by Russian subjects.

59. RGIA, f. 23, op. 28, d. 525, ll. 1–76. The firm was founded in 1901 by a German subject of Polish origin. By 1913, the entire administration was composed of Russian subjects, including the owner Avgust Elsner. The firm claimed losses of 2 million rubles, including 110,000 rubles in wine and liquor. The insurance company refused to pay and the government never granted compensation.

60. *Russkie vedomosti*, 3 June 1915, 4.

61. GARF, f. 102, op. 73, d. 235, ll. 1–21; RGB, Otdel rukopisei, f. 261, kor. 20, d. 6, l. 43ob, 50ob; GARF, f. 102, OO, op. 245, d. 246 part 1, ll. 51–54ob (Memo by Chelnokov, 4 June 1915).

62. GARF, f. 601, op. 1, d. 615 (Memo of Prince Iusupov on the need to deport German and Austrian subjects from Moscow and Petrograd and halt their acceptance into Russian subjecthood, 5–7 July 1915).

63. The following is an abridged version of the original transcript. RGVIA, f. 2005, op. 1, d. 24, ll. 414–417 (Memorandum of the extraordinary meeting of the Council of Ministers at Stavka, 14 June 1915).

64. GARF, f. 102, II, op. 75, d. 10 part 4, l. 1, 5ob. Tensions ran so high between the ministries that the Ministry of Finance intentionally did not inform the MVD of the dates of the committee meetings, even though an MVD representative was supposed to be present according to the law establishing the committees. For instructions to the committee set up to determine losses to individuals in the pogrom, see O. I. Averbakh, *Zakonodatel'nye akty vyzvannye voinoiu 1914–1917 gg.* 3 (Petrograd: Elektro-Tip. N. Ia. Stoikovoi, 1915–1918), 556–600.

65. While by late 1916 the committee had received 763 applications for compensation totaling 26 million rubles, it only recognized 11 million, most in the form of interest-free loans rather than outright grants or subsidies. This was only a fraction of the total damages, as the restrictive rules barred many people from even registering a claim. The claims registered by the committee were almost entirely

from Russian subjects; only thirteen claims from enemy subjects were registered, and of these, only a handful were recognized as deserving of state funds. Actual payment was dragged out, and as late as October 1917 not a single payment had yet been made. It was only after the German victory and the onerous Brest-Litovsk Treaty that the committee, which continued to exist under the Bolshevik regime, was forced to accelerate the pace of its work. The total bill was not yet calculated by June 1918, but probably exceeded 75 million rubles. GARF, f. r-546, op. 1, d. 1, ll. 1–168 (documents of the Ministry of Finance Committee to determine losses suffered as a result of the Moscow pogrom). An important part of both the compensation and blame debates came with a landmark lawsuit the paper manufacturer K. Sheibler, a Russian subject of Belgian origins, brought against Adrianov, Maklakov, and Iusupov for 215,000 rubles damage. The suit created a big stir in the press as an unprecedented event—a private citizen bringing a suit against such prominent and formerly powerful members of the government. I was unable to determine whether a ruling was ever issued in the case, which had not yet been resolved in early 1917. GARF, f. 102 II , op. 75, d. 10 part 4, l. 37 and "Isk k byvsh. ministru N. A. Maklakovu," *Utro Rossii*, 30 November 1915.

66. See Panayi, "Anti-German Riots."

67. See for example, *Svod otchetov fabrichnykh inspektorov za 1914 god, za 1915 god, za 1916 god* (Petrograd, 1915–1917); Fleer, *Rabochee dvizhenie*, 20–25; I. T. Scherbina, *Rabochee dvizhenie na Ukraine v period pervoi mirovoi imperialisticheskoi voiny. Jul' 1914–fevral' 1917 g.: Sbornik dokumentov i materialov* (Kiev: Naukova Dumka, 1966), 21.

68. For a large collection of such reports, see GARF, f. 58, op. 5, d. 399, especially, ll. 6, 28, 38, 83, 84ob.

69. DAKhO, f. 3, op. 287, d. 4416, l. 24 (Khar'kov governor's report to the Department of Police, 19 September 1914). I thank Mark Baker for this reference.

70. DAKhO, f. 3, op. 287, d. 5038, l. 19 (Khar'kov governor's monthly report to the Department of Police, 21 July 1915).

71. For a collection of reports, see GARF, f. 102, op. 245, d. 247.

72. GARF, f. 102, OO, op. 245, d. 246 part 1, l. 102.

73. GARF, f. 102, OO, op. 245, d. 247, ll. 1–3.

74. Ibid., l. 12.

75. RGIAgM, f. 16, op. 153, d. 33, ll. 1, 15, 22, 29.

76. GARF, f. 102, OO, op. 245, d. 247, ll. 61–63.

77. Ibid., l. 13.

78. RGVIA, f. 1759, op. 3, d. 1420; GARF, f. 102, op. 245, d. 247, l. 27.

79. For a collection of such reports throughout the country, see GARF, f. 102, II, op. 73, d. 162, ll. 3–155.

80. GARF, f. 102, op. 245, d. 247, l. 14.

81. GARF, f. 102, IV, op. 75, d. 4, part 3, T. 2, ll. 1–3.

82. GARF, f. 58, op. 5, d. 389 contains a series of such reports from the chiefs of regional gendarme administrations.

83. Irina Kuptsova, *Khudozhestvennaia intelligentsiia Rossii: razmezhevaniia i iskhod* (St. Petersburg: Nestor, 1996).

84. RGIA, f. 23, op. 28, d. 545, ll. 1–2.

85. RGVIA, f. 2005, op. 1, d. 24, l. 407 (Minister of Foreign Affairs to Minister of Trade and Industry, 23 September 1915).

86. For a large file of gendarme reports from the various districts of Moscow Province illustrating this trend, see GARF, f. 58, op. 5, d. 399.

87. RGB, Otdel rukopisei, f. 261, kor. 20, d. 6, l. 50ob; GARF, f. 270, op. 1, d. 129.

88. GARF, f. 102, op. 265 (perliastratsiia), d. 1042, l. 17 (I. Vostorgov to A. A. Vyrubova, n.d.).

89. Among the most drastic purges were those in Tver' and Riazan'. Empress Alexandra wrote to Nicholas II in August 1915 that there had been an order to remove officers with German names from their posts. Bernard Pares, *Letters of the Tsaritsa to the Tsar, 1914–1916* (London: Duckworth, 1923), 118.

90. RGIA, f. 1483, op. 1, d. 14, ll. 343–350. The fact that his father was an Austrian Jew was prominently noted in the summary of his case. His brother Elias, also a Russian subject, was deported "under suspicion of spying" earlier in the war, and the Sixth Army strongly argued that this alone was sufficient reason to fire Emil.

91. GARF, f. 102, op. 265 (perliustratsiia), d. 1042, l. 18 (intercepted letter of soldier K. I. Vogan, n.d.).

92. GARF, f. 102, op. 245, d. 247, l. 20 (secret report of the Novgorod gendarme administration to the Department of Police, 17 June 1915).

3. Nationalizing the Commercial and Industrial Economy

1. John McKay, *Pioneers for Profit: Foreign Entrepreneurship and Russian Industrialization, 1885–1913* (Chicago: University of Chicago Press, 1970), 28, 37; L. Ia. Eventov, *Inostrannye kapitaly v russkoi promyshlennosti* (Moscow, 1931), 20; P. V. Ol', *Inostrannye kapitaly v narodnom khoziaistve dovoennoi Rossii* (Leningrad, 1925), 12–13. For a radical critique of Ol's methodology, see Fred Carstensen, "Foreign Participation in Russian Economic Life: Notes on British Enterprise, 1865–1914" in Gregory Guroff and Fred Carstensen, eds., *Entrepreneurship in Imperial Russia and the Soviet Union* (Princeton: Princeton University Press, 1983), 142–146. Carstensen claims that if one takes gold flows into account, then the net influx of capital may have been much more modest than Ol's figures suggest. But he does not contest the general importance of "foreign enterprise—capital, technique, and personnel" in Russian industrialization.

2. Nadezhda Grigor'evna Abramova, "Istochnikovedcheskie problemy izucheniia germanskikh kapitalov v promyshlennosti dorevoliutsionnoi Rossii" (Kand. diss., Moscow State University, 1983), 186–187.

3. Thomas C. Owen, *Russian Corporate Capitalism from Peter the Great to Perestroika* (New York: Oxford University Press, 1995), 182. This statistic is based on a survey of 14,131 corporate founders from 1821–1913.

4. B. Ischchanian, *Die ausländischen Elemente in der russischen Volkswirtschaft* (Berlin: Franz Siemenroth, 1913). Ischchanian's figures were based on surveys in the 1890s. The absolute numbers of foreigners in these positions had risen by 1914, but the relative share of foreigners had fallen substantially.

5. Owen, *Russian Corporate Capitalism*, 187.

6. Steven Charles Ellis, "Management in the Industrialization of Russia, 1861–1917" (Ph.D. diss., Duke University, 1980), 175, 185–198; cited in Owen, *Russian Corporate Capitalism*, 72.

7. For an overview of historiographical trends on this issue, see Geoffrey Jones and Grigorii Gerenstain, introduction to *Foreign Capital in Russia* by P. V. Ol' (New York: Garland, 1983).

8. Ischchanian, *Die ausländischen Elemente*, 290–291.

9. All four of John McKay's case studies show quite extensive transfer of managerial authority to Russian personnel. Vol'fgang Sartor concludes that the Shpis family, entering the fourth generation by 1914, had become assimilated into imperial Russian life. Carstensen's case studies of British enterprises reveal less willingness among British firms to hire Russian managerial and technical staff, but he argues that British firms tended to be relatively active in training Russian personnel and with time allowed Russians to rise to all but the highest positions. Erik Amburger found that his ancestors, who controlled a broad set of firms, assimilated slowly, but that by the eve of the war assimilation was well under way. Several family members served in the Russian army and married Orthodox Russians. Fursenko, in a rare diversion from the Soviet historiographical line, asserts strongly that Nobel, an oil firm with several foreign shareholders, was Russian and made independent decisions outside Rockefeller's or other "hostile foreigners'" control. See McKay, *Pioneers for Profit;* Vol'fgang Sartor, "Torgovyi dom 'Shpis': Dokumental'noe nasledie dinastii nemetskikh predprinimatelei v Rossii (1846–1915 gg.)," *Otechestvennaia istoriia* 2 (1997): 174–183; Carstensen, "Foreign Participation in Russian Economic Life," 140–158; Erik Amburger, *Deutsche in Staat, Wirtschaft und Gesellschaft Russlands: Die Familie Amburger in St. Petersburg 1770–1920* (Wiesbaden: Otto Harrassowitz, 1986), 178–185; A. A. Fursenko, "Mozhno li schitat' kompaniiu nobelia russkim kontsernom?" in *Issledovaniia po sotsial'no-politicheskoi istorii Rossii,* vol. 12 of *Akademiia nauk SSSR Institut istorii SSSR Leningradskoe otdelenie, Trudy* (Leningrad: Nauka, 1971), 352–361.

10. Owen, *Russian Corporate Capitalism,* 188. These figures cover managers in the ten leading cities of the empire.

11. Anders Henriksson, "Nationalism, Assimilation and Identity in Late Imperial Russia: The St. Petersburg Germans, 1906–1914," *The Russian Review* 52 (July 1993): 341–353. The leading demographer V. M. Kabuzan comes to a similar conclusion for the empire as a whole, that the process of assimilation accelerated in the early twentieth century. V. M. Kabuzan, "Nemetskoe naselenie v Rossii v XVIII—nachale XX veka (Chislennost' i razmeshchenie)," *Voprosy istorii* 12 (1989): 28. See also James H. Bater, *St. Petersburg: Industrialization and Theory* (Montreal: McGill University Press, 1976), 376–378.

12. For an overview of the AIT's views on the issue see its official journal, *Promyshlennost' i torgovlia.* On the organization, see Ruth Amende Roosa, "Russian Industrialists during World War I: The Interaction of Economics and Politics," in Guroff and Carstensen, eds., *Entrepreneurship in Imperial Russia,* 159–187.

13. "Likvidatsiia nepriatel'skogo vladeniia russkimi aktsiiami," *Promyshlennost' i torgovlia,* 4 February 1917, 103–106.

14. Ischchanian, *Die ausländischen Elemente,* 295.

15. For a recent account of the early stages of this institutional struggle, see V. L. Stepanov, *N. Kh. Bunge: Sud'ba reformatora* (Moscow: Rosspen, 1998).

16. Kh. D. Gurevich, *Evreiskaia zhizn'* 2 (May 1915): 15–20.

17. RGIA, f. 821, op. 150, d. 172, l. 18 (Report on the national and religious composition of employees in private commercial stock companies and banks, April 1914).

18. Thomas Owen analyzes the concession system in his *The Corporation under Russian Law, 1800–1917: A Study in Tsarist Economic Policy* (Cambridge: Cambridge University Press, 1991).

19. Owen, *The Corporation*, 118–132. Such restrictions on landholding were thereby applied to areas throughout the empire, not just in the western regions where the restrictive land laws discussed in the following chapter applied.

20. In an argument with the Ministry of Foreign Affairs, the Ministry of Trade and Industry prevailed with the argument that "granting the right to operate in Russia is not an automatic privilege, and the former citizenship of a firm can be used as a factor in deciding whether to grant such permission." Under this rule, the right to operate in Russia was withdrawn from 14 large firms in 1915 and 18 in 1916. RGIA, f. 1276, op. 12, d. 1472, l. 3 (*Osobyi zhurnal Soveta ministrov*, 5, 9 June 1915).

21. See Muriel Joffe, "Regional Rivalry and Economic Nationalism: The Central Industrial Region Industrialists' Strategy for the Development of the Russian Economy, 1880s-1914," *Russian History/Histoire Russe* 11, no. 4 (Winter 1984): 389–421; Alfred Rieber, *Merchants and Entrepreneurs in Imperial Russia* (Chapel Hill: University of North Carolina Press, 1982); Thomas C. Owen, "Impediments to a Bourgeois Consciousness in Russia, 1880–1905: The Estate Structure, Ethnic Diversity, and Economic Regionalism," 75–92 in Edith W. Clowes, Samuel D. Kassow, and James L. West, eds., *Between Tsar and People: Educated Society and the Quest for Public Identity in Late Imperial Russia* (Princeton: Princeton University Press, 1991), 75–92.

22. Owen, *Russian Corporate Capitalism*, 126–138.

23. Hans Rogger, "Nationalism and the State: A Russian Dilemma," *Comparative Studies in Society and History* 4, no. 3 (The Hague: 1961–1962): 253–264.

24. On this point, see Roman Szporluk, *Communism and Nationalism: Karl Marx versus Friedrich List* (New York: Oxford University Press, 1988).

25. "Russkie poddannye v Germanii i Avstro-vengrii vo vremia voiny," *Russkie vedomosti*, 22 July 1914, 2.

26. Edwin Borchard, "Enemy Private Property," *American Journal of International Law* 18, no. 2 (April, 1924), 523; James A. Gathings, *International Law and American Treatment of Alien Enemy Property* (Washington D.C.: American Council on Public Affairs, 1940), vi.

27. Boris E. Nolde, *Russia in the Economic War* (New Haven: Yale University Press, 1928), 8.

28. Nolde, *Russia in the Economic War*, 9–10; *Osobyi zhurnal Soveta ministrov*, 23 August 1914.

29. Panikos Panayi, *The Enemy in Our Midst: Germans in Britain during the First World War* (New York: Berg, 1991), 134–137; GARF, f. 102, II, op. 71, d. 80, ll. 1, 55.

30. *Sbornik uzakonenii, rasporiazhenii, raziasnenii i tsirkuliarov ob ogranichenii prav nepriiatel'skikh poddannykh i o pravitel'stvennom nadzore za torgovo-promyshlennymi predpriiatiiami* (Petrograd, 1915), 3.

31. Only in early 1916 did Britain and France begin to move toward the sequestration of enemy-alien property on a large scale, and neither country moved toward permanent liquidation or transfer of property rights as did Russia. Likewise, neither Germany nor Austria engaged in the permanent liquidation of enemy-subject properties within their countries. Both instead primarily used tempo-

rary transfer through sequestration. RGIA, f. 1483, op. 1, d. 9, ll. 288–292 (*Osobyi zhurnal Soveta ministrov,* 24 October 1916); RGIA, f. 23, op. 7, d. 369, l. 9; RGIA, f. 1413, op. 1, d. 1, ll. 22ob-23ob; Rudolf Dix, *Deutsche Internationalisten in der Grossen Sozialistischen Oktoberrevolution* (Berlin: Dietz, 1987), 103.

32. For definitions of these practices, see: Ia. M. Bukshpan, *Voenno-khoziaistvennaia politika* (Moscow: Gos. Izd., 1929), 119–121; and *Rekvizitsiia: konfiskatsiia* (Petrograd: Evakuatsionno-rekvizitsionnyi Otdel Tsentral'nogo Voenno-Promyshlennogo Komiteta, 1916), 21–81. Kuzmin-Karavaev argued that confiscation had no justification in civil law and had long disappeared from the criminal code in his "Voprosy vnutrennei zhizni," *Vestnik Evropy* (March 1916): 327.

33. The army command was well aware of this distinction. In the case of a sugar beet company, Ianushkevich ruled for confiscation over sequestration to avoid the question of compensation at the end of the war. Ianushkevich informed his generals in a number of letters that they should use confiscation rather than sequestration whenever possible. RGVIA, f. 2005, op. 1, d. 25, ll. 523–24. For a full legal discussion of sequestration, see Vladimir Rozenberg, *Sovremennye pravootnosheniia k nepriiatel'skim poddannym: s prilozheniem uzakonenii po etomu predmetu* (Petrograd, 1915), 69–75.

34. GARF, f. 102, II, op. 71, d. 80, ll. 16, 91 (MVD Memo, with excerpts from the *Pravila o mestnostiakh, obiavliaemykh sostoiashchimy na voennom polozhenii,* Art. 19 and *Pravil o merakh k okhraneniiu gosudarstvennogo poriadka i obshchestvennogo spokoistva,* Art. 26).

35. Ibid., l. 47.

36. Ibid., l. 51.

37. RGVIA, f. 2005, op. 1, d. 25, ll. 523–24.

38. GARF, f. 102, II, op. 71, d. 80, l. 113; RGVIA, f. 2005, op. 1, d. 101, l. 73ob, 79; GARF, f. 270, op. 1, d. 91, l. 128. Eduard von Dellingshausen, *Im Dienste der Heimat! Erinnerungen des Freiherrn Eduard von Dellingshausen ehem. Ritterschaftshauptmanns von Estland* (Stuttgart: Ausland und Heimat Verlags Aktiengesellschaft, 1930), 193.

39. RGVIA, f. 1759, op. 3, d. 1410, l. 59.

40. GARF, f. 102, II., op. 71, l. 172 (Association of Southern Coal and Steel Producers to Maklakov, 23 October 1914).

41. GARF, f. 102, II., op. 71, d. 80, l. 158ob.

42. Ibid., l. 167.

43. *Birzhevye vedomosti,* 1 October 1914, 1; GARF, f. 102, II, op. 71, l. 80.

44. RGVIA, f. 2005, op. 1, d. 25, l. 17 (Goremykin to Ianushkevich, 23 September 1914).

45. RGVIA, f. 2005, op. 1, d. 25, ll. 21–25.

46. RGIA, f. 1483, op. 1, d. 9, l. 22 (*Osobyi zhurnal Soveta ministrov,* 12 July 1916).

47. GARF, f. 215, op. 1, d. 250, ll. 2–30.

48. The Baltic and Kiev governors were particularly active. By October 1916, 36 trade and industrial firms had been sequestered in Kiev province. The Committee for the Fight against German Dominance then raised the concern that sequestration of so many firms might not be as certain to lead to permanent change of ownership as liquidation under existing laws. The Kiev governor assured the com-

mittee that of the 36 firms, twenty had already been transferred to Russians and another six closed and dismantled, and that he would ensure that all these cases moved to formal liquidation as soon as possible. The large number of sequestrations was in part designed to prevent the sale or transfer of firms while they were being investigated for enemy-subject involvement. RGIA, f. 1483, op. 1, d. 22, ll. 89–91 (Minister of Trade and Industry to Committee for the Fight against German Dominance, 5 December 1916).

49. As late as October 1914, Foreign Minister Sazonov gave a long speech outlining the case against taking such measures. He cited fears that the enemy powers would retaliate, that it would create a bad impression among neutral countries and Russia's allies, that the principle of private property would be undermined, and that Russian workers and industrial production could be seriously affected. *Osobyi zhurnal Soveta ministrov*, 7 October 1914.

50. RGIA, f. 1278, op. 7, d. 160, l. 3 (Ministry of Finance memo on the January 11, 1915 law, 10 September 1915).

51. This somewhat arbitrary distinction reflected both the early focus on individuals engaged in "non-productive" pursuits and the initially cautious approach to liquidating the larger industrial firms. Rozenberg, *Sovremennye pravootnosheniia*, 73–75.

52. The original interpretation defining the "nationality" of a firm was issued by the Minister of Justice: "The nationality [natsional'nost'] of a firm is defined not by the composition of its participants and members of its administration, but by the order of foundation of the firm or partnership. If the charter and statutes regulating its activity were confirmed under Russian laws, then the organization is considered a Russian organization." *Osobyi zhurnal Soveta ministrov*, 7 October 1914.

53. RGIA, f. 23, op. 28, d. 3178, ll. 1–2ob (Memo of the Liquidation Division of the People's Commissariat of Trade and Industry on the situation of firms liquidated according to official decrees, n.d. [late 1917]). Vogel's figures for the results through 1916 are only slightly lower, suggesting that most firms of this type were expropriated quickly. Adolf von Vogel, *Der Wirtschaftskrieg, herausgegeben vom Königlichen Institut für Seeverkehr und Weltwirtschaft an der Universität Kiel*, Part II (Jena: Kommissionsverlag von Gustav Fischer, 1918), 56. Nolde uses Vogel's 1916 figures in *Russia in the Economic War*, 81.

54. This estimate of the size of firms affected is based on a report by Minister of Finance Bark on 3 November 1915. By that date, 1,102 firms with 32,328 workers and a turnover of 106 million rubles had come under the January decree. RGIA, f. 1276, op. 11, d. 1211, l. 5.

55. L. M. Zaitsev, *Poddannye vrazhdebnogo gosudarstva i russkie sudy* (Kiev: Petr Barskii, 1915), 1–16. S. Dobrin, "Voprosy ministra iustitsii prav. senatu o prave nepriiatel'skikh poddannykh na sudebnuiu zashchitu," *Pravo: Ezhenedel'naia iuridicheskaia gazeta* 6 (8 February 1915): 345–355.

56. The government was quite responsive to specific accusations against firms in the press. Often reports in *Novoe vremia* or *Vechernee vremia* precipitated official correspondence and investigations of firms to find out if there was enemy-subject involvement or business ties with Germany. For example, the investigation and liquidation of the Tiudor generator factory began with Rezanov raising questions about "suspicious" connections of the firm in Berlin in his book:

Aleksandr S. Rezanov, *Nemetskoe shpionstvo (Kniga sostavlena po dannym sudebnoi praktiki i drugim istochnikam* (Petrograd: M. A. Suvorin, 1915); RGIA, f. 1483, op. 1, d. 35, ll. 49–53.

57. RGIA, f. 1483, op. 1, d. 29, ll. 12ob-15.

58. One example of such an exemption applied to the chemical firm Liudvig Rabenek. It was founded in 1879 and had 4.5 million rubles capital in 1914. Rabenek and his family members were to be fired from their management and directorship posts according to the December 1915 law; the firm was placed under state oversight and the question of liquidation was under discussion when General Ipatiev of the Artillery Department intervened with a strong letter in support of the Rabeneks and their firm. Ipatiev pointed out that the firm produced almost entirely for defense, and that the Rabeneks were "fully Russian in spirit." The Committee for the Fight against German Dominance heard Rabenek's case and ruled that he could be exempted from all limitations. RGIA, f. 1483, op. 1, d. 14, ll. 118–126 (*Zhurnal osobogo komiteta po bor'be s nemetskim zasil'em*, 25 August 1916).

59. This clause, it is worth noting, made a mockery of one of the major justifications for the laws—that they were intended to remove enemy-alien control over strategic parts of the economy—because the firms could purportedly use this control to engage in spying or espionage. Obviously, from this point of view, firms working in the crucial defense sector would be the most dangerous.

60. The issue became a major one in the press, which mercilessly attacked the government for purported German influence in high circles and consequent protection of German businesses. See V. Rosenberg, "Fiktivnaia peredacha predpriiatii," *Torgovo-promyshlennaia gazeta*, 17 January 1916, no. 13.

61. RGIA, f. 23, op. 28, d. 3178, ll. 1–2ob; on the Provisional Government's policies, see L. E. Shepelev, "Aktsionernoe zakonodatel'stvo Vremennogo pravitel'stva," *Issledovaniia po sotsial'no-politicheskoi istorii Rossii*, vol. 12 of *Akademiia nauk SSSR Institut istorii SSSR Leningradskoe otdelenie, Trudy* (Leningrad: Nauka, 1971), 369–381.

62. RGIA, f. 23, op. 27, d. 674, ll. 1–32, 33–35ob; for lists of firms subject to government oversight along with the names and dates of appointment for each inspector, see *Paevye aktsionernye obshchestva v Rossii, 1915–1917*.

63. RGIA, f. 23, op. 27, d. 675, ll. 31, 3–7ob (Ministry of Trade and Industry [MTiP] instructions to the state inspectors, 30 March 1916 and Memo, n.d.).

64. "Likvidatsiia nepriatel'skogo vladeniia russkimi aktsiamy," *Promyshlennost' i torgovlia* 5 (4 February 1917): 105. The Association sent a similar memo to the Council of Ministers a week before the law was implemented. RGIA, f. 1276, op. 13, d. 69, l. 22 (AIT to Council of Ministers, 30 January 1917).

65. RGIA, f. 1483, op. 1, d. 10, ll. 69–70 (Memo of the Committee for the Fight against German Dominance, February 1917).

66. RGIA, f. 23, op. 7, d. 3194, l. 3 (Circular of the RFSR division for the compensation of losses caused by the war to the liquidation team, 10 October 1918); RGIA, f. 23, op. 28, d. 3179, l. 39 (List of 79 firms liquidated by an unspecified 1918 deadline).

67. Total stock capital figures are from McKay, *Pioneers for Profit*, 28.

68. The files of this department are to be found in RGIA, f. 23 op. 28 (Osoboe deloproizvodstvo po pravitel'stvennomu nadzoru za torgovo-promyshlennymi predpriiatiiami). The opis has 3,118 files covering the varied activities of the state

administrators from investigations of alleged enemy-subject involvement to oversight and liquidation. For an overview of this institution and its powers see Abramova, "Istochnikovedcheskie problemy."

69. For the memoirs of an administrator who served briefly in early 1916 as an inspector, see RGB, Otdel rukopisei, f. 261, kor. 20, d. 6, ll. 108–110.

70. *Osobyi zhurnal Soveta ministrov,* 29 March 1915; V. S. Diakin, *Germanskie kapitaly v Rossii: Elektroindustriia i elektricheskii transport* (Leningrad: Nauka, 1971), 219; Abramova, "Istochnikovedcheskie problemy," 166.

71. RGIA, f. 23, op. 28, d. 3178, ll. 35–40ob (Protocol of the meeting of the temporary administrations and liquidation committees in Petrograd, 15 November 1915).

72. RGIA, f. 1276, op. 10, d. 336 (On the influx of workers of the yellow race); Eric Lohr, "Enemy Alien Politics within the Russian Empire during World War I" (Ph.D. diss., Harvard University, 1999), 86–92.

73. RGIA, f. 23, op. 27, d. 673, l. 32 (Ministry of Trade and Industry Circular to State Inspectors, 9 February 1917).

74. The best survey of these trends remains S. O. Zagorsky, *State Control of Industry in Russia during the War* (New Haven: Yale University Press, 1928). For example, administrators imposed accounting and pricing techniques such as attempting to set prices 10% above an "inherent" value of the product, a basic principle of later Soviet pricing. RGIA, f. 23, op. 28, d. 3178, l. 41 (Protocol of the meeting of special management and liquidation committees, 27 January 1917).

75. RGIA, f. 1483, op. 1, d. 10, l. 118.

76. Diakin, *Germanskie kapitaly v Rossii;* "Germaniia i Russkaia elektrotekhnicheskaia promyshlennost'," *Golos Moskvy,* 2 September 1914.

77. RGVIA, f. 1759, op. 4, d. 1673, l. 798.

78. Kniaz' Vsevolod Nikolaevich Shakhovskoi, *"Sic transit gloria mundi" (Tak prokhodit mirskaia slava) 1893–1917 gg.* (Paris: Self-published, 1952), 173.

79. Arkhiv vneshnoi politiki Rossiskoi Imperii (AVPRI), Otdel pechati, op. 477, d. 608, l. 13.

80. RGIA, f. 1284, op. 190, d. 212, l. 11ob.

81. RGIA, f. 1483, op. 1, d. 10, ll. 109–110 (*Osobyi zhurnal Soveta ministrov,* 23 December 1916, 10 and 27 January 1917).

82. Diakin, *Germanskie kapitaly,* 221.

83. *Promyshlennost' i torgovlia,* 14 January 1917, 24; Diakin, *Germanskie kapitaly,* 222–223. The Russian financiers N. A. Vtorov and N. N. Konshin acquired a 34% stake in the company.

84. RGIA, f. 1276, op. 12, d. 1440, l. 44 ("O zakrytii 'Kievskogo elektricheskogo obshchestva,'" *Osobyi zhurnal Soveta ministrov,* 4 March 1916); RGIA, f. 1276, op. 12, d. 1464, l. 12.

85. RGIA, f. 23, op. 27, d. 673, l. 8 (Secret circular from the Ministry of Trade and Industry to state inspectors, 15 October 1916).

86. RGIA, f. 1276, op. 12, d. 1464, ll. 1–12 (Memo of the MTiP special administration for government oversight over trade-industrial firms, 13 May 1916). The MTiP declared that sequestration was insufficient since "it did not ensure that at war's end the firms would not return to enemy [sic] hands."

87. RGIA, f. 1483, op. 1, d. 9, l. 383 (*Osobyi zhurnal Soveta ministrov,* 2 December 1916).

88. GARF, f. 102, d. 307, d. 122, ll. 2–3 (*Zhurnal osobogo komiteta po bor'be s nemetskim zasil'em*, 24 November 1916).

89. RGIA, f. 1276, 13, 70, ll. 1–9ob.

90. See, for example, RGIA f. 23, op. 27, d. 681, ll. 2–6.

91. Lothar Deeg, *Kunst & Albers Wladiwostok: Die Geschichte eines deutschen Handelshouses im russischen Fernen Osten 1864–1924* (Tubingen: Klartext, 1996), 189.

92. GARF, f. 1791, op. 2, d. 433, l. 3.

93. RGIA, f. 1276, op. 13, d. 70, ll. 1–9 (Ministry of Trade and Industry memo, August 4, 1916).

94. RGIA, f. 1276, op. 12, d. 1493, l. 16–18.

95. Ibid., ll. 1–2.

96. RGVIA, f. 2000s, op. 1, d. 8317, ll. 1–3.

97. RGIA, f. 1276, op. 13, d. 70, ll. 15–20ob. The property of the firm was nationalized in 1925, its branches and offices forced to close in 1930, and all other activities ended in 1939.

98. Alexander Bauermeister, *Spies Break Through: Memoirs of a German Secret Service Officer* (London: Constable, 1934). On the widespread sense within the military that spying was extensive in the Far East and counterintelligence weak before the war, see I. V. Derevianko, "Shpionov lovit' bylo nekomu," *Voenno-istoricheskii zhurnal* 12 (1993): 51–53.

99. Another much publicized sequestration of a firm entirely owned by Russian subjects was that of the Putilov Works in Petrograd. It was ostensibly sequestered because of corruption within the management and failure to produce for defense at full capacity. A major element in the agitation for sequestration was worker dissatisfaction with one of the directors, Karl Shpann, and with other foremen and managers of German descent. In a letter to the Society of 1914, a group of workers at the plant demanded its sequestration "in order to save it from the Germanophile banks which supplied it with raw materials" and to "purge the management of Germans, whom Karl Shpann had protected." GARF, f. 579, op. 1, d. 2527, l. 1. On the sequestration of Putilov see Jonathan A. Grant, *Big Business in Russia: The Putilov Company in Late Imperial Russia, 1868–1917* (Pittsburg: University of Pittsburg Press, 1999), esp. 119.

100. Fred Carstensen, *American Enterprise in Foreign Markets: Singer and International Harvester in Imperial Russia* (New Haven: Yale University Press, 1984), 80, 91.

101. The letter and reports of counterintelligence and police officials on it are contained in GARF, f. 102, op. 73, II, d. 162, ll. 220–227.

102. RGVIA, f. 1759, op. 3 dop., d. 1413, l. 282.

103. This accusation was also central to the press campaign against Singer. See GARF, f. 102, op. 73, II, d. 162, l. 67; "Loial'nost' Ko. Zinger," *Novoe vremia*, 29 July 1915.

104. GARF, f. 102, op. 73, II, d. 162, l. 200; Carstensen, *American Enterprise in Foreign Markets*, 80.

105. GARF, f. 102, op. 73, II, d. 162, ll. 41–44.

106. Ibid., ll. 16, 48, 64–66. These documents include requests from the Arkhangel'sk, Khabarovsk, Tula, Tiflis, Astrakhan, and Irkutsk governors, all of whom mentioned articles in the press and requested authority to search and close branches of Singer in their jurisdictions.

107. GARF, f. 102, op. 73, II, d. 162, l. 132 (Kazan' Governor Boiarskii to Department of Police, 10 September 1915).

108. RGIA, f. 23, op. 28, d. 806, l. 43 (Report of the state inspector of the Baku central office of the Singer Company, n.d. [late 1915]). The state inspector at the Baku Singer Regional Headquarters, which had 71 stores under its control, reported that in 1915 there had been a marked effort to "clear out the German and Jewish elements (*pochistit'sia ot nemetskogo i evreiskogo elementa*)" from these Singer branches.

109. For example, see GARF, f. 102, op. 73, II, d. 162, l. 28 (Tula governor order to officials in the province, 4 July 1915).

110. GARF, f. 102, op. 73, II, d. 162, ll. 76–103ob, 176.

111. Ibid., ll. 135–138ob; "Po voprosu o priniatii osobykh mer v otnoshenii aktsionernogo obshchestva Kompanii shveinykh mashin Zinger predstavlenie Upravleniia Voennogo ministerstva ot 25 August 1915," *Osobyi zhurnal Soveta ministrov*, 18 September 1915.

112. *Aktsionerno-paevye predpriiatiia Rossii* (Petrograd: Ministerstvo Finansov, 1917), 375. The firm, prosperous and rapidly growing prior to the war, suffered losses of 1.2 million rubles in 1914 and 9.4 million rubles in 1915.

113. RGIA, f. 23, op. 28, d. 806, l. 6 (Report of the state inspector for the regional headquarters of Singer in Tiflis, 7 December 1916).

114. RGIA, f. 23, op. 28, d. 806, l. 26 (Report of the state inspector of Singer in Odessa, 12 December 1915).

115. Among others, the American firm Treugol'nik (Triangle) underwent a similar ordeal. RGIA, f. 23, op. 27, d. 681, l. 2.

116. RGIA, f. 23, op. 28, d. 3178, ll. 1–6; Nolde, *Russia in the Economic War*, 175–176.

117. A Bolshevik committee in early 1918 estimated that enemy-subject trade and industrial firms worth a total of 2.35 billion rubles had been liquidated, primarily under legislation passed under the old regime. According to this estimate, 2 billion rubles out of this total belonged to German subjects. These totals excluded the entire area under enemy occupation, Ukraine and Poland. It should be noted that these are the only summary figures I was able to find, and there is no way to verify their accuracy. GARF, f. r-546, op. 1, d. 70, l. 52 (Memo on possible claims by Germany against Russia compiled by the Bolshevik committee on financial questions linked to the Brest-Litovsk treaty negotiations, n.d.). One can get an idea of the scale of this program by comparing these figures with estimates of the results of nationalization of all industry under the Bolsheviks. At the end of 1918, the Society of Industrialists and Factory Owners estimated that the Bolsheviks had nationalized 1,100 corporations with a founding capital of 3 billion rubles. D. A. Kovalenko, *Oboronnaia promyshlennost' Sovetskoi Rossii v 1918–1920* (Moscow: Nauka, 1970), 156. Another indication of the scale of the program can be found in the financial treaty supplement to the Brest-Litovsk peace treaty which was signed on August 27, 1918. It required the Bolshevik state to pay compensation for all the damages suffered by enemy subjects from the beginning of the war through the date of the treaty. Although there were no separate figures for this category, "losses suffered by civilian individuals" and "for confiscation" totaled 4 billion marks. *Sovetsko-Germanskie otnosheniia* 1, 615–617, 640.

118. RGIA, f. 23, op. 27, d. 689 (Records of the standing committee of the Ministry of Trade and Industry, 1916–1918); RGIA, f. 23, op. 28, d. 3194, l. 1 (Circular

of RFSR People's Commissariat of Trade and Industry Liquidation Section to temporary administrators, liquidation committees and liquidators of enemy firms, 22 July 1918).

119. While the nationalization of heavy industry was clearly one of the central tenets and goals of Marxism, according to Silvana Malle, in the first six months after Bolshevik seizure of power, nationalization was driven more by the spontaneous actions of revolutionaries, workers, and lower-level Bolshevik officials than by a coherent policy from above. In fact, Lenin displayed remarkable reluctance to proceed with a decree on the nationalization of both domestic and foreign heavy industry, fearing a collapse of domestic production. The shift from the early policy of "state capitalism" to "war communism" in June 1918 has often been attributed to the threat of civil war, but the enemy-alien issue played a role too. The liquidation of enemy-alien properties under the previous two regimes limited Lenin's options. Moreover, by a serious blunder, German negotiators at Brest-Litovsk in June 1918 agreed that "land, mines, industrial and commercial establishments and shares [shall be] restored to enemy nationals . . . except property which has been taken over by the state." The blunder was to allow this exemption for any properties acquired by the state before July 1, 1918, giving the Bolshevik regime a week which it used to frantically nationalize every last bit of enemy shares and properties in the economy in order to avoid the requirement of compensation. In chaotic and rapid fashion, a list of 1,100 firms—including all the remaining firms with even a small amount of enemy ownership—was compiled and their nationalization decreed on June 28, on the very eve of the July 1 deadline. In this way, at least the precipitate cause of the Bolshevik decree on nationalization was the Brest agreement on the consequences of the World War I campaign against enemy aliens. GARF, f. r-393, op. 7, d. 1; Nolde, *Russia in the Economic War,* 180; Kovalenko, *Oboronnaia promyshlennost',* 153–155; Silvana Malle, *The Economic Organization of War Communism, 1918–1921* (Cambridge: Cambridge University Press, 1985), 59–61; RGIA, f. 23, op. 28, d. 3194, l. 1; *V. I. Lenin vo glave velikogo stroitel'stva: Sbornik vospominanii o deiatel'nosti V. I. Lenina na khoziaistvennom fronte* (Moscow: Gos. izd., 1960), 63–64.

4. Nationalizing the Land

1. Hans Rogger, "Government, Jews, Peasants, and Land in Post–Emancipation Russia," *Cahiers du Monde Russe et Soviétique* 17, no. 1 (1976), 1–11.

2. By 1897, the Jewish share of landholding and leasing fell to only 1.4% and 3.9%, respectively, in the twelve provinces for which there is reliable data. Both shares fell by over 50% from levels prior to the implementation of the Temporary Laws in 1882. See I. M. Bikerman, *Cherta evreiskoi osedlosti* (St. Petersburg, 1911), 44–45.

3. Rogger, *Jewish Policies and Right-Wing Politics in Imperial Russia* (Berkeley: University of California Press, 1986), 143.

4. Michael Cherniavsky, *Prologue to Revolution: Notes of A. N. Iakhontov on the Secret Meetings of the Council of Ministers, 1915* (Upper Saddle River, N.J.: Prentice Hall, 1967), 56–72.

5. For excellent accounts of the interrelationships between the Polish question and the land issue, see Witold Rodkiewicz, *Russian Nationality Policy in the*

Western Provinces of the Empire (1863–1905) (Lublin: Scientific Society of Lublin, 1998); Daniel Beauvois, *La Bataille de la terre en Ukraine, 1863–1924: Les Polonais et les conflits socio-ethniques* (Lille: Presses universitaires de Lille, 1993).

6. RGVIA, f. 2005, op. 1, d. 28, l. 126 (Goremykin to Ianushkevich, 20 June 1915); RGVIA, f. 2003, op. 2, d. 539; RGVIA, f. 2005, op. 1, d. 155, l. 12; Waldemar Giesbrecht, "Die Verbannung der Wolhyniendeutschen, 1915/1916," *Wolhynische Hefte* 3 (1984): 62; Alexander Prusin, "Russian Occupation Policies and Anti-Semitism in Eastern Galicia, 1914–1915," in Marshall Poe and Eric Lohr, eds., *Military and Society in Russian History, 1450–1917* (Leiden, The Netherlands: Brill, 2002).

7. Andreas Kappeler, *Russland als Vielvölkerreich: Entstehung, Geschichte, Zerfall* (Munich: C. H. Beck, 1992).

8. Ironically, many of these estates were transferred to Baltic German nobles, who were officially defined as Russian in the late nineteenth century. Louis Lubliner, *Les Confiscations des Biens des Polonais sous le Regne de L'Empereur Nicolas Ier suivi de Tableaux Nominatifs et Alphabeétiques* (Brussels: C. Muquardt, 1861); RGIA, f. 821, op. 150, d. 358, ll. 1–6 (Lists of German families granted estates in the Kingdom of Poland, n.d.). Nearly all the dates of the grants were in the 1830s and 1860s—following the two Polish uprisings.

9. A. N. Pypin, "Pol'skii vopros v Russkoi literature," *Vestnik Evropy* 1 (1881): 703–736.

10. Rodkiewicz, *Russian Nationality Policy*, 58.

11. RGIA, f. 1284, op. 190, d. 307, ll. 1–4 (Memo, MVD Department of General Affairs, 16 October 1914).

12. On May 1, 1905, a new law weakened limits on Poles slightly by allowing Poles to acquire land from individuals of Polish origin and up to 60 *desiatin* from non-Poles for industrial purposes. GARF, f. 102, II, op. 73, ch. 1, d. 63, l. 2ob (Introduction to the Duma proposal to eliminate legal limits on Poles within the empire, 2 September 1915).

13. Like much else, rather than unequivocally abolish the laws, the Provisional Government suspended them until elections to the Constituent Assembly. GARF, f. r-546, op. 1, d. 9, ll. 19, 23.

14. For example, see RGIA, f. 1284, op. 190, d. 323, ll. 1–3ob (Volynia governor to Khvostov, 17 January 1916).

15. For the history of German colonists and their landholding patterns up to 1914, see Detlef Brandes, *Von den Zaren Adoptiert: Die Deutschen Kolonisten und die Balkansiedler in Neurussland und Bessarabien 1751–1914* (Munich: R. Oldenbourg Verlag, 1993); Dietmar Neutatz, *Die "deutsche Frage" im Schwarzmeergebiet und in Wolhynien: Politik, Wirtschaft, Mentalitäten und Alltag im Spannungsfeld von Nationalismus und Modernisierung (1856–1914)* (Stuttgart: Franz Steiner Verlag, 1993); James Long, *From Privileged to Dispossessed: The Volga Germans, 1860–1917* (Lincoln: University of Nebraska Press, 1988).

16. Neutatz, *Die "deutsche Frage"*; Terry Martin, "The German Question in Russia, 1848–1896," *Russian History/Histoire Russe* 18, no. 4 (Winter 1991): 403–413.

17. Rodkiewicz, *Russian Nationality Policy*, 61.

18. The case in Crimea was similar. Discrimination against Crimean Tatars in the decade after the Crimean War contributed to the migration to Turkey of nearly

200,000 Tatars by 1863. Many of the emigrants' lands were purchased by German migrants from Ukrainian and Polish areas of the Russian Empire. V. V. Obolenskii, *Mezhdunarodnye i mezhkontinental'nye migratsii v dovoennoi Rossii i SSSR* (Moscow: Ts.S.U. SSSR, 1928), 77.

19. GARF, f. 215, op. 1, d. 524 (Confidential MVD memo, 22 August 1914); M. I. Mysh, *Ob inostrantsakh v Rossii: Sbornik uzakonenii, traktatov i konventsii, s otnosiashchimsia k nim pravitel'stvennymi i sudebnymi raziasneniiami,* 2nd ed. (St. Petersburg, 1911), 33–34; Rodkiewicz, *Russian Nationality Policy,* 73–78.

20. R. P. Bartlett, "Colonists, 'Gastarbeiter' and the Problems of Agriculture in Postemancipation Russia," *Slavonic and East European Review* 60 (1982): 547–571.

21. Ingeborg Fleischhauer, "The Germans' Role in Tsarist Russia," in Ingeborg Fleischhauer and Benjamin Pinkus, eds., *The Soviet Germans: Past and Present* (London: C. Hurst, 1986), 20, 22; Benjamin Pinkus and Ingeborg Fleischhauer, *Die Deutschen in der Sowjetunion* (Baden-Baden: Nomos Verlagsgesellschaft, 1987), 96.

22. Neutatz, *Die "deutsche Frage,"* 261, 265, 160, 86. The land tenure and inheritance patterns among German colonists contributed to their relative success throughout most of the empire, leading to German landholdings averaging between two and three times larger than the imperial norm. An instructive contrast is provided by the Volga provinces of Samara and Saratov, where German colonists had adopted the Russian communal pattern of land tenure by the early nineteenth century. Colonists in the Volga region, unlike colonists elsewhere, suffered a rapid decline in the average size of their landholdings in the late nineteenth and early twentieth centuries as their population grew. See Long, *From Privileged to Dispossessed,* 110–137.

23. Available figures indicate that on average 70% of all new German acquisitions came from the gentry rather than from Slavic peasants. The exception was Siberia, where nearly all of the roughly one million *desiatin* acquired by German settlers came from the resettlement administration in purchase and long-term lease. RGIA, f. 391, op. 5, d. 316 (On the liquidation of German land in Siberia, 1911–1917).

24. In 1895, the restrictions were made applicable only to individuals acquiring Russian subjecthood after 1895. An important law of May 1, 1905, curtailed the power of local officials to prevent acquisition of land by foreigners if there was no specific law banning such transactions. RGIA, f. 1284, op. 190, d. 307, l. 72.

25. Bartlett, "Colonists, 'Gastarbeiter'," 547–571.

26. This was more true in the western and southern German settlements than in the Volga region, where communal forms of ownership prevailed among colonists.

27. Dorothy Atkinson, *The End of the Russian Land Commune, 1905–1930* (Stanford: Stanford University Press, 1983), 53. There is an interesting parallel between the dispersal of the German colonies to foster the spread of agricultural innovations through the demonstration effect, and the Stolypin reform's support for individual *khutoriani* in a checkerboard pattern throughout the countryside to demonstrate the benefits of private property. Judith Pallot, *Land Reform in Russia, 1906–1917: Peasant Responses to Stolypin's Project of Rural Transformation* (Oxford: Clarendon Press, 1999), 64, 103–104; Bartlett, "Colonists, 'Gastarbeiter'."

28. For an account of the failures of the reform, see Pallot, *Land Reform.*

29. RGIA, f. 396, op. 7, d. 453, l. 8.

30. Christoph Schmidt, *Russische Presse und Deutsches Reich, 1905–1914* (Cologne: Böhlau Verlag, 1988), 100–108. Nearly all the German-colonist and Baltic-German Duma deputies were members of the Octobrist Party.

31. Neutatz, *Die "deutsche Frage,"* 185.

32. Ibid., 190. Even as late as 1913, several major newspapers on the Right defended the colonists, including *Golos Rusi* and *Kievlianin.* RGIA, f. 391, op. 5, d. 316, l. 103.

33. Schmidt, *Russische Presse,* 106–108.

34. Such maps also became part of public discourse through their publication in newspapers and pamphlets. For maps of colonists according to population density published in the press along with articles pointing out the threats the colonists posed to Russian interests, see RGIA, f. 1483, op. 1, d. 29, 119, and a collection of articles from the newspaper Novoe vremia: A. Rennikov, *Zoloto Reina: O nemtsakh v Rossii* (Petrograd: A. S. Suvorin, 1915).

35. The maps and statistics are found in RGIA, f. 391, op. 5, d. 316, ll. 1–350. They revealed that internal migration, mostly from the New Russia provinces of South Ukraine, had brought nearly 25,000 German colonists to three districts of the Omsk region, where they made up nearly 5% of the population and held 430,101 *desiatin* by 1911.

36. RGIA, f. 391, op. 5, d. 316, l. 107. Typically, the report was very negative on the capabilities of Russian peasants to compete with Germans without the intervention of coercive state action.

37. For examples of the new fixation on demographic breakdowns of the population in the immediate prewar years, see the collections of articles published in A. P. Tupin, *Pribaltiiskii krai i voina: Materialy iz russkoi pechati za avgust, sentiabr' i oktiabr' 1914 g.* (Petrograd: Izd. A. P. Tupina, 1914); Rennikov, *Zoloto Reina.* On the importance of these shifts, see Peter Holquist, "To Count, To Extract, To Exterminate: Population Statistics and Population Politics in Late Imperial and Soviet Russia," in Ronald Grigor Suny and Terry Martin, eds., *A State of Nations: Empire and Nation-Making in the Age of Lenin and Stalin* (Oxford: Oxford University Press, 2001), 111–144; Kate Brown, "A Biography of No Place: The Ukrainian Borderlands and the Making of Nation-Space" (Ph.D. diss., University of Washington, 2000).

38. Prominent officials who carried out wartime measures against enemy aliens had gained important experience by implementing prewar limitations. For example, N. P. Kharlamov, as director of the chancery of the Warsaw governor general, was responsible for the oversight of foreigners in the prewar years. GARF, f. 215, op. 1, d. 429, l. 40.

39. William W. Hagen, *Germans, Poles and Jews: The Nationality Conflict in the Prussian East, 1772–1914* (Chicago: University of Chicago Press, 1980), 134.

40. Hagen, *Germans, Poles and Jews,* 192, 320. Hagen explicitly links this prewar transformation of nationality practice to Hitler's later comment in *Mein Kampf* that "Germanization can only be applied to soil and never to people."

41. One example was the decision of Russian authorities to continue to enforce German bans on land acquisition by Poles in East Prussia, during the brief Russian occupation in 1914. RGVIA, f. 2005, op. 1, d. 29, ll. 48–51.

42. For a good analysis of the controversy, see V. N. Durdenevskii, "Germanskoe Dvupoddanstvo," *Problemy velikoi Rossii,* 1916, no. 11, pp. 10–12; no. 13, pp. 11–13; no. 15, pp. 9–10. For the law, see Wilhelm Cahn, *Reichs- und staatsangehörigkeitsgesetz vom 22. Juli 1913, erläutert mit Benutzung amtlicher Quellen und unter vergleichender Berücksichtigung der ausländischen Gesetzgebung,* 4th ed. (Berlin: J. Guttentag, 1914).

43. Fritz Fischer, *Germany's War Aims in the First World War* (New York: W. W. Norton, 1967), 115; Imanuel Geiss, *Der polnische Grenzstreifen 1914–1918: Ein Beitrag zur deutschen Kriegszielpolitik im Ersten Weltkrieg* (Lübeck: Matthiesen Verlag, 1960); Vejas Liulevicius, *War Land on the Eastern Front: Culture, National Identity and German Occupation in World War I* (Cambridge: Cambridge University Press, 2000); Werner Basler, *Deutschlands Annexionspolitik in Polen und im Baltikum, 1914–1918* (Berlin: Rütten & Loening, 1962).

44. Tupin, *Pribaltiiskii krai i voina,* 139. Nationalist Baltic German landlords brought as many as 20,000 German peasants from the Volga and Ukraine into the Baltic region from 1906 to 1910 as part of an attempt to alter the demographics of land ownership and population in the provinces. Nikolaus Arndt, "Umsiedlung wolyniendeutscher Kolonisten ins Baltikum, 1907–1913," *Wolhynische Hefte* 5 (1988): 91–214; Jürgen von Hehn, "Das baltische Deutschtum zwischen den Revolutionen 1905–1917," in Andrew Ezergailis and Gert von Pistohlkors, eds., *Die baltischen Provinzen Russlands zwischen den Revolutionen von 1905–1917* (Cologne: Bohlau, 1982): 20–42.

45. For a summary of the issue which reveals how keenly aware the Russian public was of Pan-German publications, see the reprint of V. Ia. Fan der Flit's 1909 article: "Vse Nemetskoe dvizhenie kak faktor Evropeiskoi voiny," *Izvestiia Ministerstva inostrannykh del* 4 (1915); A. P. T[upin], "Vnutrennie izvestiia: Pravda o pribaltiiskikh kolonistakh" *Novoe vremia,* 28 August 1916.

46. See, for example, N. D. Polivanov, *O nemetskom zasilii: Broshiura Shtabom verkhovnogo glavnokomanduiushchego otpravlena na peredovye pozitsii,* 12th ed. (Petrograd, 1917); RGIA, f. 1284, op. 190, d. 307.

47. For an argument over the relative strength of property rights in the *longue durée* of Russian history, see the exchange between Richard Pipes and George G. Weickhardt: "Was There Private Property in Muscovite Russia?," *Slavic Review* 53, no. 2 (Summer 1994): 524–538. On the weakness of the Russian concept of private property prior to 1905 in relation to Europe, see Richard Wortman, "Property, Populism, and Political Culture," in Olga Crisp and Linda Edmondson, eds., *Civil Rights in Imperial Russia* (Oxford: Clarendon Press, 1989), 13–32.

48. Karl Lindeman, *Prekrashchenie zemlevladeniia i zemlepol'zovaniia poselian sobstvennikov. Ukazy 2 fevralia i 13 dekabria 1915 goda i 10, 15 iiulia i 19 avgusta 1916 goda i ikh vliianie na ekonomicheskoe sostoianie iuzhnoi Rossii* (Moscow: K.L. Men'shova, 1917), 50.

49. In a sense, the fact that citizenship and legal protection of property rights were not firmly established made the controversy over their establishment and violation more contentious, interesting, and important, a point that Andrzej Walicki makes for the broader related issues of liberalism and law in his *Legal Philosophies of Russian Liberalism* (Notre Dame: University of Notre Dame Press, 1992), 1–7. Once the idea of universal citizenship began to come into practice during the Great Reforms and especially with the promulgation of the Fundamental Laws in 1906,

issues of the property rights of one subset of the population were much more readily translated into issues of principle, of the rights of all citizens. Prior to these developments, guarantees of colonist lands and rights were much less a national issue, as colonists were not citizens but members of an estate under its own complete set of laws and regulations. For the last codification of colonist regulations, see "Ustav o koloniiakh inostrantsev v Imperii 1857 g." in *Istoriia rossiiskikh nemtsev v dokumentakh (1763–1992 gg)* (Moscow: Mezhdunarodnyi institut gumanitarnykh programm, 1993), 22–36. Article 166 explicitly confirmed that "colonists are allowed, for the expansion and improvement of their economy, to purchase and in general to obtain land from private individuals in ownership." In 1874, however, when "colonists" as a distinct category were abolished, they were brought under all-imperial laws. This made their rights of land ownership, at least in principle, a matter of all-imperial legislation and concern.

50. An important exception is the study of grain requisition policies, through which the state imposed extensive measures limiting the free sale of grain and turned at times to outright expropriation of grain stocks. See Lars Lih, *Bread and Authority in Russia, 1914–1921* (Berkeley: University of California Press, 1990), 9–15, 49–51.

51. *Sbornik uzakonenii, rasporiazhenii, raziasnenii i tsirkuliarov ob ogranichenii prav nepriiatel'skikh poddannykh i o pravitel'stvennom nadzore za torgovo-promyshlennymi predpriiatiiami* (Petrograd: Tip. Ministerstva finansov, 1915), 5–6; GARF, f. r-546, op. 1, d. 9, l. 19.

52. GARF, f. 215, op. 1, d. 524, ll. 1–3.

53. GARF, f. 102, II, op. 73, d. 351, ll. 40–42.

54. RGVIA, f. 2005, op. 1, d. 24, l. 3 (Grand Duke Nikolai Nikolaevich to Goremykin, 11 November 1914 [*sic:* the date of the original letter was October 3, 1914]).

55. "Po voprosu o polozhenii nepriiatel'skikh poddanykh v Rossii," *Osobyi zhurnal Soveta ministrov* (7 October 1914): 1–10; RGVIA, f. 2005, op. 1, d. 24, ll. 4–10, esp. ll. 6–8 (Goremykin to Ianushkevich, 14 October 1914); Article 19, pt. 18 of the *Pravila o mestnostiakh, obiavliaemykh sostoiashchimi na voennom polozhenii* gave military officials the right to sequester real estate, freeze assets and income from any property, the owners of which were engaged in criminal activities, or when "allowing the activity of such [would] cause dangerous consequences for social order." Civilian authorities had similar powers under the state of extraordinary security, which was valid for most provinces for the duration of the war. However, civilian authorities were constrained to a far greater degree by other civilian legislation. GARF, f. 102, II, op. 71, d. 80, l. 91.

56. RGVIA, f. 2003, op. 2, d. 539, l. 12ob.

57. RGVIA, f. 2005, op. 1, d. 24, l. 305.

58. *Razdel Aziatskoi Turtsii: Po sekretnym dokumentam b. Ministerstva inostrannykh del* (Moscow: Izd. Litizdata NKID, 1924), 360–361; Avetis Amaiakonich Arutiunian, "Pervaia mirovaia voina i armianskie bezhentsy (1914–1917)" (Kand. diss., Akademiia nauk Armianskoi SSR, Institut Istorii, 1989), 58–74.

59. GARF, f. 215, op. 1, d. 524, ll. 99–103ob.

60. According to Giesbrecht, the deportations were often accompanied by Cossacks riding into town and local Ukrainians and Jews gathering to buy up farm

machinery, livestock, and household items at a sharp discount. Giesbrecht, "Die Verbannung der Wolhyniendeutschen," 52; Alfred Krueger, *Die Fluchtlinge von Wolhynien: Der Leidensweg russlanddeutcher Siedler, 1915–1918* (Plauen: Günther-Wolff, 1937).

61. This decision was preceded by the practice of sequestering properties of colonists and enemy subjects who had "hidden themselves abroad" (i.e., were out of the country on the outbreak of war). Such sequestrations began in September 1914. No summary statistics are available, but the number of such sequestered properties was significant. RGVIA, f. 2005, op. 1, d. 24, l. 305.

62. RGIA, f. 1483, op. 1, d. 32, l. 1 (Report of the Zhitomir regional notary archive on the liquidation of German landholding, n.d.).

63. GARF, f. 215, op. 1, d. 460, l. 21.

64. RGVIA, f. 2005, op. 1, d. 28, l. 137 (Ivanov to Ianushkevich, 19 June 1915).

65. Hans Jurgen Seraphim, *Rodungssiedler, Agrarverfassung und Wirtschaftsentwicklung des deutschen Bauerntums in Wolhynien* (Berlin: Paul Parey, 1938), 77.

66. GARF, f. 579, op. 1, d. 2615, l. 1 (Report on the Conference of German Settler-Landowners in Moscow, 20–22 April 1917); Gosudarstvennaia Duma, *Stenograficheskie otchety* 4, session 4, meeting 45, 30 March 1916, col. 658; Lindeman, *Prekrashchenie*, 24.

67. Lindeman, *Prekrashchenie*, 21–22. In July 1916, the commander of supply for the Northern Front ordered the immediate sequestration of all deported colonists' lands and properties that had not yet been sequestered. RGVIA, f. 1932, op. 12, d. 92, l. 255ob.

68. Lindeman, *Prekrashchenie*, 24. Lindeman estimated the value of this land at 40 million rubles.

69. RGVIA, f. 2005, op. 1, d. 28, ll. 178–180.

70. Ibid., ll. 99–100.

71. RGIA, f. 1483, op. 1, d. 14, l. 163.

72. RGVIA, f. 2005, op. 1, d. 28, l. 137 (Ivanov to Ianushkevich, 19 June 1915).

73. The following is based on the provisions of the three decrees, which are published in *Sbornik uzakonenii, rasporiazhenii, raziasnenii i tsirkuliarov*, 15–30. Article 87 gave the government and tsar the power to issue decrees while the Duma was out of session. In principle, such decrees were to lose force if not explicitly confirmed by the Duma during its next session. In practice, none of the laws affecting enemy-alien landholdings ever came to vote in the Duma. However, this does not mean that a majority in the Duma disapproved of the measures. In fact, in June 1916, the Progressive Bloc prevented the Right from bringing the decrees to the floor for discussion for fear that they would pass. Because they were never confirmed by the Duma, they technically never became laws (*zakony*), and thus should be referred to as decrees (*ukazy*).

74. The law covered the following provinces: the ten Polish provinces, plus Petrograd, Estland, Lifland, Kurland, Kovno, Grodno, Vilna, Minsk, Volynia, Podolia, Bessarabia, Kherson, Taurida, Ekaterinoslav, the Don Cossack region, the whole of the Caucasus, Finland, and the area under the governor general of the Amur.

75. *Sbornik uzakonenii, rasporiazhenii, raziasnenii i tsirkuliarov*, 25. A *versta* (plural: *versty, verst*) is equivalent to 1.07 kilometers.

76. RGVIA, f. 2005, op. 1, d. 29, l. 82.

77. "Voprosy vnutrennei zhizni," *Vestnik Evropy* (April 1915): 342–343.

78. RGIA, f. 1483, op. 1, d. 32, ll. 4–6 (Memo signed by V. M. Liubanskii, n.d.). The Volynia governor reiterated the argument in early 1916: RGIA, f. 1284, op. 190, d. 323, ll. 1–3ob (Volynia governor to A. N. Khvostov, 17 January 1916).

79. RGB, Otdel rukopisei, f. 261, kor. 20, d. 6, l. 87; *Osobyi zhurnal Soveta ministrov* (2 August 1915): 1–5.

80. RGB, Otdel rukopisei, f. 261, kor. 20, d. 6, l. 87.

81. RGIA, f. 1483, op. 1, d. 32, l. 9. A bill to ensure that colonist lands were transferred to soldiers was introduced into the Duma on August 5, 1915. The shortness of the Duma sessions and disagreement among deputies on the issue prevented it from ever reaching the floor for a vote. RGIA, f. 1483, op. 1, d. 29, l. 18. The proposal was discussed in early 1916, again without result. See Gosudarstvennaia Duma, *Stenograficheskie otchety*, 29 February 1916, col. 2455.

82. Tsentral'nyi derzhavnyi arkhiv Ukrainy, f. 385, op. 2, spr. 139, ark. 6. Thanks to Alex Dillon for generously sharing his notes on this report.

83. "V Pribaltiiskom krae," *Novoe vremia*, 3 July 1916, cited in RGIA, f. 1483, op. 1, d. 25, l. 83.

84. "Nemtsy-Kolonisty Zalog Zemel'" *Russkoe Slovo*, 15 July 1916; RGIA, f. 1483, op. 1, d. 25, l. 84.

85. One *desiatina* (plural: *desiatiny, desiatin*) = 1.093 hectares = 2.7 acres. Gosudarstvennaia duma, *Stenograficheskie otchety* 4, 4, 5th session, (3 August 1915): 434–435. It should be noted that Shcherbatov did not oppose the goal of expropriating German lands. He merely wanted a reasonable approach, with full consideration of potential damages to Russia's wartime economy.

86. For a good analysis of the law, see "Po povodu zakona 13-ogo dekabria 1915 g." *Zhurnal Ministerstva iustitsii* 4 (1916): 209–219.

87. RGIA, f. 391, op. 5, d. 316 (Memo on the liquidation of German land in Siberia, n.d.); RGVIA, f. 2005, op. 1, d. 27, ll. 37–40.

88. "On the expansion of the limitations relating to land ownership . . . to all the provinces and regions of the Russian state," *Osobyi zhurnal Soveta ministrov*, 10 and 31 January 1917, signed by the tsar on 6 February 1917; RGIA, f. 1483, op. 1, d. 10, l. 88.

89. RGIA, f. 1483, op. 1, d. 10, l. 82.

90. *Osobyi zhurnal Soveta ministrov*, 2 August 1915, 1–5.

91. GARF, f. 579, op. 1, dd. 2608–2612.

92. GARF, f. 579, op. 1, d. 2610, l. 1.

93. GARF, f. 1483, op. 1, d. 20, l. 7. In the unlikely event that prices at auction exceeded prices that Peasant Bank appraisers set, the bank typically reversed such sales, exercising its right to purchase at the lower price.

94. In 1916, two extraordinary allocations of 200,000 rubles and over a hundred appraisers and additional office support staff were granted to local officials to help with the process. RGIA, f. 1483, op. 1, d. 9, ll. 36–37.

95. RGIA, f. 1483, op. 1, d. 16, l. 386. For detailed summary data on the implementation of the laws by province up to May 30, 1916, see GARF, f. r-393, op. 1, d. 7, ll. 26–28.

96. GARF, f. 215, op. 1, d. 452, ll. 24, 115.

97. Neutatz, *Die "deutsche Frage,"* 261.

98. GARF, f. 102, II, op. 73, d. 34, l. 124. Lindeman, *Prekrashchenie*, 303–305.

The average size of a leaseholding appears from his limited data to have been about 25 *desiatin*.

99. This figure is very inexact, and is based on the assumption that in the areas subject to the February and December decrees an additional 20% of the lands subject to the expropriatory decrees was held in lease. Using the conservative Peasant Bank figure of 3.7 million *desiatin* published in lists for expropriation, one can surmise that an additional 750,000 *desiatin* were held in lease. One of the reasons for the paucity of official statistics on leaseholdings was that lease agreements were almost entirely private contracts, not always formally reported. The breaking of a lease was a private action, and thus statistics were not as easily compiled, especially during the chaos and dislocation of the war years.

100. Including these later expansions of the expropriatory decrees could bring the estimates as high as one million individuals with 9–10 million *desiatin*. To recap, these estimates include: 3.7 million *desiatin* within the empire; 3 million in occupied and reoccupied areas; 750,000 in lease; 750,000 in Siberia, and one million in the Volga provinces.

101. This amounted to roughly 14% of the total area of land remaining in communal landholding. S. M. Dubrovskii, *Stolypinskaia zemel'naia reforma: Iz istorii sel'skogo khoziaistva Rossii v nachale XX veka* (Moscow: Akademiia nauk SSSR, Institut istorii, 1963), 574–576; Atkinson, *The End of the Russian Land Commune*, 76.

102. Sonja Striegnitz comes to a similar conclusion in her study of the Volga region during the war. See "Der Weltkrieg und die Wolgakolonisten: Die Regierungspolitik und die Tendenzen der Gesellschaftlichen Entwicklung," in Dittmar Dahlmann and Ralph Tuchtenhagen, eds., *Zwischen Reform und Revolution: Die Deutschen an der Wolga 1860–1917* (Essen: Klartext, 1994), 145–146.

103. G. A. Nozdrin, "Natsional'naia nemetskaia blagotvoritel'nost' v Sibiri vo vtoroi polovine XIX–nachale XX vv." in L. M. Goriushkin, ed., *Zarubezhnye ekonomicheskie i kul'turnye sviazi Sibiri (XVIII–XX vv.)* (Novosibirsk: RAN Sibirskoe otdelenie Institut Istorii, 1995), 148–149.

104. Lindeman, *Prekrashchenie*, 163.

105. Gosudarstvennaia duma, *Stenograficheskie otchety* 4, no. 4 (3 August 1915), 500–508.

106. RGIA, f. 1483, op. 1, d. 23, ll. 4–10; RGIA, f. 1278, op. 7, d. 587, l. 3. The language of the relevant decrees merely allowed the postponement of their expropriation until the end of the war. Moreover, enemy subjects of Slavic origin never received exemption from the requirement that all enemy-subject leases be terminated. Finally, exemptions granted to enemy subjects of favored ethnicity were not universally applied. For example, as late as December 1916, the Ekaterinoslav governor reported that since there was no explicit law exempting Armenian enemy subjects from the expropriatory decrees, he was continuing to expropriate them. RGIA, f. 1483, op. 1, d. 14, l. 406.

107. Peter Gatrell, "Refugees in the Russian Empire, 1914–1917: Population Displacement and Social Identity," in Edward Acton, Vladimir Iu. Cherniaev, and William G. Rosenberg, eds., *Critical Companion to the Russian Revolution, 1914–1921* (Bloomington: Indiana University Press, 1997), 554–564.

108. RGIA, f. 1483, op. 1, d. 36, l. 91 (Taurida governor to Maklakov, 13 March 1915).

109. Nozdrin, "Natsional'naia nemetskaia," 147–150.

110. Lindeman, *Prekrashchenie*, 360.

111. For tables showing the deficit and surplus provinces see N. D. Kondratiev, *Rynok khlebov i ego regulirovanie vo vremia voiny i revoliutsii* (Moscow: Nauka, 1991), 95–97. For an overview of agriculture and the Germans' role in the Black Sea region, see Brandes, *Von den Zaren*; Neutatz, *Die "deutsche Frage."*

112. Lih, *Bread and Authority*, 9–11; George Yaney, *The Urge to Mobilize: Agrarian Reform in Russia, 1861–1930* (Urbana: University of Illinois Press, 1982): 408–419; Petr B. Struve, *Food Supply in Russia during the World War* (New Haven: Yale University Press, 1930), 460.

113. GARF, f. 102, II, op. 75, d. 29, ll. 75 ff. Slavic prisoners and internees were used for labor in much larger proportion than Germans. Officers, according to international agreements, were not required to work. The POW workers were let out for work in teams with police or military guards.

114. Lindeman, *Prekrashchenie*, 30. The intention of this order was to ensure that the expropriated lands would remain available for distribution to valorous soldiers at the end of the war.

115. *Sbornik uzakonenii, rasporiazhenii, raziasnenii i tsirkuliarov ob ogranichenii prav nepriiatel'skikh poddannykh*, 32–33.

116. Lindeman, *Prekrashchenie*, 52; David Rempel, "The Expropriation of the German Colonists in South Russia during the Great War," *Journal of Modern History* (March, 1932): 64.

117. Kondratiev, *Rynok khlebov*, 121. According to Kondratiev's figures, the total area under seed in the empire fell by 2.6 million *desiatin* in 1915, not including areas occupied by the enemy. Lindeman's estimate of 1.5 million, if accurate, would mean that over half of this decline was caused by the expropriation program.

118. Lindeman, *Prekrashchenie*, 82. Kamenskii was a prominent member of the Octobrist Party's central committee and had a long history of defending religious tolerance and Mennonite rights. See Terry Martin, *The Mennonites and the Russian State Duma, 1905–1914*, The Donald W. Treadgold Papers in Russian, East European and Central Asian Studies, no. 4 (Seattle: Henry M. Jackson School of International Studies, University of Washington, 1996): 38–39. Kharlamov went even further, claiming that 2 million *desiatin* of German land would go unplanted in Kherson province alone. RGB, Otdel rukopisei, f. 261, kor. 20, d. 6, l. 100.

119. Alexis N. Antsiferov, et al., *Russian Agriculture during the War* (New Haven: Yale University Press, 1930), 183. The actual decline from 1915 to 1916 was 18% (903 million poods). No figures are readily available for the decline in German areas under seed for 1916. The issue is worthy of further research, as this land likely made up a significant proportion of this decline. It is important to note, however, that the actual impact of these declines upon the domestic supply of grain is a complex issue. The war stopped nearly all export of grain, reducing export levels from an average of 718 million poods between 1909 and 1913 to only an average of 25 million poods. Nearly the entire decline in grain output during the war was offset by the decline in exports. This does not devalue the importance of the decline in German grain production, however, since there was a marked decline in production of private owners oriented toward the imperial market and a huge shift to smaller-scale communal production. As German farmers, especially in the south and west, were disproportionately private owners, producing disproportionately

large amounts for the market, their expropriation made a substantial contribution to the decline in the amount of grain available to the domestic market.

120. RGB, Otdel rukopisei, f. 261, kor. 20, d. 6, l. 86ob.

121. Lindeman, *Prekrashchenie*, 322.

122. RGIA, f. 1483, op. 1, d. 5, l. 150.

123. RGIA, f. 23, op. 28, d. 3203, ll. 1–2. Most of these firms had from ten to 200 workers, although firms as large as a Kiev beet sugar plant with 1,100 workers were also listed.

124. Lindeman, *Prekrashchenie*, 80, citing P. V. Kamenskii's speech to the State Council on March 24, 1916.

125. RGIA, f. 1483, op. 1, d. 22, l. 24.

126. Lindeman, *Prekrashchenie*, 198.

127. GARF, f. 215, op. 1, d. 161, l. 27.

128. RGB, Otdel rukopisei, f. 261, kor. 20, d. 6, l. 94. The decree included the ambiguous phrase: "and in general, employees."

129. The MVD sent prominent officials to areas with substantial enemy-alien populations with instructions to oversee and enforce the implementation of the laws. RGB, Otdel rukopisei, f. 261, kor. 20, d. 6, ll. 94–102.

130. GARF, f. 1800, op. 1, d. 65 (*Osobyi zhurnal Soveta ministrov*, 3 June 1916). For an overview of Bulgarian immigration to the Russian Empire see Elena Khadzhinikolova, *Belgarskite preselnitsi v iuzhnite oblasti na Rusiia, 1856–1877* (Sofiia: Nauka, 1987).

131. RGIA, f. 1483, op. 1, d. 14, l. 264.

132. GARF, f. 579, op. 1, d. 2610, ll. 1–2.

133. Rempel, "The Expropriation," 65. The Volynia Zemstvo also petitioned on behalf of a group of Russian small credit organizations which were owed over 2 million rubles by expropriated colonists. RGIA, f. 1483, op. 1, d. 22, l. 15 ("Dolgi nemtsev-kolonistov," *Russkoe slovo*, 16 July 1915).

134. Lindeman, *Prekrashchenie*, 234–249, includes extensive data on such contributions. See also Karl Lindeman, *Von den deutschen Kolonisten in Russland: Ergebnisse einer Studienreise 1919–1921* (Stuttgart: Ausland und Heimat Verlags-Aktsiengesellschaft, 1924).

135. Lindeman, *Prekrashchenie*, 184–193.

136. Fleischhauer, *Die Deutschen im Zarenreich*, 514.

137. RGIA, f. 23, op. 28, d. 3148, ll. 32–35.

138. See GARF, f. 102, II, op. 73, d. 34, ll. 1–6.

139. RGIA, f. 23, op. 28, d. 3148, ll. 1–15ob. The lists included over one hundred mills and factories per province in Ekaterinoslav, Taurida, and Kherson, and smaller numbers in other provinces throughout the country.

140. RGIA, f. 1483, op. 1, d. 9, ll. 275–282.

141. RGIA, f. 1278, op. 7, d. 584, l. 3; RGIA, f. 1483, op. 1, d. 9, ll. 16–19; "O nekotorykh merakh k podderzhaniiu khoziaistva na podlezhashchikh likvidatsii kolonistskikh zemel'," *Osobyi zhurnal Soveta ministrov*, signed by tsar on 10 July 1916.

142. RGIA, f. 1483, op. 1, d. 23, l. 42.

143. RGB, Otdel rukopisei, f. 261, kor. 20, d. 6.

144. Based on Peasant Bank data of January 1, 1917. RGIA, f. 1483, op. 1, d. 16, l. 386.

145. RGIA, f. 1483, op. 1, d. 16, l. 390.

146. *Novoe vremia*, 9 February 1917, 4, cited in Rempel, "The Expropriation," 63.

147. Lindeman, *Prekrashchenie*, 358.

148. GARF, f. r-546, op. 1, d. 24, ll. 5–5ob.

149. The figure of 2 million is based on the Peasant Bank figures for January 1, 1917, March 1, 1917, and separate newspaper reports of additional sales at auction not included in these figures (250,000 *desiatin*). It is meant as a rough estimate only. It should be noted that this figure is substantially higher than figures cited by leading historians of the Russian-Germans. For example, Fleischhauer claims that only about 500,000–600,000 *desiatin*) were expropriated during the war. The figures cited by Nolde underestimate the results of the program, as he cites publications only from the summer of 1916, before the most active implementation period, which began in the fall. Sobolev, who cites the 1 January 1917 figures, concentrates only on the activity of the Peasant Bank, disregarding sales by auction, army sequestration, and the ending of leases. Thus he too underestimates the scope of the planned property transfer. Nolde, *Russia in the Economic War*, 114; I. G. Sobolev, "Krest'ianskii pozemel'nyi bank i bor'ba s 'nemetskim zasil'em' v agrarnoi sfere (1915–1917)," *Vestnik sanktpeterburgskogo universiteta*, ser. 2, vyp. 3, no. 16 (1992): 24–29; Fleischhauer, "The Germans' Role," 27.

150. Several of the provinces where the Stolypin reform was most successful (Ekaterinoslav, Khar'kov, Kherson, Samara, Saratov, Taurida) were also major areas of German settlement. Pallot, *Land Reform*, 44, 97, 103.

151. RGIA, f. 1483, op. 1, d. 32, ll. 167–172. Interestingly, in this memo, the Volynia governor expressed a similar view himself, proposing that the only way to allow Russians to compete with Germans was to incorporate the Germans' individual holdings into Russian peasant communes and institutions. According to Kharlamov, who oversaw implementation of the expropriatory decrees in southern Russia, the belief among peasants became widespread during the war that "Germans acquired *khutory* illegally," and thus that they were not entitled to them. GPB, Otdel rukopisei, f. 261, kor. 20, d. 6, l. 3.

152. If one includes the years 1907–1909, then the figures for German expropriations come to nearly half the total amount of land transferred to private ownership in 1907–1915. Atkinson, *The End of the Russian Land Commune*, 76, 78. Recent scholarship on the Stolypin reforms has stressed their coercive, "administrative utopian" nature, as a project to radically transform the countryside, with the intimation that this was a precursor to Soviet methods. The campaign against enemy-alien properties can be read along these lines—though with quite a different evaluation of the Stolypin reforms—as a radical coercive project targeting private ownership and an entire enemy population in the countryside in ways that prefigured Bolshevik approaches to rule in the countryside. Yaney, *The Urge to Mobilize*; Pallot, *Land Reform*; Yanni Kotsonis, *Making Peasants Backward: Agricultural Cooperatives and the Agrarian Question in Russia, 1861–1914* (New York: St. Martin's Press, 1999).

5. Forced Migrations

1. RGVIA, f. 1759, op. 4, d. 1693, l. 1.

2. GARF, f. 102, op. 260, d. 269, l. 2 (MVD circular to governors and city governors, 29 July 1914). GARF, f. 215, op. 1, d. 432, ll. 34–35ob.

3. RGVIA, f. 2005, op. 1, d. 24, l. 1 (MVD circular to provincial and city governors, signed by Maklakov, 11 August 1914); GARF, f. 215, op. 1, d. 174, l. 159.

4. GARF, f. 215, op. 1, d. 174, l. 352 (Memorandum, confirmed by General Zhilinskii, 3 August 1914); GARF, f. 215, op. 1, d. 432, l. 35ob.

5. RGVIA, f. 2005, op. 1, d. 24, ll. 30–32 (Goremykin to Ianushkevich, 19 October 1914).

6. The actual implementation was much faster near the front than in the interior of the country. Reports from governors to the MVD on the progress of implementation show that by September 1914, approximately half of the identified foreigners owing military service in enemy countries within central Russian provinces had been deported. GARF, f. 102, II, op. 71, d. 102 (1914), ll. 1–10; 15–127; *Deutsche und das Orenburger Gebiet (Sammelung der Materialien der wissenschaftlichen Gebietskonferenz zum 250 Jahrestag des Orenburger Gouvernements und zum 60. Jahretag des Orenburger Gebiets) den 17 Dez 1994* (Orenburg, 1994), 25–26. By October 31, 1914, an investigation by three members of the tsar's suite presented far from complete data for the number of enemy-subject deportees then under police oversight in only 11 provinces. They indicated that 35,000 enemy subjects were already under police oversight in these provinces, of which well over half owed military service in enemy countries. (This data included only 7,500 Ottoman subjects since their deportation had been under way only for the week after Turkey entered the war.) Exact estimates of the number of enemy-subject males of service age deported during the war are not available, but already by January 1915, the Department of Police reported that it had 55,580 enemy subjects under police oversight in 19 different internal Russian provinces. Two of the largest internment camps for enemy-subject males of draft age were in Vologda and Orenburg, where respectively about 5,000 and 10,000 were interned. GARF, f. 102, II, op. 71, d. 102 (1914), ll. 15–127.

7. Richard B. Speed, III, *Prisoners, Diplomats, and the Great War: A Study in the Diplomacy of Captivity* (London: Greenwood Press, 1990), 141–153.

8. GARF, f. 215, op. 1, d. 174, l. 180.

9. For a full account of the exchanges and a discussion of departures from the country, see Eric Lohr, "Enemy Alien Politics Within the Russian Empire During World War I" (Ph.D. diss., Harvard University, 1999), 92–99.

10. RGVIA, f. 2049, op. 1, d. 644, l. 133; Sergei Nelipovich, "Repressii protiv poddannykh 'tsentral'nykh derzhav'," *Voenno-istoricheskii zhurnal* 6 (1996): 33.

11. GARF, f. 270, op 1, d. 91, l. 46 (Chief of Lifland Gendarme Administration to Dzhunkovskii, 4 September 1914).

12. RGVIA, f. 2005, op. 1, d. 24, l. 3. The issue of enemy atrocities was a major theme in official propaganda and in the Russian press. German and Austrian atrocities did take place on the Eastern Front. Most, however, dealt with the treatment of Russian prisoners of war rather than civilians. The most famous was the Austrian camp at Talerhof, where Russian POWs were treated quite brutally. See *Talergofskii al'manakh: propamiatnaia kniga avstriiskikh zhestokostei, izuverstv i nasilii nad karpato-russkim narodom vo vremia vsemirnoi voiny 1914–1917 gg.* (L'vov: Izd. "Talergofskogo komiteta," 1924–25).

13. RGVIA, f. 2005, op. 1, d. 24, l. 67; RGVIA, f. 1932, op. 12, d. 67, ll. 2–2ob.

14. GARF, f. 215, 1, 432, l. 61.

15. RGVIA, f. 2005, op. 1, d. 24, l. 12; GARF, f. 215, op. 1, d. 524.

16. On February 9, 1915, the Ruling Senate confirmed the September decision to deny enemy subjects access to the courts, at the same time ruling that Russian subjects would retain the right to sue enemy subjects. Thus trials in civil suits against enemy subjects were held without the presence of the accused. RGIA, f. 1483, op. 1, d. 14, l. 151; L. M. Zaitsev, *Poddannye vrazhdebnogo gosudarstva i russkie sudy* (Kiev: "Petr Barskii v Kieve", 1915); S. Dobrin, "Voprosy ministra iustitsii prav. Senatu o prave nepriiatel'skikh poddannykh na sudebnuiu zashchitu," *Pravo: ezhenedel'naia iuridicheskaia gazeta* 6 (8 February 1915): 345–356; GARF, f. 215, op. 1, d. 432, l. 29 (Circular to governors, signed Dzhunkovskii, 21 September 1914).

17. RGVIA, f. 2005, op. 1, d. 20, l. 375; Nelipovich, "Repressii protiv," 37.

18. RGVIA, f. 2005, op. 1, d. 24, l. 133 (Ianushkevich to Fan der Flit, 20 December 1914).

19. AVPRI, f. 323, op. 617, d. 80, l. 28 (Ianushkevich to Fan der Flit, 5 January 1915). Within the following weeks, Ianushkevich allowed Czechs and Slovaks to be exempted if they presented proof of their nationality from the Czech and Slovak committee, and if background checks showed unquestionable reliability. Enemy aliens of French or Italian origins were also allowed to be exempted on a similar basis. But he did not allow exemptions for any other Slavic nationalities, unless they were in the process of applying for Russian subjecthood, and acceptance looked likely. Broader exemptions for Slavs came later and are discussed below.

20. RGVIA, f. 2005, op. 1, d. 14, l. 214; GARF, f. 102, op. 260, d. 263, l. 27 (MVD circular, 11 January 1915).

21. RGVIA, f. 2000s, op. 1, d. 4430, ll. 52, 61 (Secret Report to the Main Administration of the General Staff, 24 April 1916).

22. GARF, f. 601, op. 1, d. 615 (Memo of Prince Iusupov on the need to deport German and Austrian subjects from Moscow and Petersburg [sic] and halt their acceptance into Russian subjecthood, 5–7 July 1915).

23. RGVIA, f. 2005, op. 1, d. 101, l. 37 (Memo from Counterintelligence to Army Headquarters, 15 October 1914).

24. RGVIA, f. 1759, op. 3, d. 1421, l. 45.

25. On August 1, 1917, the Galician-Bukovinian Committee estimated that 120,000 civilians had been deported from Galicia and Bukovina to the Russian Empire during the war, 43,000 of whom were Ukrainian or Polish. AVPRI, f. 138, op. 475, d. 428, l. 91. At least 50,000 civilians, perhaps as many as 100,000, were deported from East Prussia, including large numbers of women and elderly. RGVIA, f. 2005, op. 1, d. 24, l. 215 (Maklakov to Ianushkevich, 6 January 1915). On the basis of available evidence, I am unable to estimate the number of civilians deported from occupied parts of Bulgaria, Rumania, and the Ottoman Empire.

26. Bauer et al., *Die Nationalitäten*, 211; Obolenskii, *Mezhdnarodnye*, 108, 110.

27. GARF, f. 215, op. 1, d. 432, l. 239 (Memo on the number of enemy subjects deported from the city of Warsaw by 1 June 1915).

28. Nelipovich, "Repressii protiv," 37.

29. GARF, f. 1791, op. 2, d. 393, l. 54.

30. Speed, *Prisoners, Diplomats, and the Great War,* 141–153.

31. For an overview, see J. Spiropulos, *Ausweisung und Internierung Feindlicher Staatsangehöriger* (Leipzig: Rossberg'sche Verlagsbuchhandlung, 1922).

32. RGVIA, f. 2005, op. 1, d. 101, l. 140; RGVIA, f. 1932, op. 12, d. 67, ll. 1–3.

33. RGVIA, f. 2005, op. 1, d. 28, l. 78 (Ianushkevich to Oranovskii, 26 December 1914).

34. RGVIA, f. 2005, op. 1, d. 28, l. 84 (Engalychev to Ianushkevich, 11 January 1915).

35. Ibid., l. 83 (Ianushkevich to Ruzskii, 5 January 1915).

36. GARF, f. 215, op. 1, d. 460, l. 21 (Engalychev circular to nine governors, 16 January 1915).

37. RGVIA, f. 2005, op. 1, d. 28, ll. 238–239.

38. According to the 1897 census, the total German-speaking population of the Kingdom of Poland was 407,700, making up 4.3% of the population. By 1914, their number had grown to over half a million, making up 5.6% of the population. V. M. Kabuzan, "Nemetskoe naselenie v Rossii v XVIII—Nachale XX veka (Chislennost' i razmeshchenie)," *Voprosy istorii* 12 (1989): 28. In 1907 there were 115,726 German Protestants in towns and cities and 417,385 in rural areas. RGIA, f. 1284, op. 190, d. 307, ll. 14–15ob.

39. RGVIA, f. 1932, op. 12, d. 67, l. 3.

40. RGVIA, f. 2005, op. 1, d. 28, l. 84 (Engalychev to Ianushkevich, 11 January 1915).

41. Ibid.

42. GARF, f. 215, op. 1, d. 524, ll. 102–103ob (Special conference, 25 January– 2 February 1915).

43. GARF, f. 215, op. 1, d. 460, l. 21.

44. RGVIA, f. 2005, op. 1, d. 28, l. 97 (Ivanov to Ianushkevich, n.d.).

45. Ibid., l. 103 (Ianushkevich to Warsaw governor general, 11 February 1915).

46. In one case, the Polish aid committee in Warsaw complained that thousands of Polish-speaking Protestants with German names were being deported, even though they had fully assimilated into Polish culture. GARF, f. 215, op. 1, d. 524, ll. 132–33 (Residents' committee for aid to the population of Warsaw to governor general of Warsaw, 20 February 1915).

47. RGVIA, f. 2005, op. 1, d. 28, l. 94 (Ianushkevich to N. V. Ivanov, 15 January 1915).

48. RGIA, f. 465, op. 1, d. 13, ll. 20–40ob.

49. Daniel Graf, "The Reign of the Generals: Military Government in Western Russia, 1914–1915" (Ph.D. diss., University of Nebraska, 1972), 138–141.

50. GARF, f. 102, II, op. 111, d. 224, ll. 222–224 (Special conference on measures in connection with the clearing by troops of regions of the Northern and Southwest Fronts, confirmed by the Supreme Commander [Grand Duke Nikolai Nikolaevich], 24 June 1915).

51. RGVIA, f. 1759, op. 3, d. 1421, l. 33.

52. RGVIA, f. 2005, op. 1, d. 28, l. 136.

53. GARF, f. 102, II, op. 71, l. 111.

54. GARF, f. 102, II, op. 111, d. 224, ll. 222–224.

55. Mikhail Konstantinovich Lemke, *250 dnei v tsarskoi stavke (25 sent.–2 iiulia 1916)* (Petrograd: Gosud. Izd., 1920), 626.

56. RGVIA, f. 2005, op. 1, d. 28, ll. 232–235 (Ivanov to Alekseev, 23 October 1915; Alekseev to Ivanov, 24 October 1915).

57. V. Miakotin, "Nabroski sovremennosti. Likvidatsiia nemetskogo

zemlevladeniia," *Russkie zapiski*, nos. 2–3 (February-March 1917): 300; Karl Linde-man, *Prekrashchenie zemlevladeniia i zemlepol'zovaniia poselian sobstvennikov. Ukazy 2 fevralia i 13 dekabria 1915 goda i 10, 15 iiulia i 19 avgusta 1916 goda i ikh vliianie na ekonomicheskoe sostoianie iuzhnoi Rossii* (Moscow: K.L. Men'shova, 1917), 20.

58. RGIA, f. 1483, op. 1, d. 25, l. 96; "Zhizn' v Rige," *Rech'*, 5 August 1916; GARF, f. 102, II, op. 71, d. 111A, ll. 55, 61, 420. The first deportation order affect-ing the Girshengof settlement was implemented on May 4, 1916.

59. Lindeman, *Prekrashchenie*, 21.

60. RGVIA, f. 2005, op. 1, d. 28, l. 265 (Brusilov to Ianushkevich, 23 June 1916); GARF, 102, II, op. 71, d. 111A, ll. 164, 167.

61. Bakhmetieff Archives, Columbia University, Bark Memoirs, chapter 14, 43.

62. RGVIA, f. 2005, op. 1, d. 155.

63. Altschuler cites a figure of 500,000–600,000 Jews deported and expelled during the war. Frankel estimates that one million Jews were expelled by the end of 1915. M. Altshuler, "Russia and Her Jews. The Impact of the 1914 War," *The Wiener Library Bulletin* 27, no. 30/31 (1973): 14; Jonathan Frankel, ed., *Studies in Contemporary Jewry: An Annual* 4, *The Jews and the European Crisis, 1914–1921* (Bloomington: Indiana University Press, 1988), 6.

64. "Iz chernoi knigi rossiiskogo evreistva," *Evreiskaia starina* 10 (1918): 233; GARF, f. 9458, op. 1, d. 145, ll. 67–70; "Dokumenty o presledovanii," 247–248.

65. RGVIA, f. 1932, op. 12, d. 67, ll. 27–35.

66. "Dokumenty o presledovanii," 250.

67. "Iz 'chernoi knigi'," 236; Graf, "The Reign of the Generals," 143.

68. YIVO, New York, Mowshowitz Collection, 13094.

69. RGVIA, f. 1932, op. 12, d. 67, l. 48 (Popov to Commander of Dvinsk Mili-tary District [17 March 1915]).

70. RGVIA, f. 1932, op. 12, d. 67, l. 54 (Danilov to Tumanov, 11 April 1915).

71. Ibid., ll. 24–27, 38 (Kurlov to Danilov, 27 April 1915).

72. RGVIA, f. 1932, op. 12, d. 67, l. 166 (Report of the Kurland governor, 7 June 1915); RGVIA, f. 2005, op. 1, d. 153, l. 601 (Rabbi Girshovich to Grand Duke Nikolai Nikolaevich, 28 April 1915).

73. Graf, "The Reign of the Generals," 127.

74. "Iz chernoi knigi," 240.

75. GARF, f. 1467, op. 1, d. 635, ll. 10–11 (On the topic of mass deportation [*pogolovnoe vyselenie*] by order of military authorities of Jews from the western bor-der provinces within the theater of military activity, signed by Goremykin, 15 May 1915).

76. RGVIA, f. 2003, op. 2, d. 991, ll. 33–34.

77. RGVIA, f. 1759, op. 3, d. 1422, l. 7 (Dzhunkovskii to Commander of Kiev Military District, 10 February 1915); RGVIA, f. 1932, op. 12, d. 67, ll. 35, 40, 43.

78. RGVIA, f. 1932, op. 12, d. 67, l. 95 (Poltava governor to Commander of Dvinsk Military District, 8 May 1915).

79. GARF, f. 1467, op. 1, d. 635, ll. 10–11.

80. RGVIA, f. 1932, op. 12, d. 67, ll. 146, 211.

81. For an account of the opposition of government ministers to army poli-cies toward the Jews, see Michael Cherniavsky, *Prologue to a Revolution: Notes of A. N. Iakhontov on the Secret Meetings of the Council of Ministers, 1915* (Upper Saddle

River, N.J.: Prentice Hall, 1967), 56–64; *Sovet ministrov Rossiiskoi Imperii v gody pervoi mirovoi voiny. Bumagi A. N. Iakhontova (Zapisi zasedanii i perepiska)* (St. Petersburg: Sankt-Peterburgskii filial Instituta Rossiiskoi istorii Rossiiskoi Akademii Nauk, 1999), 163–164.

82. RGVIA, f. 1932, op. 12, d. 67, l. 138 (Alekseev to all commanders on the Northwest Front, 8 May 1915); Cherniavsky, *Prologue to Revolution,* 56–64.

83. RGVIA, f. 1932, op. 12, d. 67, l. 141 (Danilov to army commanders and Warsaw governor general, 9 May 1915). In practice, railroad administrators, local officials, and the army all made it very difficult for deported Jews to return to their homes. Ibid., ll. 269–272.

84. Ibid., l. 183.

85. Ibid., ll. 193–194.

86. Ibid., ll. 216–227 (Correspondence between Grigor'ev, Tumanov, and Ivanov, 24–25 May 1915).

87. RGIA, f. 465, op. 1, d. 13, l. 21; RGVIA, f. 1932, op. 12, d. 67, l. 302; Volodymyr Serhiichuk, *Pohromy v Ukraini, 1914–1920* (Kyiv: Vyd-vo im. O. Telihy, 1998), 104–105; "*Dokumenty o presledovanii,*" 249–250.

88. RGVIA, f. 2003, op. 2, d. 539, l. 21 (Reports of the governor general of Galicia, 28 August 1914–1 July 1915). The practice itself has some analogs in the tradition of *krugovaia poruka* (collective responsibility) in medieval Russian politics and war, a fact which opponents pointed to as evidence of the "medieval barbarity" of the regime and illegality of its policies toward Jews. "Iz chernoi knigi," 225–226, 264.

89. RGVIA, f. 2021, op. 1, d. 20, l. 9 (Vilna deportation stage (*etapnyi*) commander to the commander of the Northwest Front, 1 June 1915).

90. For an example of one such form, see "Dokumenty o presledovanii," 256.

91. RGVIA, f. 1932, op. 12, d. 67, l. 302. For this and other documents on army policies toward Jews during World War I see Eric Lohr, "Novye dokumenty o rossiiskoi armii i evreiakh vo vremena Pervoi mirovoi voiny," *Vestnik evreiskogo universiteta v Moskve* [forthcoming, 2003].

92. GARF, f. 102, II, op. 71, d. 123, l. 4; RGVIA, f. 1759, op. 3, d. 1422, ll. 22, 60–88; RGVIA, f. 1932, op. 12, d. 67, l. 290.

93. In fact, no formal bureaucratic body to coordinate hostage-taking was formed until September 1915; once formed, it focused on hostages taken from occupied territories, mostly dealing with diplomatic correspondence on the issue rather than coordinating conditions of oversight and punishments for Russian-subject hostages. AVPRI, f. 323, op. 617, d. 83, l. 61; f. 157, op. 455a, d. 238, T. 3.

94. RGVIA, f. 2005, op. 1, d. 80, ll. 670ob, 728; RGVIA f. 2005, op. 1, d. 28, l. 319.

95. RGVIA, f. 1343, op. 8, d. 305, ll. 102–111, 113.

96. For a discussion of recent scholarship on the issue of government responsibility for pogroms in the Russian Empire before World War I, see John D. Klier and Shlomo Lambroza, eds., *Pogroms: Anti-Jewish Violence in Modern Russian History* (Cambridge: Cambridge University Press, 1992), esp. 315. On the basis of their studies of earlier pogroms (1881–1884 and 1902–1906), the contributors to this volume conclude that high-level *civilian* authorities neither ordered nor approved of pogroms as a policy.

97. GARF, F 215, op. 1, d. 524, ll. 2–3 (Acting governor general of Warsaw to Council of Ministers, 6 September 1914).

98. Cherniavsky, *Prologue to Revolution*, 56–74; *Sovet Ministrov*, 169, 204–205, 211–212.

99. "Iz chernoi knigi," 233; "Dokumenty o presledovanii," 247.

100. RGVIA, f. 2005, op. 1, d. 24, l. 305.

101. GARF, f. 9458, op. 1, d. 163, ll. 4–4ob (Shadovo, Kovno Province, n.d. [report submitted by a Shadovo resident to Duma deputy Bomash]).

102. Duma deputy Bomash's files (GARF, f. 9458, op. 1) contain dozens of reports similar to the one summarized above.

103. The following is based on reports of this type, gathered by the Collegium of Jewish Social Activists, an interparty group of leading Jewish politicians. The group collected copies of official documents and reports from the communities affected. GARF, f. 9458, op. 1, d. 163; YIVO, New York, Mowshowitz Collection, 13090–13245; "Iz chernoi knigi," 231–296. For a report based primarily on this material, see American Jewish Committee, *The Jews in the Eastern War Zone* (New York, 1916).

104. "Iz chernoi knigi," pp. 218–219.

105. On the problem of wartime inflation, with some discussion of its impact on relations between nationalities, see Iurii I. Kir'ianov, "Massovye vystupleniia na pochve dorogovizny v Rossii (1914-fevral' 1917 g.)," *Otechestvennaia istoriia* 1 (1993): 3–18.

106. YIVO, New York, Mowshowitz Collection, 13197, 13200.

107. F. Golczewski, *Polnisch-Jüdische Beziehungen, 1881–1922* (Wiesbaden, 1981), 106–120.

108. YIVO, New York, Mowshowitz Collection, 13214.

109. More research needs to be done on the deportations of Germans before any firm assertions about violence can be made. An eyewitness to the German deportations from Volynia claims fairly extensive violence by Cossacks following a similar pattern to the Jewish expulsions. Alfred Krueger, *Die Flüchtlinge von Wolhynien: Der Leidensweg russlanddeutscher Siedler, 1915–1918* (Plauen: Günther-Wolff, 1937). A poorly footnoted study that seems to be based on eyewitness accounts also claims extensive violence: Waldemar Giesbrecht, "Die Verbannung der Wolhyniendeutschen, 1915/1916," *Wolhynische Hefte* 3 (1984): 43–97; 4 (1986): 9–97; 5 (1988): 6–62.

110. GARF, f. 102, II, op. 71, d. 111A, ll. 41–42, 67–69.

111. The army command insisted that no previously deported individuals be allowed to return without its explicit permission in each individual case. As the procedure for this required a full investigation of each individual to assure his or her reliability, this policy in effect blocked all returns until this requirement was abandoned during late summer 1917. RGVIA, f. 2005, op. 1, d. 28, ll. 316–318; RGVIA, f. 2032, op. 1, d. 281, l. 408 (A. M. Dragomirov to *Stavka*, 15 May 1917); RGVIA, f. 2049, op. 1, d. 452, ll. 117–130.

112. RGVIA, f. 2005, op. 1, d. 28, ll. 319–22 (Correspondence between *Stavka* and the Chief of the Chancery for civilian administration of the armies of the Southwest Front, 31 August 1917); GARF, f. 1791, op. 2, d. 413, ll. 1–19 (Correspondence between governors, MVD, and Army Headquarters, April–September 1917). For a general overview of pogroms against Jews, Germans, foreigners, and others during 1917, see V. V. Kanishchev, *Russkii bunt—bessmyslennyi i besposhchadnyi: Pogromnoe dvizhenie v gorodakh Rossii v 1917–1918 gg.* (Tambov: Tambovskaia gos. univ. imeni G. R. Derzhavina, 1995).

113. GARF, f. 1791, op. 2, d. 413, l. 9 (Zhitomir provincial commissar to Army Headquarters, 21 September 1917); l. 14 (MVD to Army Headquarters, 24 April 1917).

114. GARF, f. 1791, op. 2, d. 413, l. 12; *Saratower Deutsche Zeitung* (28 September 1917): 1, 4.

115. AVPRI, f. 157, op. 455a, d. 236 T. 1, ll. 10–17, 20 (Viatka governor to the Ministry of Foreign Affairs, 26 April 1917; Report of escapee from Viatka province to the Swedish Red Cross, n.d).

116. RGVIA, f. 1932, op. 12, d. 67, ll. 24–27, 38, 166.

117. YIVO, New York, Mowshowitz Collection, 13141.

118. See Hans Rogger, "Conclusion and Overview," in Klier and Lambroza, eds., *Pogroms: Anti-Jewish Violence,* 314–362. Edward H. Judge makes a similar point in his "Urban Growth and Anti-Semitism in Russian Moldavia" in Edward H. Judge and James Y. Simms, Jr., eds., *Modernization and Revolution: Dilemmas of Progress in Late Imperial Russia* (New York: Columbia University Press, 1992), 43–57. For a recent review of the pogroms in Ukraine, see Henry Abramson, *A Prayer for the Government: Ukrainians and Jews in Revolutionary Times, 1917–1920* (Cambridge, Mass.,: Harvard University Press, 1999), 109–140. According to Peter Gatrell, two-fifths of all displaced Jews moved to areas of the Russian Empire that had previously been closed to them. Peter Gatrell, *A Whole Empire Walking: Refugees in Russia during World War I* (Bloomington: Indiana University Press, 1999), 146.

119. RGVIA, f. 1932, op. 12, d. 64, ll. 534–536. Unfortunately, this is the only document regarding deportation policies toward gypsies that I found in the archives. There is also to my knowledge no secondary literature on this important topic. It remains unknown how and whether the order was implemented.

120. GARF, f. 406 (old numbering) 1791 (new numbering), op. 2, d. 404, ll. 1–48, esp. 46, 48. See also Lohr, "Enemy Alien Politics," 104.

121. RGVIA, f. 1218, op. 1, d. 155, l. 93 (Dzhunkovskii to Khar'kov governor 15 January 1915). See also Gosudarstvennaia duma, *Stenograficheskie otchety* 4, session 4, meeting 1, col. 129; meeting 2, cols. 153–54, 187; meeting 10, col. 829.

122. GARF, f. 102, II, op. 73, d. 83, l. 6.

123. RGVIA, f. 1218, op. 1, d. 155, ll. 5–132.

124. Ibid., l. 26.

125. Ibid., l. 77ob (Nizhnii Novgorod governor to Dzhunkovskii, 18 January 1915).

126. RGVIA, f. 2018, op. 1, d. 95, l. 41. Nargen Island is located in the Caspian Sea about five miles from Baku.

127. Malkhaz Makarovich Sioradze, "Batumskaia oblast' v imperialisticheskikh planakh zapadnykh derzhav (1914–1921 gg.)" (Kand. diss., Tblisi, 1986), 79.

128. RGIA, f. 1276, op. 19, d. 1061, ll. 1–4 (Pederson to A. P. Nikol'skii, 17 January 1915).

129. Sioradze, "Batumskaia oblast'," 60–78; Robert Conrood, "The Duma's Attitude toward War-time Problems of Minority Groups," *American Slavic and East European Review* 13 (1954): 44.

130. RGIA, f. 1276, op. 19, d. 1061, ll. 61–62.

131. Deportations of Russian-subject Muslims from the provinces continued right up to September 10, 1915, when an order was finally issued to stop them.

RGVIA, 1218, op. 1, d. 155, l. 150 (Tiflis governor to the director of MVD, 10 September 1915). The investigation of alleged Adzhar treason was not closed until January 26, 1918, by order of the Caucasus Commissariat. Sioradze, "Batumskaia oblast'," 79.

132. RGVIA, f. 1932, op. 12, d. 34, l. 1.

133. M. D. Bonch-Bruyevich, *From Tsarist General to Red Army Commander* (Moscow: Progress, 1966), 63–65.

134. The Petrograd Military District reported that the Sixth Army alone received 2,500 denunciations in the first three months of the war. RGVIA, f. 2005, op. 1, d. 101, l. 37 (Memo from the Petrograd Military District counter-intelligence, 15 October 1914).

135. Ibid., ll. 1–30 (Ianushkevich to Lodyzhenskii, n.d. [1914]).

136. See for example, the brochure "Shpiony ot religii" in GARF, f. 579, op. 1, d. 2598. The personal files of Pavel Miliukov, who became a vocal defender of their rights, contain a wealth of evidence on the repressions. For an example of the press agitation, see a collection of articles in *Novoe vremia* by A. Selitrennikov [pseud. A. Rennikov], *Zoloto Reina: O nemtsakh v Rossii* (Petrograd: A. S. Suvorin, 1915). The assertion that the religious groups were closely linked to Germany is tenuous at best. By 1914, most of the groups had become largely Russian in membership and leadership. GARF, f. 579, op. 1, d. 2592.

137. GARF, f. 579, op. 1, d. 2597, ll. 1–2. Many *stundists* were fired from positions of responsibility and deported under the simple accusation of spreading their faith. See RGIA, f. 1282, op. 1, d. 1142, ll. 14–20.

138. RGVIA, f. 2005, op. 1, d. 24, l. 172 (MVD Department of Spiritual Affairs circular, 22 November 1914). A decision of the Ruling Senate in November 1914 officially granted the MVD the right to fire and deport leaders of these denominations. RGIA, f. 821, op. 150, d. 33, l. 12 (Maklakov circular to provincial and city governors, 13 November 1914).

139. RGIA, f. 821, op. 150, d. 360, l. 2; "Nemtsy-pastory v Rossii," *Golos Rusi*, no. 356 (1914). The campaign was also quite intense in the Polish provinces. The paper *Privislenskii krai* frequently included notices of German pastors being deported for "Germanofil'stvo." RGIA, f. 821, op. 150, d. 360, ll. 20–23; RGIA, f. 821, op. 150, d. 357 (Alphabetical list of pastors removed from their positions and deported for anti-government and Germanophile activity, 1915–1916).

140. GARF, f. 215, op. 1, d. 524, ll. 132–33.

141. Seppo Zetterberg, *Die Liga der Fremdvölker Russlands 1916–1918. Ein beitrag zu Deutschlands antirussischen propagandakrieg unter den fremdvölkern Russlands im ersten Weltkrieg*, vol. 8 of *Studia Historica* (Helsinki, 1978). For an overview of a comprehensive police program to suppress the Ukrainian national movement and intelligentsiia, see RGIA, Pechatnaia zapiska 410, no. 262, "Zapiska ob ukrainskom dvizhenii za 1914–1916 gody s kratkim ocherkom istorii etogo dvizheniia, kak separatisko-revoliutsionnogo techeniia sredi naseleniia Malorossii."

142. RGIA, f. 821, op. 150, d. 256 (Book of Catholic priests deported to east for anti-government actions, 1914–16).

143. Eduard Freiherr von Stackelberg-Sutlem, *Aus meinem Leben: Die Kriegsjahre 1914–1918: Verschickung nach Sibirien* (Hannover-Döhren: Verlag Harro von Hirschheydt, 1964); Jakob Stach, *Schicksalsjahre der Russlanddeutschen: Erlebnisse eines deutschen Pastors, 1916–1922* (Bonn: Stiftung Ostdeutscher

Kulturrat, 1983). RGVIA, f. 2003, op. 2, d. 991, ll. 46–50 (Bonch Bruevich to Ianushkevich, 12 June 1915).

144. The frequent use of this term is in some ways suggestive of common features with later Soviet ethnic cleansing. Terry Martin has claimed the use of the term *ochishchenie* was indeed similar in intent and meaning to ethnic cleansing in his study of ethnic deportations in the 1930s. Terry Martin, "The Origins of Soviet Ethnic Cleansing," *The Journal of Modern History* 70 (December 1998): 815–817. The term has several meanings, including the "cleansing, purging or removal of a foreign or unwanted element," but it was also commonly used by military commanders simply to mean the clearing of territory of enemy troops. Although this specific term originally had a strictly military and security meaning, as the practice of forced migration evolved, it expanded beyond its restricted military origins and came closer to the ethos of modern ethnic cleansing, with its intent to permanently transform the demographic makeup of territories, to make them more national. Moreover, deportation orders often used terms suggesting that deportees were dangerous, diseased, unhealthy elements that needed to be removed. The high incidence of epidemics among deportees from the horrible conditions in the trains only added to these notions. See "General ot infanterii N.N. Ianushkevich: 'Nemetskuiu pakost' uvolit' i bez nezhnostei: deportatsii v Rossii 1914–1918 gg.," *Voenno-istoricheskii zhurnal* 1 (1997): 42–53; RGVIA, f. 1218, op. 1, d. 155, ll. 5–132.

145. RGVIA, f. 2005, op. 1, d. 24, l. 348.

146. GARF, f. 1791, op. 2, d. 413 (Petition from a group of German farmers who had been deported from a Polish province to Khar'kov to the Council of Worker and Soldier Deputies, 21 May 1917); Giesbrecht, "Die Verbannung," 3 (1984): 69.

147. The following is based on RGVIA, f. 2018, op. 1, d. 155, ll. 50, 63–70, 87.

148. RGVIA, f. 970, op. 3, d. 1872, ll. 82–85 (Report of Dashkov to the tsar, January 1915).

149. See, for example, GARF, f. 102, II, op. 73, d. 235, l. 23; RGVIA, f. 1218, op. 1, d. 155, l. 77ob.

150. Christoph Schmidt, *Russische Presse und Deutsches Reich, 1905–1914* (Cologne: Böhlau Verlag, 1988), 100–108; Terry Martin, *The Mennonites and the Russian State Duma, 1905–1914*, The Donald W. Treadgold Papers in Russian, East European and Central Asian Studies, no. 4 (Seattle: Henry M. Jackson School of International Studies, University of Washington: 1996).

151. *Volkszeitung* (Saratov), 6 August 1914, 1.

152. Parallel to the deportations was the threat that land expropriations would be extended to the Volga and other German communities, a threat which became a reality in January 1917. Sonja Striegnitz, "Der Weltkrieg und die Wolgakolonisten: Die Regierungspolitik und die Tendenzen der gesellschaftlichen Entwicklung," in Dittmar Dahlmann and Ralph Tuchtenhagen, eds., *Zwischen Reform und Revolution: Die Deutschen an der Wolga 1860–1917* (Essen: Klartext, 1994), 146.

153. GARF, f. 102, II, op. 71, d. 111A, l. 118 (MVD circular to governors, military governors, and uezd officials, 3 December 1915).

154. This was the case in Perm Province. GARF, f. 102, II, op. 71, d. 111A, l. 149 (Lifland Marshal of the Nobility to B. V. Shtiurmer, 9 June 1916).

155. RGVIA, f. 2005, op. 1, d. 28, l. 206. See, for example, Johannes

Schleuning's personal evolution by comparing what he wrote about his identity during and after the war. Johannes Schleuning, *Aus tiefster Not: Schicksale der deutschen Kolonisten in Russland* (Berlin: Carl Flemming and C. E. Wiskott, 1922); *In Kampf und Todesnot: Die Tragödie des Russlanddeutschtums* (Berlin: Bernard & Graefe Verlag, 1931).

156. Before the war, there had been some cooperation between German Duma representatives from the different areas of settlement and Baltic German members, most notably in the German Group of the Octobrist faction. A 1908 meeting of representatives of all German organizations in Russia failed to overcome the deep divisions between various communities and achieve its goal of creating a single organization. During the war, Karl Lindeman and Duma member Liuts actively communicated with the various German communities and organized a lobby for their interests in Moscow and Petrograd. See Lindeman, *Prekrashchenie*, and police reports of their activities in GARF, f. 102, II, op. 73, d. 351, ll. 184, 203–204; GARF, f. 102, II, op. 73, d. 351, l. 204 (Chief of the Kuban Oblast' Gendarme Administration to MVD Department of Police, 30 November 1916); Ingeborg Fleischhauer, *Die Deutschen im Zarenreich: Zwei Jahrhunderte deutsch-russische Kulturgemeinschaft* (Stuttgart: Deutsche Verlags-Anstalt, 1986), 385.

157. GARF, f. 579, op. 1, d. 2615. Several regional congresses were held in Odessa, Moscow, Saratov, and other places during May. GARF, f. 1791, op. 2, d. 496, l. 154 (Request of the representatives of the Congress of Russian Germans in the South of Russia to G.E. L'vov, 5 June 1917).

158. GARF, f. 579, op. 1, d. 2615.

159. *Saratower Deutsche Zeitung*, 28 September 1917.

160. Inge Pardon and Waleri Shurawljow, eds., *Lager, Front oder Heimat. Deutsche Kriegsgefangene in Sowjetrussland 1917 bis 1920*, vol. 1 (Munich: LKG Saur, 1994).

161. For an excellent study of the burst of communal activism and aid work, see Steven J. Zipperstein, "The Politics of Relief: The Transformation of Russian Jewish Communal Life during the First World War" in Frankel, ed., *Studies in Contemporary Jewry: An Annual IV*, 22–40. For a memoir of such activity, see Jacob Frumkin, Gregor Aronson, and Alexis Goldenweiser, eds., *Russian Jewry (1860–1917)* (New York: A. S. Barnes, 1966), 74–110. For the activities of associations and mobilization of ethnic and other communities to provide aid for all refugees, see Gatrell, *A Whole Empire Walking*.

162. The concept of the "mobilization of ethnicity" during the war is developed in Mark von Hagen, "The Great War," 34–57.

163. The first categorical exemptions affected very small groups of individuals. On July 31, 1914, in response to a French petition, enemy subjects who could prove French nationality and former residence in Alsace or Lorraine were exempted. When Italy entered the war on the Russian side, a similar exemption was granted for Austrian subjects of Italian nationality. Most major deportation orders throughout the war included a phrase allowing exemption for these nationalities. Despite the early acceptance of the principle of allowing exemptions for these groups, in practice it was often unclear, and the ambassadors of Russia's allies were active throughout the war, lobbying to be sure that these groups were exempted from every major deportation order. For example, on January 9, 1915, French Ambassador Paleologue angrily demanded exemption for ethnic French, Belgian, and

Rumanian enemy subjects after several of each nationality had been deported from Petrograd. RGVIA, f. 970, op. 3, d. 1872, l. 50; RGVIA, f. 2005, op. 1, d. 24, l. 205.

164. The views of these Right Kadet liberals were developed by Peter Struve and others in *Russkaia mysl'*, which Struve edited, and *Moskovskii ezhenedel'nik*, edited by liberal philosopher Evgenii Trubetskoi. See A. Fischel, *Der Panslawismus bis zum Weltkrieg* (Stuttgart: Cotta, 1919).

165. GARF, f. 270, op. 1, d. 99, l. 26.

166. RGVIA, f. 970, op. 3, d. 1872, l. 51. The units were to form in the Kiev Military District. Policies toward prisoners of war taken in the field of battle moved quickly toward differentiated treatment for those of Slavic origins. Already on September 26, 1914, the War Ministry began to separate Czechs, Slovaks, Serbs, Alsace-Lotharinians, Italians, and Romanians from Germans in the camps, give them better clothing and material conditions, allow them to live in private apartments in internal provinces rather than in camps, and gave them lighter work. AVPRI, f. 323, op. 617, d. 80, 11, 13 (Main Administration of the General Staff to MID, 26 September 1914). Although the Ministry of Foreign Affairs proposed granting Poles similar privileges on October 9, 1914, Poles never officially received such privileges. The policy of allowing Slavs to join national units and thereby gain freedom from internment proceeded very slowly. As late as January 1, 1916, army headquarters estimated that only 2,400 individuals, mostly Serbs, had been freed on this basis. RGVIA, f. 2000s, op. 6, d. 162, ll. 1–6ob. Richard Speed estimates that during the entire course of the war, only 10% of the approximately 200,000 Slavic POWs in Russia joined military units. Speed, *Prisoners, Diplomats, and the Great War,* 121.

167. RGVIA, f. 2005, op. 1, d. 23, l. 139.

168. RGVIA, f. 1759, op. 3, d. 1421, l. 53.

169. RGVIA, f. 2005, op. 1, d. 24, l. 395.

170. RGVIA, f. 2005, op. 1, d. 20, ll. 6, 142; RGVIA, f. 2005, op. 1, d. 24, ll. 38–50; RGVIA, f. 2005, op. 1, d. 22, l. 21. There were approximately 200,000 individuals of Czech origin living in the Russian Empire on the outbreak of war, about 70,000 in agricultural colonies in Ukraine. Over half the Czech population had come to Russia in the last three decades of the old regime, and many of these had not naturalized. Kovba, "Ches'ka emigratsiia na ukraini," 70–74.

171. Ibid., l. 265. The voluntary surrender of an Austrian unit with 1,100 Czechs under Radko Dmitriev was noted at army headquarters as proof that the Czechs were loyal to Russia. RGVIA, f. 2003, op. 2, d. 544, l. 48.

172. RGVIA, f. 2005, op. 1, d. 24, l. 399 (Savich to Alekseev, 27 September 1915). His justification was that they might be forced to serve in enemy armies.

173. RGIA, f. 821, op. 150, d. 294, l. 23ob.

174. Arutiunian, "Pervaia mirovaia voina," 33.

175. For example: GARF, f. 1791, op. 2, d. 404, l. 5; RGIA, f. 1483, op. 1, d. 14, ll. 404, 406; RGIA, f. 1284, op. 190, d. 344, ll. 1–3.

176. RGIA, f. 1483, op. 1, d. 23, ll. 8–9.

177. GARF, f. 1791, op. 2, d. 414, ll. 7, 10, 13, 15–20.

178. GARF, f. 406 (old numbering) 1791 (new numbering), op. 2, d. 404, ll. 31–41. The Laz were a small minority group linguistically closest to the Mingrelians. For a brief account of the large emigration of Laz to Turkey after the annexation of Kars and Batumi by the Russian Empire, see Justin McCarthy, *Death and Exile: The*

Ethnic Cleansing of Ottoman Muslims, 1821–1922 (Princeton: The Darwin Press, 1995), 114–116.

179. GARF, f. 406 (old numbering) 1791 (new numbering), op. 2, d. 404, ll. 1–48, esp. 46, 48.

180. GARF, f. 215, op. 1, d. 432, l. 36.

181. AVPRI, f. 323, op. 617, d. 80 (Minister of Foreign Affairs Sazonov to Minister of War Sukhomlinov, 9 October 1914).

182. GARF, f. 215, op. 1, d. 174, l. 160 (MVD circular to governors, signed by Maklakov, n.d. [August 1914]).

183. RGVIA, f. 2000s, op. 1, d. 4430, l. 7 (Ianushkevich to Count Velopol'skii, 7 February 1915); RGVIA, f. 2005, op. 1, d. 24, l. 237 (Ianushkevich to Warsaw governor general, 16 January 1915).

184. RGVIA, f. 2005, op. 1, d. 24, ll. 294–297 (Polish Aid Society to *Stavka*, 15 January 1915).

185. Ibid. (Polish division of the All-Russian Aid Organization for Slavic prisoners to Prince Tumanov, 2 January 1914 [*sic* (1915)]).

186. RGVIA, f. 2005, op. 1, d. 23, ll. 45–76.

187. GARF, f. 1791, op. 2, d. 330, ll. 37, 39, 49, 58, 69. Even after the law was removed, the military insisted that written approval be required from Army Headquarters in each individual case, substantially slowing the return of deported Poles to their homelands.

188. Spontaneous returns of deportees began in the spring of 1917, but did not become truly massive until summer 1918, when thousands of deportees were reported moving along railroads. GARF, f. r-393 op. 1, d. 66, ll. 13–14.

189. RGVIA, f. 2005, op. 1, d. 24, ll. 403, 405.

190. Ibid., l. 407 (Minister of Foreign Affairs to Minister of Trade and Industry, September 1915).

191. RGIA, f. 1276, op. 12, d. 1469, ll. 1–2; RGIA, f. 1483, op. 1, d. 9, ll. 9–15ob (*Osobyi zhurnal Soveta ministrov*, approved by the tsar 7 May 1916). Orders were also issued to deport all Bulgarian subjects from Moscow and Petrograd. See *Rech'*, 23 July 1916; *Russkie vedomosti*, 29 August 1916.

192. John Torpey, *The Invention of the Passport: Surveillance, Citizenship and the State* (Cambridge: Cambridge University Press, 2000), 111.

193. AVPRI, f. 157, op. 455a, d. 21b, ll. 3–22 (Ministry of Foreign Affairs correspondence with the Ministry of Internal Affairs regarding a new law on rules concerning entry and exit from the empire; "Ob ustanovlenii vremennykh pravil o vydache zagranichnykh pasportov," *Osobyi zhurnal Soveta ministrov*, 7 July 1915 (signed by the tsar, 14 July 1915). Among other changes, this law introduced the requirement of photographs for foreign passports for the first time. AVPRI, f. 157, op. 455a, d. 21a, ll. 1–325 (Petitions and correspondence on individuals entering and departing the country, 1915).

194. GARF, f. 102, II, op. 73 (part 1), d. 10 (part 36), ll. 1–117; RGIA, Pechatnaia Zapiska, 2534.

195. RGVIA, f. 2005, op. 1, d. 24, ll. 414–417 (Memorandum of the Extraordinary Meeting of the Council of Ministers at Army Headquarters, 14 June 1915).

196. In March 1915, a Polish Protestant committee pointed out that the Russian government had opposed the Polonization of ethnic German Protestants and pressured them to retain German culture in the late nineteenth century because

they were considered more loyal than the Poles. Suddenly, during the war, they were deported if they were German rather than Polish. RGVIA, f. 2005, op. 1, d. 29, ll. 60–65 (Report to the Grand Duke on the deportation of Evangelicals from the Warsaw region, 17 March 1915).

197. General Kurlov, early in the war, expressed the soon to be outmoded view that "Latvians are all, without exception, revolutionaries." He was dismissed in the summer of 1915 after sustained attacks on his "pro-German" policy in the Duma and press. GARF, f. 1467, op. 1, d. 676, l. 9ob.

198. For example, see Karl Stumpp, *Die Russlanddeutschen: zweihundert Jahre unterwegs* (Stuttgart: Verlag Landmannschaft der Deutschen aus Russland, 1982); Simon Dubnow, *History of the Jews in Russia and Poland from the Earliest Times until the Present Day*, vol. 3 (Philadelphia: The Jewish Publication Society of America, 1920); Walter Lacqueur, *Russia and Germany: A Century of Conflict* (Boston: Little Brown, 1965).

199. On the boycott, see Golczewski, *Polnisch-Jüdische Beziehungen*, 106–120.

200. RGVIA, f. 2005, op. 1, d. 24, l. 236 (Warsaw governor general to Ianushkevich, 16 January 1915).

201. RGVIA, f. 2005, op. 1, d. 20, ll. 14–18 (Matvei M. Radzivill to Ianushkevich, 29 Sept. 1914). Ironically enough, Ianushkevich himself was of Polish descent.

202. GPB, Otdel rukopisei, f. 261, kor. 20, d. 6, part 1.

203. John Armstrong makes this argument in his "Mobilized and Proletarian Diasporas," *American Political Science Review* 70, no. 2 (June 1976): 393–408.

Conclusion

1. RGVIA, f. 2003, op. 2, d. 991, ll. 96–97.

2. Gosudarstvennaia Duma, *Stenograficheskie otchety*, 14 June 1916, 5395–5396; RGIA, f. 1483, op. 1, d. 29, ll. 1–4.

3. Ibid., ll. 1–60 (Ministry of Justice materials on the project to remove special agrarian rights held by gentry in the Baltic provinces, 1916).

4. GARF, f. 1467, op. 1, d. 676, ll. 3ob–9ob (Report of General Adjutant Baranov on his investigation into the activity of General Lieutenant Kurlov regarding his service as special plenipotentiary for civilian affairs in the Baltic region from 24 November 1914 to 3 August 1915, 1916); Manfred Hagen, "Russification via 'Democratization'? Civil Service in the Baltic after 1905," *Journal of Baltic Studies* 9, no. 1 (Spring 1978): 56–65.

5. RGVIA, f. 970, op. 3, d. 1952, ll. 1–30 (Lists of generals and officers, 1 April 1914); *Ves' Petrograd*, 1916.

6. *Zhurnal "1914 god" Bor'ba s nemetskim zasil'em i vozrozhdenie Rossii*, 21 April 1916, 15; Andrew M. Verner, "What's in a Name? Of Dog-Killers, Jews and Rasputin," *Slavic Review* 53, no. 4 (Winter 1994): 1047, 1061–1065.

7. GARF, f. 102, II, op. 73, d. 351, ll. 167–173. For a discussion of the pressures felt by officials because of their German names, see Baron Rosen, *Forty Years of Diplomacy*, vol. 2 (New York: Knopf, 1922), 84–91.

8. GARF, f. 58, op. 5, d. 393, ll. 1, 38, 48, 56 (Gendarme reports from districts in Moscow Province, April–December 1916).

9. Leonid Heretz, "Russian Apocalypse 1891–1917: Popular Perceptions of

Events from the Year of Famine and Cholera to the Fall of the Tsar" (Ph.D. diss., Harvard University, 1993), 337; Orlando Figes and Boris Kolonitsky, *Interpreting the Russian Revolution: The Language and Symbols of 1917* (New Haven: Yale University Press, 1999), 9–29.

10. Allan K. Wildman, *The End of the Russian Imperial Army: The Old Army and the Soldiers Revolt (March–April 1917)* (Princeton: Princeton University Press, 1980), 92.

11. Figes and Kolonitskii, *Interpreting the Russian Revolution*, 161–163.

12. GARF, f. 102, II, op. 73, d. 351, l. 51 (Bashmakov to Khvostov, 16 October 1916).

13. GARF, f. 58, op. 5, d. 399, ll. 123, 168, 172, 175–182, 246.

14. On the speech, see Aleksandr S. Rezanov, *Shturmovoi Signal P. N. Miliukova: s prilozheniem polnogo teksta rechi, proiznesennoi Miliukovym v zasedanii Gosud. Dumy 1 noiabria 1916 g.* (Paris: Izdanie avtora, 1924). For gendarme reports on the spread of copies of the speech, rumors about it, and its impact on public opinion, see GARF, f. 58, op. 5, d. 399, l. 234 ff.

15. Richard Pipes, *The Russian Revolution* (New York: Vintage Books, 1990), 255. See also Figes and Kolonitskii, *Interpreting the Russian Revolution*, 9–29; Aleksandr Solzhenitsyn, *November 1916: The Red Wheel/Knot II* (New York: Farrar, Straus and Giroux, 1999), 785.

16. One of the major issues of discussion in the closed Kadet Party conferences of 1915 that led to that party's move back into open oppositional activity was the army's forced expulsions of Jews and other minorities. RGIA, Pechatnaia zapiska 310; "Iz chernoi knigi rossiiskogo evreistva," *Evreiskaia starina* 10 (1918): 197–227.

17. "Postanovlenie Vremennogo Pravitel'stva o priostanovlenii ispolneniia uzakonenii o zemlevladenii i zemlepol'zovanii avstriiskikh, vengerskikh i germanskikh vykhodtsev" in N. F. Bugai and V. A. Mikhailov, eds., *Istoriia rossiiskikh nemtsev v dokumentakh (1763–1992)* (Moscow: RAU Korporatsiia, 1993), 54–56; for correspondence relating to the implementation of this decree, see RGIA, f. 23, op. 27, d. 675, ll. 3–19; Owen, *The Corporation*, 89.

18. On this process, see the documents in Inge Pardon and Waleri Shurawljow, eds., *Lager, Front oder Heimat. Deutsche Kriegsgefangene in Sowjetrussland 1917 bis 1920*, vol. 1 (Munich: LKG Saur, 1994).

19. Steven J. Zipperstein, "The Politics of Relief: The Transformation of Russian Jewish Communal Life during the First World War," in Jonathan Frankel, ed., *Studies in Contemporary Jewry: An Annual IV: The Jews and the European Crisis, 1914–1921* (Oxford: Oxford University Press, 1988): 22–40.

20. Peter Gatrell, *A Whole Empire Walking: Refugees in Russia during World War I* (Bloomington: Indiana University Press, 1999), 141–170; "Vom Zweiten deutschen Kongress des Volgagebiets, 19–22 September 1917," *Saratower Deutsche Zeitung*, 28 September 1917, p. 1; Zipperstein, "The Politics of Relief," pp. 22–40.

21. Lars Lih, *Bread and Authority in Russia, 1914–1921* (Berkeley: University of California Press, 1990); Peter Holquist, "'Information Is the Alpha and Omega of Our Work': Bolshevik Surveillance in Its Pan-European Context," *The Journal of Modern History* 69 (September 1997): 415–450; Holquist, "To Count, to Extract," 111–144; Yanni Kotsonis, *Making Peasants Backward*.

22. One reason that previous studies of Russian nationalism stress what was

missing rather than what was there is that the main comparisons have been implicitly or explicitly made primarily with Western European nation-states rather than with the continental empires.

23. Donald Quataert, *Social Disintegration and Popular Resistance in the Ottoman Empire, 1881–1908: Reactions to European Economic Penetration* (New York: New York University Press, 1983), esp. 121–155.

24. Joseph Rothschild makes the point that nationalization in East Europe after World War I was greatly facilitated where "'alien' landlords and entrepreneurs could be expropriated for the benefit of 'native' peasants and bureaucrats." Joseph Rothschild, *East Central Europe between the Two World Wars* (Seattle: University of Washington Press, 1974), 12.

25. For the most complete account of both the promotion of national cultures and mass deportations of select nationalities, see Terry Martin, *The Affirmative Action Empire: Nations and Nationalism in the Soviet Union, 1923–1939* (Ithaca: Cornell University Press, 2001); Terry Martin, "The Origins of Soviet Ethnic Cleansing," *Journal of Modern History* 70, no. 4 (1998): 813–861. On Soviet deportations during World War II, see N. F. Bugai, *The Deportation of Peoples in the Soviet Union*, (New York: Nova Science Publishers, 1996); A. M. Nekrich, *The Punished Peoples: The Deportation and Fate of Soviet Minorities at the End of the Second World War* (New York: Norton, 1978).

26. Richard B. Day, *Leon Trotsky and the Politics of Economic Isolation* (Cambridge: Cambridge University Press, 1973).

27. Roman Szporluk, *Communism and Nationalism: Karl Marx versus Friedrich List* (Oxford: Oxford University Press, 1988), 225.

28. Andrzej Walicki, *The Controversy over Capitalism: Studies in the Social Philosophy of the Russian Populists* (Notre Dame: University of Notre Dame Press, 1969), 132–194; *The Slavophile Controversy: History of a Conservative Utopia in Nineteenth-Century Russian Thought* (Notre Dame: University of Notre Dame Press, 1989); Leszek Kolakowski, *Main Currents of Marxism: Its Origins, Growth, and Dissolution*, 3 vol. (Oxford: Oxford University Press, 1978–1981), esp. vol. 3.

Archival Sources

Arkhiv Vneshnei Politiki Rossiiskoi Imperii (AVPRI), Moscow

f. 133 Kantseliariia Ministerstva inostrannykh del
f. 135 Osobyi politicheskii otdel
f. 140 Otdel pechati i osvedomleniia
f. 155 II Departament (Departament vnutrennikh snoshenii)
f. 157 Pravovoi departament
f. 160 Otdel o voennoplennykh
f. 323 Diplomaticheskaia kantseliariia pri Stavke
f. 340 Kollektsiia dokumental'nykh materialov iz lichnykh arkhivov chinovnikov
  MID op. 610 Nolde, B. E.

Derzhavnyi Arkhiv Kharkivskoi Oblasti (DAKhO), Kharkov

f. 3 Kantseliariia Khar'kovskogo gubernatora: sekretnoe otdelenie

Gosudarstvennyi Arkhiv Rossiiskoi Federatsii (GARF), Moscow

f. 63 Moskovskoe okhrannoe otdelenie
f. 102 Departament politsii Ministerstva vnutrennikh del
  —Osobyi otdel (OO)
  —II Deloproizvodstvo
  —VI Deloproizvodstvo
  —IX Deloproizvodstvo
f. 110 Shtab otdel'nogo korpusa zhandarmov
f. 116 Vserossiiskii dubrovinskii soiuz russkogo naroda
f. 117 Russkii narodnyi soiuz imeni Mikhaila Arkhangela

f. r-130 Sovet narodnykh komissarov, 1917

f. 215 Kantseliariia Varshavskogo general-gubernatora

f. r-375 Voenno-revoliutsionnyi komitet pri stavke verkhovnogo
glavnokomanduiushchego

f. r-393 Narodnyi komissariat vnutrennikh del

f. r-546 Osobyi otdel po finansovym voprosam, stoiashchim v sviazi s
osushchestvleniem Brestskogo Dogovora pri departamenta gos.
kaznacheistva narodnogo komissariata finansov, 1918

f. 573 Meiendorfy, barony. Aleksandr Feliksovich, tov. predsedatelia III i IV dumy

f. 579 Miliukov, Pavel Nikolaevich

f. 601 Nikolai II

f. 671 Nikolai Nikolaevich (mladshii)

f. 826 Dzhunkovskii, Vladimir F.

f. 1339 Kanseliariia Lomzhinskogo gubernatora

f. 1467 Chrezvychainaia sledstvennaia komissiia dlia rassledovaniia
protivozakonnykh po dolzhnosti deistvii byvshikh ministrov i prochikh
vyshchikh dolzhnostnykh lits (ChSK)

f. 1790 Ministerstvo iustitsii Vremennogo pravitel'stva

f. 1791 Glavnoe upravlenie po delam militsii

f. 1797 Ministerstvo zemledeliia Vremennogo pravitel'stva

f. r-1218 Narodnyi komissariat po delam narodnostei Rossii

f. 3333 Tsentral'naia kollegiia po delam plennykh i bezhentsev (Tsentroplenbezh)

f. 9458 Bomash, Meer Khaimovich

Rossiiskii gosudarstvennyi istoricheskii arkhiv g. Moskvy (RGIAgM)

f. 3 Moskovskaia kupecheskaia uprava

f. 16 Moskovskii general-gubernator

f. 17 Kantseliariia Moskovskogo gubernatora

f. 46 Kantseliariia Moskovskogo gradonachal'nika

f. 143 Moskovskii birzhevoi komitet

ROSSIISKII GOSUDARSTVENNYI ISTORICHESKII ARKHIV (RGIA), ST. PETERSBURG

f. 23 Ministerstvo torgovli i promyshlennosti

f. 30 Komitet po ogranicheniiu snabzheniia i torgovli nepriiatelia Ministerstvo
torgovli i promyshlennosti (MTiP)

f. 32 Sovet s"ezdov predstavitelei promyshlennosti i torgovli

f. 40 Vsepoddanneishchie doklady po chasti torgovli i promyshlennosti (kollektsiia)

f. 126 Vserossiiskii s"ezd obshchestv zavodchikov i fabrikantov

f. 398 Departament zemledeliia (pri MTiP)

f. 468 Kabinet e. i. v.

f. 472 Kantseliariia ministerstva (Imperatorskogo dvora)

f. 560 Obshchaia kantseliariia ministra finansov

f. 563 Komitet finansov

f. 592 Gosudarstvennyi krest'ianskii pozemel'nyi bank

f. 593 Gosudarstvennyi dvorianskii zemel'nyi bank

f. 788 Voennaia tsenzura pri Petrogradskom komitete po delam pechati Glavnogo upravleniia po delam pechati

f. 796 Kantseliariia Synoda

f. 821 Departament dukhovnykh del inostrannykh ispovedanii

f. 828 General'naia evangelichesko-liuteranskaia konsistoriia (MVD)

f. 1276 Sovet ministrov

f. 1278 Gosudarstvennaia duma

f. 1281 Sovet ministra (MVD)

f. 1282 Kantseliariia ministra (MVD)

f. 1284 Departament obshchikh del (MVD)

f. 1291 Zemskii otdel (MVD)

f. 1322 Osoboe soveshchanie po ustroistvu bezhentsev

f. 1360 O-vo povsemestnostnoi pomoshchi postradavshim na voine soldatam i ikh sem'iam

f. 1405 Ministerstvo iustitsii

f. 1413 Osobyi mezhduvedomstvennyi komitet dlia ucheta ubytkov, ponesennykh v sviazi s voinoi russkimi poddannymi vne Rossii i dlia ucheta ubytkov nepriiatel'skikh poddannykh v Rossii MF (pri Ministerstve finansov)

f. 1425 Dokumenty torgovo-promyshlennykh aktsionernykh obshchestv i tovarishchestv (kollektsiia)

f. 1483 Osobyi komitet po bor'be s nemetskim zasil'em

f. 1647 Mansyrev, Serafim Petrovich

Pechatnaia zapiska 310, "Voennaia tsenzura i evreiskii vopros, n/d [early 1916]"

Pechatnaia zapiska 468, "K voprosu o prave poddannykh vrazhdebnykh gosudarstv na sudebnuiu zashchitu v Rossii vo vremia voiny"

Pechatnaia zapiska 470, 471 [Collections of documents on the deportation of foreigners]

Pechatnaia zapiska 1199, "Svedeniia o deiatel'nosti krest'ianskogo pozemel'nogo banka 1910, 1914, 1915, 1916"

Rossiiskii voenno-istoricheskii arkhiv (RGVIA), Moscow

f. 239, op. 1 Bonch-Bruevich, M. D.

f. 400 Glavnyi shtab

f. 970 Voenno-pokhodnaia kantseliariia e. i. v. pri imperatorskoi glavnoi kvartire

f. 1300 Shtab Kavkazskogo voennogo okruga

f. 1343 Shtab Petrogradskogo voennogo okruga

f. 1396 Shtab Turkestanskogo voennogo okruga

f. 1558 Shtab Priamurskogo voennogo okruga

f. 1606 Shtab Moskovskogo voennogo okruga

f. 1720 Shtab Kazan'skogo voennogo okruga

f. 1759 Shtab Kievskogo voennogo okruga

f. 1915 Shtab Minskogo voennogo okruga

f. 1932 Shtab Dvinskogo voennogo okruga

f. 2000s Glavnoe upravlenie general'nogo shtaba (GUGSh)

f. 2003 Shtab verkhovnogo glavnokomanduiushchego (*Stavka*)

f. 2004 Upravlenie nachal'nika voennykh soobshchenii na teatre voennykh deistvii

f. 2005 Voenno-politicheskoe i grazhdanskoe upravlenie pri verkhovnom glavnokomanduiushchem
f. 2007 Polevoi shtab kazach'ikh voisk pri verkhovnom glavnokomanduiushchem
f. 2015 Upravlenie voennogo komissara vremennogo pravitel'stva pri verkhovnom glavnokomanduiushchem
f. 2018 Upravlenie verkhovnogo nachal'nika sanitarnoi i evakuatsionnoi chasti pri shtabe verkhovnogo glavnokomanduiushchego
f. 2019 Shtab Severo-zapadnogo fronta
f. 2021 Upravlenie nachal'nika voennykh soobshchenii armii Severo-zapadnogo fronta
f. 2048 Shtab glavnokomanduiushchego armiiami Zapadnogo fronta
f. 2049 Kantseliariia glavnogo nachal'nika snabzhenii armii Zapadnogo fronta
f. 2050 Upravlenie nachal'nika voennykh soobshchenii armii Zapadnogo fronta
f. 2067 Shtab glavnokomanuiushchego armiiami Iugo-zapadnogo fronta
f. 2031 Shtab glavnokomanduiushchego armiiami Severnogo fronta
f. 2048 Shtab glavnokomanduiushchego armiiami Zapadnogo fronta
f. 2068 Kantseliariia glavnogo nachal'nika snabzhenii armii Iugo-zapadnogo fronta
f. 2070 Upravlenie nachal'nika voennykh soobshchenii armii Iugo-zapadnogo fronta
f. 2100 Shtab glavnokomanduiushchego voiskami Kavkazskogo fronta
f. 2101 Upravlenie nachal'nika voennykh soobshchenii voisk Kavkazskogo fronta
f. 2102 Upravlenie nachal'nika sanitarnoi chasti voisk Kavkazskogo fronta
f. 2126 Shtab 6-i armii
f. 2144 Shtab 10-i armii
f. 2168 Shtab kavkazskoi armii
f. 2169 Upravlenie nachal'nika voennykh soobshchenii Kavkazskoi armii
f. 12651 Glavnoe upravlenie rossiiskogo obshchestva Krasnogo kresta

Bakhmetieff Archive, Columbia University, New York.

Bark, Petr L'vovich. Memoirs

National Archives, Washington D.C.

Listen und Fragebögen aus Russland ausgewanderter Reichsdeutscher, angelegt durch das Deutsche Auslandsinstitut Stuttgart: German Records, T-81, R. 630–632.

Rossiiskaia gosudarstvennaia biblioteka (RGB), Manuscript Division, Moscow.

Otdel rukopisei, f. 261, kor. 20, d. 6, Kharlamov, Nikolai Petrovich, "Zapiski biurokrata: Vospominaniia 'Bor'ba s nemetskim zasil'em vo vremia russko-germanskoi voiny 1914–1916 gg.'"

YIVO Archives, New York.

Lucien Wolf and David Mowshowitch Collection

Periodicals

Aktsionerno-paevye predpriiatiia Rossii
Arkhiv russkoi revoliutsii
Byloe
Birzhevye vedomosti
Evreiskaia nedelia
Evreiskaia zhizn'
Ezhegodnik Ministerstva inostrannykh del
Flugblatt des Moskauer Verbands russischer Staatsbürger deutscher Nationalität
Golos Moskvy
Golos Rossii
Iskry. Iliustrirovannyi khudozhestvenno-literaturnyi zhurnal s karikaturami
Izvestiia Ministerstva inostrannykh del
Korennik: Monarkhicheskii-patrioticheskii ezhenedel'nik
Krasnyi arkhiv
*Moskauer Nachtrichten: Organ des Moskauer Verbandes russ. Staatsbürger dt.
    Nationalitätat*
Moskovskie vedomosti
Moskower deutsche Zeitung
Natsional'nye problemy
Novoe vremia
Novyi voskhod
Osobyi zhurnal Soveta ministrov
Petrograder Herold
Petrograder Zeitung
Promyshlennost' i torgovlia
Rech'
Rigasche Rundschau
Rizhskaia gazeta
Russkaia budushchnost'
Russkaia mysl'
Russkie vedomosti
Russkie zapiski
Russkoe znamia
Saratower deutsche Volkszeitung
Vestnik Evropy
Vestnik finansov, promyshlennosti i torgovli
Vestnik partii narodnoi svobody
Ves' Petrograd
Volkszeitung (Saratov)
Voina: Obozrenie, parodii i karikatury
Voskhod: gazeta
Vsia Moskva
Zhurnal Ministerstva iustitsii
Zhurnal "1914 god" Bor'ba s nemetskim zasil'em i vozrozhdenie Rossii

Index